THE CONTEMPORARY DISCUSSION SERIES

Death and Immortality
in the Religions
of the World

Death and Immortality in the Religions of the World

EDITED BY
PAUL AND LINDA BADHAM

A NEW ERA BOOK

PARAGON HOUSE

NEW YORK

Published in the United States by
Paragon House Publishers
2 Hammarskjöld Plaza
New York, New York 10017

A New Ecumenical Research Association Book.

Library of Congress Cataloging-in-Publication Data

Death and Immortality in The Religions of The World.

(God, The Contemporary Discussion Series)
Bibliography: p.
Includes index.
1. Future life—Comparative studies.
2. Death—Religious aspects—Comparative studies.
3. Immortality—Comparative studies. I. Badham,
Paul, II. Badham, Linda. III. Series.
BL535.D43   1987   291.2′3   86-30253
ISBN 0-913757-54-3
ISBN 0-913757-67-5 (pbk)

Contents

Death and Immortality in the Religions of the World: An Editorial Survey

PAUL and LINDA BADHAM

Introduction

All the major religions of the world have held a belief in some form of life after death. But is it possible to draw these beliefs into a unity and talk of "the teaching of world religions" concerning a future life? Moreover, if such a unity can be found can it stand in the face of contemporary philosophical analyses, and can it cohere with the well-established facts that the natural sciences have discovered? Seeking answers to various questions, an International Conference on "Death and Immortality in the Religions of the World" took place in Seoul, Korea, in August 1984, under the auspices of the 4th International God Conference. The chapters of this volume grew out of some of the papers presented there.

The first stage in this investigation was to establish just what it is that the major world religions currently teach, since this may well differ from the traditional understanding of their doctrines. To this end, we felt it important to include presentations by exponents who are from within the traditions that they describe; and where there are significant differences between various forms of a particular tradition, we have sought to obtain representatives of more than one view.

What the World Religions Teach

We begin with Kofi Asare Opoku who gives us a comprehensive overview of African tribal religious beliefs about the nature of human beings and their ultimate destiny. Essentially a mind-body dualism is presupposed, such that the human soul (*Okra*) has a divine origin and destiny. The *Okra* both preexists the physical embodiment and survives—in an incorporeal state—the body's dissolution at death. Moreover, a two-way interaction between the living and the dead is not only possible but also forms a significant element in the religion and culture of African tribal society. Some notion of divine judgment may be found, but it is seldom accompanied by belief in heaven and hell, or any kind of systematic eschatology.

We move onto Rabbi Dan Cohn-Sherbok's historical survey of Judaism. He shows that Jewish belief passed from the notion of a vague, shadow world of the dead through the idea of physical resurrection to belief in the immortality of the soul. Latterly, however, there has been a growth of a this-worldly emphasis, so that the hereafter is no longer central to Jewish life and thought. Cohn-Sherbok observes that belief in personal survival of death arose in response to the moral requirements of justice, and that the partial eclipse of a firm belief in a future life poses serious problems for contemporary Jewish theodicy.

The next two chapters describe contemporary Christian belief from two very different perspectives. Paul Badham argues that life after death is a foundational Christian belief necessarily required for the coherence of Christian theism. The expression of this belief requires both the doctrine of the resurrection of the body and the immortality of the soul. A case is made for the indispensability of the notion of the soul as providing the essential link between the person who dies and the person who is raised from the dead. Thomas McGowan takes a very different line in that he repudiates the concept of the soul and offers a radical reinterpretation of the Christian hope. He summarizes the views of some contemporary Roman Catholic writers who suggest that death is not to be seen as a curse but rather that, in the sacrament of death, each individual can attain consummation in eternal life. McGowan claims that Christianity offers a new and different life rather than a mere continuation of something like this one.

Two Islamic papers continue the discussion of "Abrahamic" religion. Sulayman Nyang draws our attention to the centrality in Islam of belief in life after death coupled with divine judgment as taught in the Quran. The good will go to paradise while sinners suffer in hell until Allah grants them mercy. Belief in the soul, created by Allah, is implicit in Islam, but we can know little concerning its nature or about the life it will lead hereafter. Salih Tug explores some of the implications of Quranic teaching as expounded by al-Ghazali. Tug suggests that, in this life, the human soul develops from a level of simple consciousness to spirituality, and that unless it reaches a certain level of development it cannot enter heavenly life. A person's state of mind at the moment of death is crucially important since change is not possible thereafter, and hence a "bad ending" is much to be feared. After death, the soul waits in Barzakh for resurrection to heaven or hell and, during this time, its thoughts will be a direct result of the life the person led on earth. After the final judgment, the souls of the righteous go to heaven while "diseased" souls are sent to hell, which is to be thought of as a "spiritual hospital" for the cure of such souls.

Turning to the Hindu tradition, Mariasusai Dhavamony provides us with a detailed account of what the various sacred scriptures of Hinduism have taught concerning death and immortality. He describes in turn the Rig Veda, Upanishads, Law Books, Mahabarata, Bhagavad Gita, Puranas, and the teaching of Mahatma Gandhi. While there are significant differences between the teachings from these various sources, the dominant trend is towards a belief that the true self (*Atman*) is unborn and never dies, and that the ultimate goal of the human spirit is to escape a continual cycle of birth, death, and rebirth and attain either absorption into the Absolute or union with God. R. Balasubramanian, on the other hand, concentrates on the Advaita-Vedanta school, which in contrast to other forms of Hinduism, teaches that immortality can be attained in this life and does not have to wait for a life beyond death because true knowledge is attainable in the present life. Nonetheless, belief in transmigration is an integral part of Advaita-Vedanta. What survives the death of the 'gross' body is a complex of the changeless and eternal 'self' together with the 'subtle' body; and it is this complex that provides continuity between successive lives. Only true knowledge of the 'self' is the key to release from the cycle of reincarnation.

Kindred views are expressed by Saeng Chandra-Ngarm in his exposition of Theravada Buddhism. A being exists in the form of a "life process" that flows endlessly on through successive reincarnations. At bodily death, a "connecting psyche" leaves the corpse, but it will enter into a new body (not necessarily human) as long as "ignorance" of the true nature of life remains. If however an individual achieves "intuitive insight," then that person becomes an "arahant," that is one who has experienced nirvana in this life; and when an arahant dies, his or her 'mental element' merges with the cosmic nirvana, achieving eternal existence.

3

Some Western Responses

The first nine chapters in this volume may be seen as accounts of beliefs about death and a future life within particular religious traditions. The remaining five authors discuss the issues in the light of philosophical analysis and/or the findings of modern science, both natural and paranormal.

Bruce Reichenbach provides a critique of Buddhist beliefs. He suggests that it is not clear how exactly the notion of rebirth is to be understood since Buddhists seem to affirm some sort of continuity—yet not an identity—between successive rebirths. Moreover, he argues that the doctrine of karma conflicts with the belief that the notion of self is a fiction. Finally, he contends that the karmic activity, which is supposed to provide an explanation for our experience of individual selves in this life, does not adequately underpin the notion of continuity, which ideas of rebirth demand, and that even if it did, mere continuity of karma is not sufficient to provide grounds for ascribing moral responsibility.

Linda Badham uses the philosophical implications of modern science to argue that the Christian hope for life after death is subject to numerous problems. She shows why belief in the literal resurrection of the flesh is no longer tenable in the light of modern knowledge and goes on to show that the recreation of a quasi-physical replica is unsatisfactory because it lacks an adequate principle of continuity between this life and the next. Hence, Christians need some concept of soul to supply the requisite link between lives. However, she argues, when such a concept is explicated, it cannot bear the weight that it must bear if it is to supply the necessary identity link. Finally, she gives a brief consideration to the alleged empirical evidence for the survival of discarnate souls on the basis of near-death studies and argues that, even if one were to embrace an explanation of such phenomena in terms of immaterial souls, that would raise more explanatory difficulties than it would solve.

Antony Flew argues the more radical case that whether or not there is life after death is not even an empirical question. Rather to understand the correct usage of person words and terms like "survive" is sufficient to rule out even the possibility of persons surviving the death of their bodies. Further, he suggests that all attempts to describe coherently what exactly survives death (and counts as the "real me") fail. Belief in the reconstitution of the body falls foul of the replica problem; astral bodies are paradoxical precisely because they must be both sufficiently substantial to be identifiable and reidentifiable and yet also sufficiently unsubstantial to slip away unnoticed at death; and since problems of the identification of immaterial souls are, Flew suggests, insoluble, there is no way to give content to the notion that persons can live after death. Finally, Flew criticizes claims that paranormal phenomena supply empirical evidence for the existence of disembodied persons, concluding that the very concepts of "psi" are just as much involved with the human body as are those of other human capacities and interests.

But just what is the nature of this paranormal data? Arthur Berger begins by describing some of the reasons for resistance to survival evidence and goes on to note the relation between religion and this evidence. He then surveys six types of the latest prima facie survival evidence: physical phenomena such as levitation, poltergeists, electronic voice phenomena, reincarnation, out-of-the-body experiences, visions of the dying, and drop-in communicators. However compelling some of the cases cited may seem, Berger points out that alternative explanations to the survival hypothesis can rarely, if ever, be ruled out completely. With this in mind, the Survival Research Foundation in Florida is setting up experiments which, if successful, would not be subject to these alternative explanations (such as the Super ESP hypothesis). Berger concludes that although materialists may continue to resist survival evidence, dualists will realize that no science or philosophy that ignores the evidence that human survival of death may indeed be a reality can stand for long.

Finally, we come to a chapter that is as concerned with Western attitudes to death, as with prospects for a future life. David Lorimer gives us an historical survey of ideas about death and the hereafter in Western thought from the Old Testament, through various religious and secular ideas, to those of the present day. Concerning life after death, he argues that paranormal data supply a real challenge to current Western materialism. Concerning death itself, he suggests that characteristically in the West, death has been almost a forbidden topic, so that a dying person is subject to a conspiracy of silence about his impending death and that modern funerals and attitudes to mourning have represented an evasion and denial of the reality of death. Lorimer contends that a right understanding of death (and hence questions relating to the meaning of life) should lead people to an integrated and more compassionate perspective.

5

Towards a Possible Synthesis

In the face of the wide diversity of views expressed in this book, it may seem reckless to suggest that any future synthesis might be possible at all. And it must be acknowledged from the outset that no world-view based on the religious experience of the human race is likely to commend itself to future generations unless it can come to terms with, and find satisfactory responses to, the challenges of philosophical analysis and scientific knowledge.

Yet we remain hopeful that a global perspective on the issues of death and immortality may indeed emerge and present a coherent and intelligible account of a possible future hope, which will draw insights from both the religious and the secular experience of the human race. Let us, therefore, consider what elements in the teachings of the world religions might go towards this future global perspective.

The first element in this scheme might be the unanimous testimony of the world religions that belief in an eternal destiny is necessary to any concept of human life serving any larger purpose than the fulfillment of the immediate aspirations we set ourselves. This religious insight is supported by the parallel secular response of some twentieth century artists, musicians, and playwrights who portray life as literally absurd precisely because no future vision appears available to them.[1]

But this pessimistic view is by no means universally shared. For other contemporary thinkers have argued that it is perfectly possible for individuals to find adequate fulfillment in the limited tasks and goals they set themselves within the possibilities perceived as open to them.[2] And this view is not simply a modern one but found expression more than two thousand years ago in the sober judgment of Ecclesiastes that "life has no meaning" and that "the best thing anyone can do is to eat and drink and enjoy what one has worked for," find fulfillment in work and marriage, and not "worry about how short life is." (Ecclesiastes 3:9, 5:18, 10:9, 5:20).

But there is a more radical religious response to the claim that a future life gives our present life meaning and purpose, for implicit in such a belief is the notion that this purpose is God's purpose for us. Yet to live a life in order to accord with the purposes of another, far from being the ultimate in human fulfillment, is potentially debasing since it removes from the individual the freedom to find satisfying goals for him- or her-self. Such a life amounts to perpetual religious immaturity. And indeed, Don Cupitt goes so far as to argue that "it is spiritually important that one should *not* believe in life after death but should instead strive to attain the goal of the spiritual life in history."[3]

Clearly such a view runs completely contrary to those elements in the religious experience of mankind that suggest, with Christianity, that God's service is "perfect freedom" or with Islam that only in "submission" to the will of Allah do we find our true selfhood, or with the Bhakti way in Hinduism that "loving devotion" to God's service is the way to human fulfillment. And in so far as these perspectives remain dominant it is likely that the religions of the world may continue to see belief in life after death as essential to a meaningful existence.

A second and arguably more important element, which seems common to the major religious traditions, is the belief that human beings are not merely creatures of flesh and blood but are composed of a physical and nonphysical element. The latter supplies the connecting link between this life and the next. Moreover there seems broad agreement that in the stage immediately following death this connecting principle lives in a mind-dependent world, even though all the religions we consider here (except possibly the African) see this as an essentially temporary stage before resurrection or reincarnation. We may note too that some notion of judgment according to the nature of our deeds in this life is present in the major religious traditions. But in contrast to earlier times in which the punishments of hell were emphasized, we may note a distinct playing-down or even rejection of such a notion, except perhaps as a temporary and reformatory stage in man's spiritual evolution. Finally, the religions of the East look forward to an ultimate destiny in which the true self is either absorbed into, or united with, God or the Ultimate in "bliss unspeakable,"[4] and this vision does not seem significantly different from that of those Christian mystics who see their final state in terms of utter oneness with God in the beatific vision. Hence, it seems entirely plausible to point to an underlying framework of belief concerning a future state in which there is already considerable agreement within mankind's religious heritage.[5]

We may note also that a significant undercurrent in religious thought stresses the importance of attaining "immortality" in this life. But this need not be interpreted as an alternative to belief in survival of bodily death for in many religious traditions it serves rather as a ground for such belief.

As to whether life after death is a realistic possibility in the light of modern knowledge, it seems to us that this hinges on belief in the reality of some essentially nonphysical part in human beings that can legitimately be identified as the "real self." Western philosophy seriously challenges the coherence of such a claim, and the findings of the natural sciences place human beings firmly within the natural order. Yet serious study of paranormal phenomena is at least suggestive of the reality and potential survival of such an immaterial entity, and this lends strong support to what seems a nigh universal religious intuition.

NOTES

1. Cf. Martin Esslin, *Absurd Drama* (Harmondsworth: Penguin, 1965), p. 13.

2. Cf. Kurt Baier, "The Meaning of Life," in Peter Angeles *Critiques of God* (New York: Prometheus, 1976).

3. Don Cupitt, *Taking Leave of God* (London: SCM, 1980), p. 10.

4. Cf. discussion of this in Rudolf Otto, *The Idea of the Holy* (Harmondsworth: Penguin, 1917, 1959), p. 53.

5. Cf. John Hick, *Death and Eternal Life* (London: Collins, 1976), chap. 21.

2

Death and Immortality in the African Religious Heritage

KOFI ASARE OPOKU

Every culture seeks to provide meaningful answers to the ultimate questions about human existence and destiny, and these answers are born out of the experiences of the people within that cultural milieu and their mature reflection on those experiences. The important consideration here is that the answers given satisfy the needs of the human spirit and provide meaning and significance to human life and destiny.

The problem of life and death has received profound attention in the African cultural heritage, and has been the basis of much philosophical reflection and religious insight. Both life and death are viewed as given by the Creator, and once life is given, death must inevitably follow, as the Akan of Ghana say: *"obra twa 'wu"*: life must needs end in death, each person lives towards death.

African mythology abounds with innumerable accounts of how death entered the world, and although these stories may at first sight appear to be "mere" accounts or myths about the origin of death, they have a level of profundity at which they clearly inform us of the conception of the human condition held by the narrators of the myths. In some of the myths, human beings did not seem to have had a choice in the matter of death: two messengers were sent by God, one with the message of life and the other with the message of death.[1] The messenger with the message of death reached mankind first and the one with the message of life arrived rather too late.

In other myths however, human beings had a choice between immortality and mortality, and they chose the latter. The reason for their choice was clear: it conformed to the essential condition of mankind. A Nupe (Nigeria) myth recounts:

In the beginning God created tortoises, men and stones, and, with the exception of the stones, he made them male and female and provided

9

them with life. However, none of the species reproduced. One day the tortoise wanted to have descendants and asked this of God, whose response was that he had granted life to the tortoise and to men but had not given them permission to have children. At this time, the story adds, men did not die; when they became old they were automatically rejuvenated. The tortoise renewed his appeal and God warned him against the danger of death which would result from a positive response on his part. But the tortoise took no notice and pressed his request. He was joined by men, who had decided to have children even at the risk of death, while the stones refused to join in with them. Thus God granted tortoises and men the ability to have posterity, and death entered the world, but the stones remained unaffected.[2]

Clearly, a choice of immortality would have led to a rejection of the human condition, and the choice of mortality affirms our nature as human beings.

Causes of Death and Religious Explanations of Death

African notions of death and immortality cannot be understood without first taking into account African conceptions of human personality.[3] Broadly speaking, the human being is made up of material and immaterial factors and either of them can cause death. There is a profoundly interactionist view of man that holds that the material and immaterial parts of man have a causal influence on each other; in other words, what happens to the soul of man affects the body, and similarly, what happens to the body affects the condition of the soul. Death, therefore, has both physical and nonphysical, or physiological and psychological causes. Since the human being is considered to be a part of the whole universe, the visible and invisible influences that the rest of creation may have on him or her are seriously taken into consideration.

Physical causes of death may include childbirth, disease, famine, injury from wild animals, accidents or injury sustained during communal or personal disputes, execution, or old age. In addition to these, there are other kinds of physical causes that modern life has added to the stock of causes. But these physical explanations alone do not adequately explain all of the phenomenon of death, and this is where religious explanations come in.[4] And in this regard, the relationship with God, the ancestors or living-dead and spirits, and fellow members of the community are of crucial significance, for these nonphysical considerations can also cause death.

A curse by an elderly person could lead to suffering and death; those who are selfish and do not have the interest of the community at heart may suffer physically, even to the point of death. The breaking of taboos and established standards of religious behavior, dishonoring the ancestors, breaking a binding oath—all may result in physical disability and death. Witchcraft, magic, and sorcery are also recognized as causes of physical suffering and death. All of these religious explanations help to answer the question why, and enable people to accept, and to come to terms with, what would otherwise remain inexplicable.

The Meaning of Death

When death occurs, the immaterial part (the soul) separates itself from the body and survives the experience of death. The survival of a part of man after death is a certainty that is not doubted as much as the fact of human existence is not doubted, and is a stark reality. In African thought, this indestructible part of man has a divine origin and is sacred, and the attribute of immortality accorded to it stems from the fact that it is considered to be a spiritual substance or entity, and not "a bundle of qualities or perceptions," which would mean that nothing would be left when the qualities and perceptions are removed. On the contrary, there remains, after death, a sub-stratum or "owner" of those qualities.[5]

To give an example from the Akan of Ghana, a human being possesses an *okra,* the part of *Onyame,* God, in every person, which is the essential part of being human.[6] Animals do not possess *okra.* The *okra* is divine in origin and has an antemundane existence and a postmortem existence. It is the presence of the *okra* that makes one a living human being and its departure from the body signifies death. At death, therefore, the *okra* returns to its source and is reunited with *Onyame.* Hence the Akan say, *"Onyame bewu na mawu"*: could God die, I will die, or I shall only die if God dies, which is a reference to the *okra,* the undying part of the human person. It is inconceivable to the Akan to imagine that the Creator could die, therefore the *okra* does not die when one dies physically. An Akan maxim also epigrammatically expresses the idea that when a man dies he is not (really) dead: *Onipa wu a, na onwui."* In other words, there is something that is eternal and indestructible in man, which continues to exist after death in the land of spirits.

The idea of death as a *return* underlies the funeral rites. The body of the person is prepared as if the person were going on a journey, and some personal belongings are put in the coffin so that the deceased may take them along. These may include the sponge, soap, comb, and towel with which the deceased was given his or her last bath, a cup or calabash for drinking water, some pieces of coins for buying things along the way, and some assorted clothing of which the deceased was particularly fond. Messages are also given to the deceased to carry to relatives in the other world, just as one sends messages with a person going on a journey. These messages are not only given verbally but are also contained in many of the dirges that are sung during funerals.[7]

Sending messages with the deceased presupposes the ability of the living to communicate with the dead, and this communication link is maintained even after burial. The deceased is believed to be united with his or her relatives who live in the abode of the dead, which is invisible but very close to that of the living. Death does not bring the deceased to a complete end. In a sense, it is only a channel through which the deceased passes to continue to live, albeit in the form of a spirit. But the dead retain features that describe them in physical terms. They maintain their identity, and there is no merging with the Absolute. In fact the deceased person:

. . . retains most of the other features which were used to describe him during his physical existence . . . he retains his personal name, and his relatives continue to recognize him as one of the members of the family. Although he no longer lives in the flesh, he continues to hold the social, political and religious status which he held while he lived physically.[8]

But although the deceased is believed to continue to live and to interact with others, there is an important sense in which death brings an end to a person's physical participation in the community. The deceased ceases to be a physical being and separates from the community, and the funeral rites that are performed are symbols of separation between the dead and the living.

This physical separation, which interrupts normal life and robs families and the society of its members, largely accounts for the negative sentiments and attitudes towards death. Thus death is seen as a wicked destroyer, a killer and an implacable enemy who frustrates human effort; it drives men to sorrow and despair, and has no respect for intelligence, position, or beauty. The sense of frustration and utter helplessness in the face of death is expressed in a Yoruba funeral dirge:

If death had requested for money, we would have given him money; if death had requested for meat, we would have bought ram for him. We made sacrifices without ceasing, yet we do not see the medicine that will prevent death from killing man. Death has done a wicked thing. Death has done a wicked thing.[9]

But the separation is only physical and does not terminate the life of the individual, and the expression of anxiety, frustration, despondency, and utter helplessness soon gives way to a more positive and lasting attitude, since the separation marks the beginning of the prolongation of the life of the individual and a change in status from a lesser to a higher authority.

A common practice among members of the immediate family of the deceased during funerals is to shave off their hair as a symbol of separation, showing that one of their members has been separated from them. But new hair will grow back, and that is an indication of the profound belief that death does not destroy life, since the growth of new hair indicates that life continues to spring up.[10]

After-death and Immortality

Death represents a transition from corporeal to incorporeal life in the religious heritage of Africa and the incorporeal life is taken to be as real as the corporeal. This attitude was held with such utter conviction that little anxiety was shown in the face of death. An authentication of this attitude could be found in Benin where servants and persons especially indulged by the king would compete with each other for the privilege of being buried alive with the body of the king when he died so that they could attend on him in the next world.[11] This firm belief in the reality of life after death represents a fundamental antidote to the threat of human extinction and the scare of nothingness, which have jointly "conspired" to render life utterly meaningless to many a modern person. In the African understanding, death does not rob life of meaning, on the contrary, it gives greater depth of meaning to life by prolonging it on the spiritual plane.[12]

Because the dead continue to live, communication with them is possible; and there are culturally accepted ways of maintaining the relationship between the living and the dead. Prayers, libations, offerings, and the observation of other religious rites are of crucial importance in this regard. And furthermore, as Zahan wrote:

Tradition for Africans is, then, a means of communicating between the dead and the living. It belongs to a vast network of communications between the two worlds which embodies "prayer" offerings, sacrifices and myths. In this relationship tradition possesses a real originality. At times it is direct, that is, it precludes any intermediary between man and the beyond. . . .At other times tradition is indirect, and in this case the human being perceives more or less clearly the reasons for his religious actions.

Whether in the form of one or the other of these two types of communication, tradition as the "word" of the dead remains the most vital link between the living and the dead.[13]

The relationship is not one-sided, for the dead, too, have a role to play in keeping it alive and real. It is a reciprocal relationship, and death, therefore, does not put a stop to one's obligation to the family and community. The dead have a duty to protect, intervene, and mediate on behalf of the living, and as it is believed that death increases one's powers, the dead are able to offer more help or assistance. This underscores the involvement of the dead in the affairs of the living; and the reciprocal permeability of the world of the living and that of the dead is accepted without disputation.

Return of the Dead

It is firmly believed that the dead come back into life and that this is in the nature of things. In African cultural practices the symbolism of death and resurrection or return to life is very pervasive. In the initiation rites, for instance, the neophytes die to their old selves and are born into new persons, they die only to be reborn. In the *Poro* initiation rites of the Mende of Sierra Leone, the young initiates are "swallowed" by the *Poro* spirit, and on the night before the end of the initiation rites, the *Poro* spirit groans like a woman in labor. Kenneth Little explains:

The initiation rite and the whole time spent in the bush which follows it symbolize the change in status. The young initiate is supposed to be "swallowed" by the [*Poro*] spirit when he enters, and separation from his parents and kinsfolk signifies death. The marks on his back are evidence of the spirit's teeth. At the end of his time, he is "delivered" by the spirit and reborn. Thus, the period in the bush marks his transition from boyhood to manhood, and as a result of the experience he emerges a fully fledged member of Mende society.[14]

In the training for the priesthood, the same symbolism prevails. Even mystical ecstasy is a death followed by resurrection.

The Zulu express the belief that the dead are reborn by burying the dead in a squatting position in a symbolic repetition of the position of the embryo in the fetal membrane, and the niche into which the dead is put is called a "navel." The dead person is received in the grave as at birth. But this symbolism also extends to other members of the family, who also participate in the death and resurrection or death and rebirth syndrome. Sundermeier wrote:

> . . . even the mourner is born again. A Zulu widow is only allowed to take baby food at the beginning of the mourning period and is slowly accustomed to a firmer diet. She is washed like a child, later gets the clothes of a bride, and after some last ritual washings which finally wash off death, receives the clothes of a grown-up.[15]

The belief that the dead come back into life and are reborn into their families is given concrete expression in the personal names that are given to children. The Yoruba, for example, have many names that suggest the return of the dead: *Iyabo,* Mother returns; *Yetunde,* Mother comes back a second time; and *Babatunde,* Father has come again. Ewe names that indicate the return of the dead are *Afetogbo,* the master has come back (given to children born after the death of a member of the family); *Degbo,* gone and returned; *Evakpo,* he has ventured to come again; and *Noviegbo,* sister has returned. Not only are parents and grown-ups believed to return; children, too, are believed to do likewise. Hence the Yoruba names, *Omotunde,* child comes back again; and *Omodeinde,* child turns back and is here. There are also other names that express the idea of waking up from sleep, for example, *Babajide,* Father wakes up and is back; and *Babatunji,* Father wakes up again.

The belief in the return of the dead and its concrete expression in personal names suggest the idea of reincarnation, but it is one that differs significantly from the conventional understanding of the word. In African belief, even though a person is said to have returned to earth and to have been reincarnated in his or her grandchildren or great grandchildren, that person nevertheless continues to live in the afterlife and to keep his or her identity. What is reincarnated are some of the dominant characteristics of the ancestor and not his soul. For each soul remains distinct and each birth represents a new soul.

Idowu describes this as a "partial reincarnation," and observes that there are "certain dominant lineage characteristics which keep occurring through births and ensuring the continuity of the vital existence of the family or clan."[16]

The Fate of the Dead

There are areas in Africa where eschatological ideas similar to those in Judaism, Christianity, or Islam are found. The Yoruba, the Dogon, and the LoDagoa (Ghana) provide interesting insights into African eschatological thought. Among the Yoruba, for example, *Olodumare* (God), is believed to mete out judgment to individuals after death and each has to give an account of his or her earthly life before *Olodumare,* who then judges accordingly. The Yoruba say, "All that we do on earth we shall account for kneeling in heaven," and "We shall state our case at the feet of *Olodumare.*"[17] What *Olodumare,* the Searcher of Hearts, who sees and knows everything, and whose judgment is sure and absolutely inescapable, judges is *"iwa,"* character. Man's well-being here on earth depends on his character, his place in the Afterlife is determined by God according to his deserts. And by good character, the Yoruba mean "chastity before marriage, hospitality, generosity, the opposite of selfishness; kindness, justice, truth and rectitude as essential virtues; avoiding stealing; keeping a covenant and avoiding falsehood; protecting the poor and weak, especially women; giving honour and respect to older people, and avoiding hypocrisy."[18]

Those whose earthly life receives the approbation of *Olodumare* are sent to *Orun rere,* where they are reunited with their kin and where there is no sorrow or suffering. Those who enter this good heaven may choose to be reborn into their families. But those who led a bad life on earth will go to *Orun apaadi,* a place of broken potsherds, where it is unbearably hot and dry, and where they will feed on centipedes and earthworms. This is why the Yoruba express the wish in the final words of farewell to a dead person:

Be sure you do not feed on centipedes
Be sure you do not feed on earthworms
What people feed on in *Orun rere*
That you should feed on.[19]

But in most African societies, there is a marked absence of such clear-cut notions of heaven and hell, although there are notions of God judging the soul after death. The Song of Divine Judgment

from the Fon of the Republic of Benin vividly describes God as the
Final Judge:

Life is like a hill,
Mawu, the Creator, made it steep and slippery,
To right and left deep waters surround it,
You cannot turn back once you start to climb.
You must climb with a load on your head.
A man's arms will not help him for it is a trial,
The world is a place of trial.
At the gates of the land of the dead,
You will pass before a searching Judge,
His justice is true and he will examine your feet,
He will know how to find every stain,
Whether visible or hidden under the skin.
If you have fallen on the way, he will know,
If the judge finds no stains on your feet,
Open your belly to joy, for you have overcome
And your belly is clean. [20]

Other African people believe that the dead go to give an account
of their earthly existence before God, and the Akan, for instance,
believe that the *okra* of the deceased goes to give an account of its
life before God and if the *okra* did not complete its destiny, it is sent
back to complete it. There is also the belief that those who led good
lives will join the ancestors, but others will not.

The Bini of Nigeria believe that God has ordered every human
being to make fourteen tours throughout this life, and that the tours
begin at birth and end at death. A person's place in the afterlife is
determined by the way he or she has lived during the fourteen
tours. As Ighodaro wrote:

His purity, his love of his neighbour and God
and his kindness will be taken into account.
A man or woman is not judged until his or her
last journey in this world, and so a person is never
in a position to determine whether he is on his first
or last tour. A man has only to presume that this may
be his last tour, and therefore all the good he can do
now, he must do them, as he may not pass this way again. [21]

Good people become ancestors and ancestorhood is a status that
is attained, and not all who die achieve it. The notion of the ancestor
hinges on important moral, social, and religious considerations,

which make the ancestors into models worthy of emulation. Those who are accorded the status have their family life on earth extended into the supersensible world, and communion and communication are held with them regularly. Through these activities the continuity and identity of the family or community over time is maintained. The world of the dead is part of our world and the afterlife is linked up with the present life of the family or community in a dynamic way.

Absence of Eschatology?

Several writers have commented on the absence of eschatological thinking in African religion. Benjamin Ray wrote:

There is little speculation about "last things"—that is, about the nature of the after life or about immortality or final judgement—for there are no "last things" towards which human life is headed. There is no vision of a culminating "end" to individual lives or to human history in general.[22]

Such viewpoints originate from the attempt, conscious or unconscious, to evaluate African religion and other religions and to view them through the prism of Western religions. This, of course, leads to gross distortions and value judgments that prevent us from fully appreciating the contribution that insights from non-Western religions and, in this particular instance, African traditional religion, can make to the present discussion. It may be worth our while to bear in mind that one cannot fully understand eschatological thinking in Western religions without taking into account the historical experiences of the Jews. As Huston Smith wrote:

Judaism, the foundational religion of the West, was instigated by a concrete historical happening—the Exodus—as the religion of India and China were not. In addition, the basic concepts of Judaism were forged while the Jews, being either displaced or oppressed, were a people in waiting—first to cross over into the promised land, then to return to Jerusalem, then for the coming of the Messiah who was to deliver them. This built into Judaism a future-oriented character that was unique until it was duplicated by Christianity. . . .[23]

The experiences of the African peoples were quite different and their notions about death and the afterlife, as well as about time, must be viewed against their historical and other experiences. It is certainly not so difficult to see why eschatological thinking could be so pronounced in the Judeo-Christian heritage, but having said this, one must hasten to add that notions of a "culminating end" to individual lives or to human history, or about time as irreversibly headed towards a destination and more often than not, to a catastrophic end, are quite contrary to the experiences of other people. And although these eschatological speculations are grounded in faith in God, African views about time and history are also grounded in faith in God. In the African world view, time has no end, neither does the world have an end. The Creator sustains the universe and there is no thought that it will come to an end.[24]

The eschatological ideas of Christianity with respect to the resurrection of the body and life in the Kingdom of God certainly help to relieve the anxiety of believers who are facing death. To a large extent, the resurrection represents a future hope, an event that will occur at the end of time. In the religious heritage of Africa, however, the fate of the dead as it relates to their return to life is a present reality that has been and is still being experienced. It is a realized experience, which is given concrete expression in life, personal names, and rituals. This realized experience, which has already occurred in this life to fulfill our deepest ontological aspirations, it is believed, will continue through time.

The life of the dead is a reality and it does not even depend on the remembrance of them by those who are living on earth, Mbiti asserts.[25] On the contrary, the dead have their own independent existence, and they do not continue to live because they are remembered in the hearts of those who have been left behind. As Idowu wrote:

. . . they do not for any reason fade into nothing or lapse into any kind of durational retirement. In the invocation of ancestors in certain African localities, the liturgy embraces those remembered and unremembered, those known and unknown. It is often said specifically, "we cannot remember all of you by name, nevertheless, we invoke you all." Further, ancestors connected with certain professions like medicine, crafts or priesthood are mentioned as far back as the first one who initiated the practice. . . . During annual festivals, or special rituals, ancestors are traced as far back as the beginning of things.[26]

African ideas about death and immortality are not intended to encourage the illusion of escaping the reality of death; on the contrary, while living in full awareness of our mortality, we are provided with its real meaning and significance within the context of the totality of human life, as well as with the tools to overcome our mortality. The genius of the African humanity reveals itself in the ideas about death and immortality even when we live in full cognizance of the transience of bodily existence. Life is not restricted to bodily existence, for the soul, which is distinct from the body and which is identified with the conscious self, continues to live after the death and disintegration of the physical body.[27]

═══ NOTES ═══

1. See Hans Abrahamsson, *The Origin of Death*, Studia Ethnographica Upsalensia, vol. 3 (Uppsala: Almquist and Wiksell, 1951); also Dominique Zahan, *The Religion, Spirituality and Thought of Traditional Africa* (Chicago: University of Chicago Press, 1979), pp. 36–52.

2. Leo Frobenius, *Atlantis*, vol. 12 (Jena: E. Diedrichs, 1928), p. 140, as cited by Dominique Zahan, *The Religion, Spirituality and Thought of Traditional Africa*, p. 41.

3. For a full discussion of African concepts of human personality, see Kofi Asare Opoku, *West African Traditional Religion* (Singapore: F. E. P. International, 1978) pp. 91–100; also E. B. Idowu, *Olodumare: God in Yoruba Belief* (London: Longman, 1962), chap. 13–14; also W. E. Abraham, *The Mind of Africa* (London: Weidenfeld and Nicolson, 1962).

4. For a discussion of African Concepts of Causality see J. O. Sodipo, "Notes on the Concept of Cause and Change in Yoruba Traditional Thought," *Second Order: An African Journal of Philosophy*, no. 2 (1973), pp. 12–20.

5. See Kwame Gyeke, "Akan Concept of Person," *International Philosophical Quarterly*, vol. 18, no. 3 (September 1978): pp. 277–287.

6. See Opoku, *West African Traditional Religion*, pp. 94–96.

7. See Joseph H. Nketia, *Funeral Dirges of the Akan People* (Achimoto, 1955).

8. J. Mugambi and N. Kirima, *The African Religious Heritage* (Nairobi: Oxford University Press, 1979), p. 101.

9. Wande Abimbola, "Burial of the Dead Among the Yoruba," *Staff Seminar Papers*, School of African and Asian Studies, (Nigeria: University of Lagos, 1968–69), pp. 108–9.

10. See John S. Mbiti, *An Introduction to African Religion* (London: Heinemann, 1975), p. 115.

11. See James G. Frazer, *The Golden Bough*, vol. 4 (London: Macmillan, 1937), p. 104; also David Lorimer, *Survival: Body, Mind and Death in the Light of Psychic Experience* (London: Routledge and Kegan Paul, 1984), p. 27.

12. Mbiti refers to the dead as "Living-dead," a term which vividly conveys the

idea that life continues after death; see his *African Religions and Philosophy* (London: Heinemann, 1969).

13. Zahan, *The Religion, Spirituality and Thought of Traditional Africa*, p. 119.

14. Kenneth Little, *The Mende of Sierra Leone* (London: Routledge and Kegan Paul, 1967), p. 119.

15. Theo Sundermeier, "Death Rites Supporting Life: The Process of Mourning in Africa," *African Theological Journal*, vol. 9, no. 3 (November 1980), p. 60; also, A. I. Berglund, *Zulu and Symbolism*, unpublished doctoral dissertation, Kapstadt, 1972.

16. E. B. Idowu, *Olodumare: God in Yoruba Belief*, p. 159.

17. E. B. Idowu, p. 199.

18. Idowu, p. 154.

19. Idowu, p. 199.

20. John V. Taylor, *The Primal Vision* (London: S. C. M., 1963), p. 179.

21. S. O. Ighodaro, "The Benin High God," *Staff Seminar Papers*, School of African and Asian Studies (Nigeria: University of Lagos, 1967–68), pp. 43–61.

22. Benjamin C. Ray, *African Religions: Symbol, Ritual and Community* (Englewood Cliffs, N. J.: Prentice Hall, 1976), p. 140.

23. One could also add the religions of Africa, like China and India, as not instigated by a concrete historical happening. T. William Hall, ed., "Accents of the World Religions," in *Introduction to the Study of Religion* (New York: Harper and Row, 1978), p. 129.

24. For further reading, see Kofi Asare Opoku, "The World View of the Akan," in *Tarikh 26*, vol. 7, no. 2, Historical Society of Nigeria, (London: Longman, 1982), pp. 61–73.

25. John S. Mbiti, *African Religions and Philosophy* (London: Heinemann, 1969), p. 33.

26. E. B. Idowu, *African Traditional Religion: A Definition* (London: S. C. M., 1973), p. 188.

27. David Lorimer, *Survival: Body, Mind and Death in the Light of Psychic Experience*, pp. 9–28.

SELECT BIBLIOGRAPHY

Abraham, W. E. *The Mind of Africa*. London: Weidenfeld and Nicolson, 1962.

Abrahamsson, Hans. *The Origin of Death*. Studia Ethnographica Upsalensia, vol. 3. Uppsala: Almquist and Wiksell, 1951.

Baumann, H. *Schopfung und Urzeit der Menschen im Mythos des Afrikanischen Völer.* Berlin: Dietrich. Reimer, 1936.

Damman, E. *Die Relgionen Afrikas*. Stuttgart: W. Kohlhammer Verlag, 1963.

Fadipe, N. A. *The Sociology of the Yoruba*. Ibadan: Ibadan University Press, 1970.

Forde, Daryll, ed. *African Worlds*. London: Oxford University Press, 1954.

Fortes, Meyer. *Oedipus and Job in West African Religion*. Cambridge: Cambridge University Press, 1959.

Griaule, Marcel. *Conversations with Ogotemmeli*. London: Oxford University Press, 1965.

Herskovits, Melville J., and Frances S. *Dahomeyan Narrative*. Evanston, Il: Northwestern University Press, 1965.

Idowu, E. B. *Olodumare: God in Yoruba Belief*. London: Longman, 1962.

———. *African Traditional Religion: A Definition*. London: S. C. M., 1973.

Little, Kenneth. *The Mende of Sierra Leone*. London: Routledge and Kegan Paul, 1967.

Lorimer, David. *Survival: Body, Mind and Death in the Light of Psychic Experience*. London: Routledge and Kegan Paul, 1984.

Mbiti, John S. *African Religions and Philosophy*. London: Heinemann, 1969.

———. *An Introduction to African Religion*. London: Heinemann, 1975.

Mugambi, J., and N. Kirima. *The African Religious Heritage*. Nairobi: Oxford University Press, 1979.

Opoku, Kofi Asare. *West African Traditional Religion*. Singapore: F. E. P. International, 1978.

———. "The World View of the Akan," in *Tarikh* 26, vol. 7, no. 2, Historical Society of Nigeria, London: Longman, 1982.

Parrinder, Geoffrey. *West African Psychology*. London: Lutherworth Press, 1951.

———. *West African Religion*. 2nd ed. London: Epworth Press, 1951.

———. *African Mythology*. London: Paul Hamlyn, 1967.

Death and Immortality in the African Religious Heritage

Ray, Benjamin C. *African Religions: Symbol, Ritual and Community.* Englewood Cliffs, N. J.: Prentice Hall, 1976.

Sawyer, Harry, and W. T. Harris. *The Springs of Mende Belief and Conduct.* Freetown: Sierra Leone University Press, 1968.

Sawyer, Harry. *God: Ancestor or Creator?* London: Longman, 1970.

Taylor, John V. *The Primal Vision.* London: S. C. M., 1963.

Zahan, Dominique. *The Religion, Sprituality and Thought of Traditional Africa.* Chicago: University of Chicago Press, 1979.

Death and Immortality in the Jewish Tradition

DANIEL COHN-SHERBOK

The Evolution of the Doctrine of the Afterlife

Until long after the exile, the Jewish people shared the view of the entire ancient world that the dead continue to exist in a shadowy realm of the nether world where they live a dull, ghostly existence. According to K. Kohler, throughout the Biblical period no ethical idea yet permeated this conception, and no attempt was made to transform the nether world into a place of divine judgment, of recompense for the good and evil deeds accomplished on earth.[1] This was so because Biblical Judaism stressed the importance of attaining a complete and blissful life with God during earthly life; there was no need to transfer the purpose of existence to the Hereafter. In the words of R. H. Charles, "So long indeed as Yahweh's jurisdiction was conceived as limited to this life, a Yahwistic eschatology of the individual could not exist; but when at last Israel reached the great truth of monotheism, the way was prepared for the moralization of the future no less than that of the present."[2] It was only then under social, economic, and political oppression that pious Jews looked beyond their bitter disappointment with this world to a future beyond the grave when virtue would receive its due reward and vice its befitting punishment.[3]

Thus, though there is no explicit reference to the Hereafter in the Old Testament, a number of expressions are used to refer to the realm of the dead. In Psalms 28:1 and 88:5, *bor* refers to a pit. In Psalms 6:6 as well as in Job 28:22 and 30:23, *mavet* is used in a similar sense. In Psalms 22:16, the expression *afar mavet* refers to the dust of death; in Exodus 15:2 and Jonah 2:7 the earth (*eretz*) is described as swallowing up the dead, and in Ezekiel 31:14 the expression *eretz tachtit* refers to the nether parts of the earth where the dead dwell. Finally, the word *she'ol* is frequently used to refer to the dwelling of the dead in the netherworld.[4] In addition, the words *ge ben hinnom*,[5] *ge hinnom,*[6] and *ge*[7] are used to refer to a cursed valley associated with fire and death where, according to Jeremiah, children were sacrificed as burnt offerings to Moloch and Baal.[8] In later rabbinic literature, the word ordinarily used for "hell" (*Gehinnom*) is derived from these names.

Though these passages point to a Biblical conception of an Afterlife, there is no indication of a clearly defined concept; it is only later in the Greco-Roman world that such a notion began to take shape. The notion of a future world in which the righteous would be compensated for the ills they suffered in this life was prompted by a failure to justify the ways of God by any other means. According to Biblical theodicy, men were promised rewards for obeying God's law and punishments were threatened for disobedience. Rewards included health, children, rainfall, a good harvest, peace, and prosperity; punishments consisted of disease, war, pestilence, failure of crops, poverty, and slavery. As time passed, however, it became clear that life did not operate in accordance with such a tidy scheme. In response to this dilemma, the rabbis developed a doctrine of reward and punishment in the Hereafter. Such a belief helped Jews to cope with suffering in this life, and it also explained, if not the presence of evil in the world, then at least the worthwhileness of creation despite the world's ills.[9]

Given that there is no explicit belief in eternal salvation in the Bible,[10] the rabbis of the post-Biblical period were faced with the difficulty of proving that the doctrine of resurrection of the dead is contained in Scripture, which they regarded as authoritative. To do this they employed certain principles of exegesis that are based on the assumption that every word in the Pentateuch was transmitted by God to Moses. Thus, for example, R. Elezar, the son of R. Jose, claimed to have refuted the Sectarians who maintained that resurrection is not a Biblical doctrine: "I said to them: 'You have falsified your Torah . . . For ye maintain that resurrection is not a Biblical doctrine, but it is written (in Numbers 15:31ff), "Because he hath despised the word of the Lord, and hath broken his commandments, that soul shall utterly be cut off, his iniquity shall be upon him. Now, seeing that he shall utterly be cut off in this world, when shall his iniquity be upon him? Surely in the next world.""[11]

Again, R. Meir asked, "Whence do we know resurrection from the Torah?"; from the verse, "Then shall Moses and the children of Israel sing this song unto the Lord" (Exodus 15:1). Not "sang," but "sing" is written. Since Moses and the children of Israel did not sing a second time in this life, the text must mean that they will sing after resurrection. Likewise it is written, "Then shall Joshua build an altar unto the Lord God of Israel" (Joshua 8:30). Not "build" but "shall build" is stated. Thus, resurrection is intimated in the Torah.[12] Similarly, R. Joshua b. Levi said: "Where is resurrection derived from the Torah?" From the verse, "Blessed are they that dwell in thy house; they shall ever praise thee." (Psalms 84:5). The text does not say "praised thee" but "shall praise thee." Thus we learn resurrection from the Torah.[13]

The Concept of Heaven

The principle qualification for entrance to heaven (Gan Eden) is to lead a good life in accordance with God's law. Conversely, the rabbis point out that by disobeying God's law one forfeits a share in the World to Come and is doomed to eternal punishment in hell (Gehinnom).[14] According to the Mishnah, there are various categories of sinners who will be damned: (1) He who says there is no resurrection of the dead prescribed in the Torah; (2) He who says that the Torah is not from heaven; (3) a heretic; (4) A reader of heretical books and one that utters a charm over a wound; (5) He who pronounces God's name by supplying vowels; (6) The generation of the flood; (7) The generation of Babel; (8) The men of Sodom; (9) The twelve spies; (10) The ten lost tribes; (11) The children of the wicked; (12) The people of an apostate city; (13) Those who have been executed by a rabbinical court unless they confess their sins before death.[15] On the basis of the discussion of these categories in the Babylonian Talmud and the remarks of sages elsewhere in rabbinic literature, Maimonides in his *Guide for the Perplexed* drew up a different list, which has been regarded by many as authoritative,[16] of those who have no share in Heaven.

The World to Come is itself divided into several stages: first, there is the time of the Messianic redemption. According to the Babylonian Talmud, the Messianic Age (Yemot Hamashiah) is to take place on earth after a period of decline and calamity and will result in a complete fulfillment of every human wish. Peace will reign throughout nature; Jerusalem will be rebuilt; and at the close of this era, the dead will be resurrected and rejoined with their souls, and a final judgment will come upon all mankind. Those who are judged righteous will enter into heaven (Gan Eden), which is portrayed in various ways in rabbinic literature.[17] One of the earliest descriptions is found in Midrash Konen, and the following extract is a representative sample of the type of elaboration in rabbinic sources:

The Gan Eden at the east measures 800,000 years (at ten miles per day or 3,650 miles per year.). There are five chambers for various classes of the righteous. The first is built of cedar, with a ceiling of transparent crystal. This is the habitation of non-Jews who become true and devoted converts to Judaism. They are headed by Obadiah the prophet and Onkelos the proselyte, who teach them the Law. The second is built of cedar, with a ceiling of fine silver. This is the habitation of the penitents, headed by Manasseh, King of Israel, who teaches them the Law.

The third chamber is built of silver and gold, ornamented with pearls. It is very spacious, and contains the best of heaven and of earth, with spices, fragance and sweet odours. In the centre of this chamber stands the Tree of Life, 500 years high. Under its shadow rest Abraham, Isaac and Jacob, the tribes, those of the Egyptian exodus, and those who died in the wilderness, headed by Moses and Aaron. There are also David and Solomon, crowned, and Chileab, as if living, attending on his father, David. Every generation of Israel is represented except that of Absalom and his confederates. Moses teaches them the Law, and Aaron gives instruction to the priests. The Tree of Life is like a ladder on which the souls of the righteous may ascend and descend. In a conclave above are seated the Patriarchs, the Ten Martyrs, and those who sacrificed their lives for the cause of His Sacred Name. These souls descend daily to the Gan Eden, to join their families and tribes, where they lounge on soft cathedrals studded with jewels. Everyone, according to his excellence, is received in audience to praise and thank the Ever-living God; and all enjoy the brilliant light of the Shekinah. The flaming sword, changing from intense heat to icy cold, and from ice to glowing coals, guards the entrance against living mortals. The size of the sword is ten years. The souls on entering paradise are bathed in the 248 rivulets of balsam and attar.

The fourth chamber is made of olive-wood and is inhabited by those who have suffered for the sake of their religion. Olives typify bitterness in taste and brilliancy in light (olive-oil), symbolizing persecution and its reward.

The fifth chamber is built of precious stones, gold and silver, surrounded by myrrh and aloes. In front of the chamber runs the river Gihon, on whose banks are planted shrubs affording perfume and aromatic incense. There are couches of gold and silver and fine drapery.

This chamber is inhabited by the Messiah of David, Elijah, and the Messiah of Ephraim. In the centre are a canopy made of the cedars of Lebanon, in the style of the Tabernacle, with posts and vessels of silver; and a settee of Lebanon wood with pillars of silver and a seat of gold, the covering thereof of purple. Within rests the Messiah, son of David. "a man of sorrows and acquainted with grief" suffering, and waiting to release Israel from the Exile. Elijah comforts and encourages him to be patient. Every Monday and Thursday, and Sabbath and on holy days the Patriarchs, Moses, Aaron, and others, call on the Messiah and condole with him, in the hope of the fast-approaching end.[18]

The Nature of Hell

As with heaven, we also find extensive and detailed descriptions of hell in Jewish literature. In the Babylonian Talmud, R. Joshua b. Levi deduces the divisions of hell from Biblical quotations: *she'ol, abaddon, be'er shahat, bor sha'on, tit ha-yawen, zel mawet,* and *erez ha-tahtit.* This Talmudic concept of the seven-fold structure of hell is greatly elaborated in midrashic literature. According to one source, it requires 300 years to traverse the height or width or the depth of each division, and it would take 6,300 years to go over a tract of land equal in extent to the seven divisions.[19] Each of these seven divisions of hell is in turn divided into seven subdivisions and in each compartment there are seven rivers of fire, and seven of hail. The width of each is 1,000 ells, its depth 1,000, and its length 300; they flow from each other and are supervised by the Angels of Destruction. Besides, in each compartment there are 7,000 caves, and in each cave there are 7,000 crevices, and in every crevice there are 7,000 scorpions. Every scorpion has 300 rings, and in every ring 7,000 pouches of venom from which flow seven rivers of deadly poison. If a man handles it, he immediately bursts, every limb is torn from his body, his bowels are cleft, and he falls upon his face.[20]

Confinement to hell is the result of disobeying God's Torah as is illustrated by the midrash concerning the evening visit of the soul to hell before it is implanted in an individual. There it sees the Angels of Destruction smiting with fiery scourges; the sinners all the while crying out, but no mercy is shown to them. The angel guides the soul and then asks: "Do you know who these are?" Unable to respond the soul listens as the angel continues: "Those who are consumed with fire were created like you. When they were put into the world, they did not observe God's Torah and His commandments. Therefore they have come to this disgrace which you see them suffer. Know, your destiny is also to depart from the world. Be just, therefore, and not wicked, that you may gain the future world."[21]

The soul was not alone in being able to see hell; a number of Biblical personages entered into its midst. Moses, for example, was guided through hell by an angel, and his journey there gives us the most complete picture of its torments:[22]

When Moses and the Angel of Hell entered Hell together, they saw men being tortured by the Angels of Destruction. Some sinners were suspended by their eyelids, some by their ears, some by their hands, and some by their tongues. In addition, women were suspended by their hair and their breasts by chains of fire. Such punishments were inflicted on the basis of the sins that were committed: those who hung by their eyes looked lustfully upon their neighbours' wives and possessions; those who hung by their ears listened to empty and vain speech and did not listen to the Torah; those who hung by their tongues spoke foolishly and slanderously; those who hung by their hands robbed and murdered their neighbours. The women who hung by their hair and breasts uncovered them in the presence of young men in order to seduce them.

In another place called Alukah Moses saw sinners suspended by their feet with their heads downward and their bodies covered with long black worms. These sinners were punished in this way because they swore falsely, profaned the Sabbath and the Holy Days, despised the sages, called their neighbours by unseemly nicknames, wronged the orphan and the widow, and bore false witness.

In another section Moses saw sinners prone on their faces with 2,000 scorpions lashing, stinging, and tormenting them. Each of these scorpions had 70,000 heads, each head 70,000 mouths, each mouth 70,000 stings, and each sting 70,000 pouches of poison and venom. So great was the pain they inflicted that the eyes of the sinners melted in their sockets. These sinners were punished in this way because they caused other Jews to lose their money, were arrogant in the community, put their neighbours to shame in public, delivered their fellow Jews into the hands of the Gentiles, denied the Torah, and maintained that God is not the creator of the world.

In another place called Tit ha-Yawen sinners stood in mud up to their navels while Angels of Destruction lashed them with fiery chains, and broke their teeth with fiery stones. These sinners were punished in this way because they ate forbidden food, lent their money at usury, wrote the name of God on amulets for Gentiles, used false weights, stole money from fellow Jews, ate on the Day of Atonement, and drank blood.

Finally, after seeing these tortures, Moses observed how sinners were burnt in the section of Hell called Abaddon. There one-half of their bodies were immersed in fire and the other in snow while worms bred in their own flesh crawled over them and the Angels of Destruction beat them incessantly. By stealth these sinners took snow and put it in their armpits to relieve the pain inflicted by the scorching fire. These sinners were punished because they committed incest, murder, idolatry, called themselves gods, and cursed their parents and teachers.

From this description it might appear that hell is reserved for those Jews who have disobeyed the Mosaic law. Such exclusivism, however, was refuted throughout rabbinic literature. For example, in *Midrash Proverbs* R. Joshua explained that gentiles are doomed to eternal punishment unless they are righteous.[23] Asked how a man can escape the judgment of hell, he replied, "Let him occupy himself with good deeds," and he pointed out that this applies to gentiles as well as Jews.

Of course, gentiles were not expected to keep all of Jewish law in order to escape hell; they were simply required to keep the Noachide Laws, that is, those laws which Noah and his descendents took upon themselves. The violation of such laws was regarded by the rabbis as repugnant to fundamental human morality, quite apart from revelation, and was a basis for confinement to hell. However, there was some disagreement as to the laws themselves. In Genesis Rabbah, Noah 34:8, for example, we read that "The sons of Noah were given seven commands: in respect of (1) idolatry, (2) incest, (3) shedding of blood, (4) profanation of the Name of God, (5) justice, (6) robbery, (7) cutting off flesh or limb from a living animal." R. Hanina also gave commands about taking blood from a living animal, R. Elazar about "diverse kinds" and mixtures (Leviticus 19:19), R. Simeon about witchcraft, and R. Johanan b. Baroka about castration (of animals). R. Assi said everything forbidden in Deuteronomy 18:10, 11 was also forbidden to the sons of Noah, because it says, "whoever does these things is an abomination unto the Lord." Nevertheless, despite this disagreement, a gentile who lived a sinful life by violating the Noachide laws was destined to be punished in hell, and conversely, if he lived in accordance with them, he could gain entry into the World to Come.[24]

This eschatological scheme, which was formulated over the centuries by innumerable rabbis, should not be seen as a flight of fancy. It was a serious attempt to explain God's ways to man. Israel was God's chosen people and had received God's promise of reward for keeping his law. Since this did not happen on earth in this life, the rabbis believed it must occur in the World to Come. Never did the rabbis relinquish the belief that God would justify Israel by destroying the power of the oppressing nations. This would come about in the Messianic Age. The individual who had died without seeing the justification of God would be resurrected to see the ultimate victory of the Jewish people. And just as the nations would be judged in the period of Messianic redemption, so would each individual. In this way the vindication of the righteous was assured in the Hereafter.

The Rejection of Traditional Eschatology

On the basis of this scheme of eternal salvation and damnation—which was at the heart of rabbinic theology throughout the centuries—it might be expected that modern Jewish theologians of all shades of religious observance and opinion would attempt to explain contemporary Jewish history in the context of traditional eschatology. This, however, has not happened: instead many Jewish writers have set aside doctrines concerning Messianic redemption, resurrection, final judgment, and reward for the righteous and punishment for the wicked. This shift in emphasis is in part due to the fact that the views expressed in the narrative sections of the Midrashim and the Talmud are not binding. All Jews are obliged to accept the Divine origin of the Law, but this is not so with regard to theological concepts and theories expounded by the rabbis. Thus it is possible for a Jew to be religiously pious without accepting all the central beliefs of mainstream Judaism. Indeed, throughout Jewish history there has been widespread confusion as to what these beliefs are. In the first century B. C., for example, the sage Hillel stated that the quintessence of Judaism could be formulated in a single principle: "that which is hateful to you, do not do to your neighbour. This is the whole of the Law; all the rest is commentary."[25] Similarly, in the second century A. D., the Council of Lydda ruled that under certain circumstances the laws of the Torah may be transgressed in order to save one's life with the exception of idolatry, murder, and unchastity.[26]

In both these cases, the center of gravity was in the ethical rather than the religious sphere. However, in the medieval period, Maimonides formulated what he considered to be the thirteen principles of the Jewish faith.[27] Other thinkers though challenged this formulation. Hasdai Crescas, Simon ben Zemah Duran, Joseph Albo, and Isaac Arami elaborated different creeds, and some thinkers, like David ben Solomon Ibn Abi Zimrah argued that it is impossible to isolate from the whole Torah essential principles of the Jewish faith. He wrote: "I do not agree that it is right to make any part of the perfect Torah into a 'principle' since the whole Torah is a 'principle' from the mouth of the Almighty."[28] Thus, when formulations of the central theological tenets of Judaism were propounded, they were not universally accepted since they were simply the opinions of individual teachers. Without a central authority whose opinion in theological matters was binding on all Jews, it has been impossible to determine the correct theological beliefs in Judaism. In the words of Solomon Schechter, "any attempt at an orderly and complete system of rabbinic theology is an impossible task."[29]

Given that there is no authoritative bedrock of Jewish theology, many modern Jewish thinkers have felt fully justified in abandoning the various elements of traditional rabbinic eschatology that they regard as untenable. The doctrine of Messianic redemption, for example, has been radically modified. In the last century, Reform Jews tended to interpret the new liberation in the Western world as the first step towards the realization of the Messianic dream. But the Messianic redemption was understood in this-worldly terms. No longer, according to this view, was it necessary for Jews to pray for a restoration in Palestine; rather they should view their own countries as Zion and their political leaders as bringing about the Messianic age. Secular Zionists, on the other hand, saw the return to Palestine as the legitimate conclusion to be drawn from the realities of Jewish life in Western countries, thereby viewing the State of Israel as a substitute for the Messiah himself. As L. Jacobs notes, "most modern Jews prefer to interpret the Messianic hope in naturalistic terms, abandoning the belief in a personal Messiah, the restoration of the sacrificial system, and to a greater or lesser degree, the idea of direct Divine intervention."[30]

Similarly, the doctrine of the resurrection of the dead has in modern times been largely replaced in both Orthodox and non-Orthodox Judaism by the belief in the immortality of the soul. The original belief in resurrection was an eschatological hope bound up with the rebirth of the nation in the Days of the Messiah, but as this Messianic concept faded into the background so also did this doctrine. For most Jews, physical resurrection is simply inconceivable in the light of a scientific understanding of the nature of the world. The late Chief Rabbi, Dr. J. H. Hertz, for example, argued that what really matters is the doctrine of the immortality of the soul. Thus he wrote: "Many and various are the folk beliefs and poetical fancies in the rabbinical writings concerning heaven, *Gan Eden,* and hell, *Gehinnom.* Our most authoritative religious guides, however, proclaim that no eye hath seen, nor can mortal fathom, what awaiteth us in the Hereafter; but that even the tarnished soul will not forever be denied spiritual bliss."[31]

In the Reform community a similar attitude prevails. In a well-known statement of the beliefs of Reform Judaism, it is stated that Reform Jews "reassert the doctrine of Judaism that the soul is immortal, grounding this belief on the Divine nature of the human spirit, which forever finds bliss in righteousness and misery in wickedness. We reject as ideas not rooted in Judaism the belief in bodily resurrection and in Gehenna and Eden (Hell and Paradise) as abodes for eternal punishment or reward."[32] The point to note about the conception of the immortal soul in both Orthodox and Reform Judaism is that it is disassociated from traditional notions of Messianic redemption and Divine judgment.

The belief in eternal punishment has also been discarded by a large number of Jews partly because of the interest in penal reform during the past century. Punishment as retaliation in a vindictive sense has been generally rejected. Thus Jacobs writes, "the value of punishment as a deterrent and for the protection of society is widely recognized. But all the stress today is on the reformatory aspects of punishment. Against such a background the whole question of reward and punishment in the theological sphere is approached in a more questioning spirit."[33] Further, the rabbinic view of hell is seen by many as morally repugnant. Jewish theologians have stressed that it is a delusion to believe that a God of love could have created a place of eternal punishment. In his commentary on the prayerbook, Chief Rabbi Hertz categorically declared, "Judaism rejects the doctrine of eternal damnation."[34] And, in *Jewish Theology,* the Reform Rabbi, K. Kohler, argued that the question whether the tortures of Hell are reconcilable with Divine mercy "is for us superfluous and superseded. Our modern conceptions of time and space admit neither a place or a world-period for the reward and punishment of souls, nor the intolerable conception of eternal joy without useful action and eternal agony without any moral purpose."[35]

Traditional rabbinic eschatology has thus lost its force for a large number of Jews in the modern period, and in consequence there has been a gradual this-worldly emphasis in Jewish thought. Significantly, this has been accompanied by a powerful attachment to the State of Israel. For many Jews, the founding of the Jewish State is the central focus of their religious and cultural identity. Jews throughout the world have deep admiration for the astonishing achievements of Israelis in reclaiming the desert and building a viable society, and great respect for the heroism of Israel's soldiers and statesmen. As a result, it is not uncommon for Jews to equate Jewishness with Zionism, and to see Judaism as fundamentally nationalistic in character; this is a far cry from the rabbinic view of history that placed the doctrine of the hereafter at the center of Jewish life and thought.

Conclusion

We can see, therefore, that the wheel has swung full circle from the faint allusions to immortality in the Biblical period that led to an elaborate development of the concept of the Hereafter in rabbinic Judaism. Whereas the rabbis put the belief in an afterlife at the center of their religious system, modern Jewish thinkers, both Orthodox and Reform, have abandoned such an other-worldly outlook, even to the point of denying the existence of such doctrines. It may be that these concepts are outmoded and should be abandoned in the light of contemporary thought, but there is no doubt that such a development raises major problems for Judaism in the modern age. The belief in the Hereafter has helped Jews make sense of the world as a creation of a good and all-powerful God and provided a source of great consolation for their travail on earth. Without the promise of Messianic redemption, resurrection, and the eventual vindication of the righteous in Paradise, Jews will face great difficulties reconciling the belief in a providential God who watches over his chosen people with the terrible events of modern Jewish history. If there is no eschatological unfolding of a Divine drama in which Jewish people will ultimately triumph, what hope can there be for the Righteous of Israel?

NOTES

1. Kaufmann Kohler, *Jewish Theology* (New York: Ktav, 1968), p. 279.

2. R. H. Charles, *A Crictical History of the Doctrine of a Future Life in Israel, in Judaism and in Christianity* (London: Adam and Charles Black, 1913), p. 157.

3. Kaufmann Kohler, *Jewish Theology,* p. 282.

4. Psalms 28:1, 88:5; Numbers 16:33; Psalms 6:6; Isaiah 38:18.

5. Joshua 18:16; 2 Kings 23:10; Jeremiah 7:31-32, 19:6, 32:35.

6. Joshua 18:16.

7. Jeremiah 2:23; 2 Chronicles 26:9; Nehemiah 2:13, 15; Nehemiah 3:13.

8. Jeremiah 7:31-32; 19:6; 32:35.

9. See Louis Jacobs, *A Jewish Theology* (New York: Behrman House, 1973).

10. See E. Jacob, *The Interpreter's Dictionary of the Bible,* vol. 2 (New York: Abingdon Press, 1962), p. 689; Kaufmann Kohler, *Jewish Theology,* p. 392.

11. Sanhedrin 90b.

12. Sanhedrin 91b.

13. Sanhedrin 91b.

14. This was originally a valley near Jerusalem where Moloch was worshipped. See Jeremiah 7:31–32, 19:6, 32:35.

15. See A. Super, *Immortality in the Babylonian Talmud* (unpublished Ph. D. thesis, 1967) pp. 103–8.

16. Maimonides, *Mishneh Torah,* Laws of Repentence III, Sections 6, 7, 8.

17. See A. Super, *Immortality in the Babylonian Talmud.*

18. A. Super, pp. 191–93.

19. Erubin 19a.

20. Louis Ginsberg, *The Legends of the Jews* (Philadelphia: Jewish Publication Society, 1968), vol. I, p. 15.

21. Louis Ginsberg, pp. 57–58.

22. Louis Ginsberg, vol. 2, pp. 310–13.

23. Midrash Proverbs, 17, 1, 42b.

24. There were some rabbis who proclaimed that God consigns gentiles en masse to hell. See C. G. Montefiore and H. Loewe, *A Rabbinic Anthology* (New York: Schocken, 1974), p. 93.

25. Shabbatt 31a.

26. Sanhedrin 74a.

27. (1) The existence of God; (2) the unity of God; (3) the incorporeality of God; (4) the eternity of God; (5) God alone is to be worshipped; (6) prophecy; (7) Moses is the greatest of the prophets; (8) the divinity of the Torah; (9) the inalterability of the Torah; (10) the omniscience of God; (11) reward and punishment; (12) the Messiah; (13) the resurrection of the dead.

28. Responsum No. 344 as quoted by Louis Jacobs, *Principles of the Jewish Faith* (London: Vallentine Mitchell, 1964), p. 24.

29. Solomon Schechter, *Aspects of Rabbinic Theology* (New York: Schocken, 1961), p. 16.

30. Louis Jacobs, *Principles of the Jewish Faith.*

31. Joseph H. Hertz, *Commentary to the Prayerbook,* p. 255.

32. W. G. Plant, *The Growth of Reform Judaism* (New York: World Union for Progressive Judaism, 1965), p. 34.

33. Louis Jacobs, *Principles of the Jewish Faith,* p. 364.

34. As quoted by Louis Jacobs, *Principles of the Jewish Faith,* p. 415.

35. Kaufmann Kohler, *Jewish Theology,* p. 309.

4

The Christian Hope Today
PAUL BADHAM

The Future Hope as a Foundational Christian Belief

Christianity came into being as a religion of salvation offering to mankind the hope of an eternal destiny beyond the grave. According to 1 Peter 1:3ff., "We have been born anew to a living hope through the resurrection of Jesus Christ from the dead, and to an inheritance which is imperishable, undefiled and unfading, kept in heaven for you." For this author the "outcome of faith" was "the salvation of your souls" (1 Peter 1:9). This view was echoed by St. Paul, who insisted that "in this hope we are saved" (Romans 8:24), and "that life and immortality" had been "brought to light through the Gospel" (2 Timothy 1:10).

When St. Paul was imprisoned for his teaching, he insisted over and over again that the hope for resurrection was the heart of his message (Acts 23:6, 24:21, 26:8), and, indeed, he told the Corinthians that "if the dead are not raised . . . our Gospel is null and void . . . and your faith has nothing in it. . . . If for this life only Christ has given us hope we of all men are most to be pitied" (1 Corinthians 15:13-19).

It would be easy to continue to cite texts for the whole of this paper for "belief in a future world is taken for granted" in all the New Testament documents.[1] "Heaven" is mentioned more than 240 times, and all the first Christians thought of heaven as their true home.[2] 1 Peter 2:11 describes the present situation of Christians on earth as that of "aliens in a foreign land" and the author of the letter to the Hebrews sees the heroes of faith as "no more than strangers or passing travellers on earth" (Hebrews 11:13). Likewise in the second century, other-worldliness was so central a characteristic of the early Christians that the author of the Epistle to Diognetus could say of them that "They spend their existence on earth but their citizenship is in heaven . . . they dwell in the world but they are not of the world."[3] It was their absolute faith in the life beyond that enabled many of the first Christians to embrace martyrdom with composure, and thereby convert their persecutors. And on the mission field it was the hope of immortality that was seen as Christianity's distinctive attraction. Thus, when the Anglo-Saxons of Northumbria debated whether or not to accept the faith, the Venerable Bede tells us that the clinching argument was that instead of this life being seen as a brief interlude between two eternal states of darkness, it could now be seen as the prelude to a yet more glorious future.[4]

Throughout the Christian centuries in Europe, belief in a future life remained the heart of all living faith. The great themes of Christian theology—incarnation, atonement, salvation, justification—all revolved around the good news of man's eternal destiny in Christ. Thus for St. Athanasius and the whole orthodox tradition, our immortality was the reason for the incarnation and for the whole work of Christ: God became what we are so that we might became immortal as he is.[5] This theme was taken up into each one of the Christian sacraments. At Baptism a Christian is said to become "an inheritor of the Kingdom of Heaven,"[6] and reference to God's everlasting Kingdom is made at the most solemn moments of confirmation, marriage, ordination, and absolution. In the Holy Communion, Christians are given "the bread of immortality" in the Orthodox Liturgy, or the bread of "eternal" or "everlasting life" in Anglican and Roman formularies, and, finally, in the Last Rites the Christian receives the Viaticum to nourish his soul for the journey through death.

Why the Future Hope Matters

This centrality of the immortal hope in the Christian tradition is not in the least surprising. After all, the essence of the Christian understanding of God is that he loves each one of us, and that within this life we can experience real fellowship and communion with God through prayer, worship, and participation in life. Yet if man can truly enter a personal relationship with God, which God values, and if each person as a unique individual really matters to the all-powerful and all-loving God, then God will not allow that individual and that relationship to be destroyed at death.

If death meant extinction, all meaning would be evacuated from the claim that God loves and cherishes each one of us, for within this life suffering, disease, and death will ultimately triumph over each individual, and the challenge of evil emerges as an insuperable barrier against any belief that God can be truly both all-powerful and all-loving. However, as John Hick has argued, if there is indeed a life after death, then the changes and chances of this world with all its potential for joy and sorrow, for good and evil, may make sense as an inevitable part of any environment in which persons can develop as free and responsible agents.[7] As a "vale of soul-making" the hardships and challenges of life can serve a larger purpose; but if there is no soul to make, no larger purpose to serve, then the fact of suffering in general, and its random character in particular, simply makes nonsense of Christian claims about God's character and power.

It should be stressed that Hick's theodicy does not in any way imply that suffering is in itself enobling or redemptive. The evidence in general would go flat against any such simplistic a view. But what this theodicy does say is that a real objective world governed by regular physical law provides an environment more suited to the development of responsible agents than would an environment in which divine intervention consistently saved humanity from the consequences of its folly, or from the heartache and challenge implicit in any finite and physical existence.

Closely related to this issue is the problem of what meaning could be attached to the claims of Christian theism if life after death were to be discarded. This problem came very much to the fore in British theology in the mid-1950s when Antony Flew challenged sophisticated Christians to say whether or not there was *any* potentially empirical fact about the nature of reality that could affect their belief in God.[8] For if nothing whatever could be held to falsify a Christian claim, then that claim must be considered vacuous and devoid of assertive meaning. The only reply to Flew's challenge that even began to be viable was Ian Crombie and John Hick's suggestion of "eschatological verification."[9]

The proponents of eschatological verification do not believe that God directly acts within the structure of physical existence. They do not appeal to such alleged factors as special providences, answered prayers, or miracles, but rather they assume that God acts in the world only through the response to him of the human individual. Hence, they agree with the nonbeliever in accepting the autonomy of the natural order. Nevertheless there remains a significant difference in attitude towards this life arising from different expectations about its ultimate goal. To a Christian believer, life is perceived as a preparation for an eternal destiny; to an atheist, life can only find fulfillment in the goals and tasks we set ourselves within the finite boundaries of our present existence. There is a real difference between these two visions, and the difference is a factual one in that the Christian vision might potentially be verified if it turned out that there was indeed a life after bodily death. Eschatological verification is thus of considerable importance to the intelligibility of Christian theism for no other response to Flew's challenge even begins to come to terms with it in presenting a case for the potentially factual character of theistic claims.

If we turn from theism in general to the more specific doctrines of Christianity, it can be argued that none of them retain any vital significance if divorced from faith in a life beyond. According to the Creeds, the Incarnation of God in Christ took place, "For us men and for our salvation." If we have no ultimate salvation, it is hard to see what purpose the doctrine serves. Likewise with the belief in the resurrection of Jesus Christ: clearly it is possible to believe in the resurrection of Jesus as an event wholly unique to him and entailing no consequences for the rest of humanity. But, in this case, it is hard to see why it should be of any interest now except as a historical belief about the founder of Christianity. By contrast, the Christian tradition itself has seen the resurrection of Jesus as important precisely as a guarantee of a destiny in which we may expect to share. Indeed, Bruce Reichenbach sees the argument from Christ's resurrection to ours as the only plausible ground for our future hope, and in this conclusion, he echoes today the original conviction of St. Paul in the first century.[10]

So far I have argued that the Christian hope has been fundamental to the life and belief of the Christian Churches throughout the ages and that it remains a vital component of any coherent theistic belief. Is this conclusion valid? Two objections spring to mind: first that ancient Judaism developed a very profound understanding of God without initially possessing any positive belief in a future life, and second that many modern Christians have ceased to believe in life after death without ceasing to believe in God. Concerning ancient Judaism my comment would be that initially God's covenant was seen as being made with Israel as a whole rather than with the individual person. While that view of the covenant existed, life after death was not considered, but as soon as a more individualistic understanding of God's relation to mankind gained ground the ancient theodicy came under increasing strain, and Israel's thought was inevitably led in a direction that must and, indeed, did lead towards a belief in a future hope.[11] Concerning contemporaries who affirm theism while denying immortality, we may note that to claim a belief in God can be an extremely nebulous affirmation as the theology and falsification debate indicated, whereas to affirm belief in a future life is to express a fairly concrete hope, even if the expression of that hope may be ill-defined and confused. In terms of any real commitment to Christianity, there has been a dramatic decline in twentieth-century Europe, and it is tempting to suggest that this may be connected with the decline in the belief in immortality in European Christianity. Certainly, at the turn of the century, both William James and Miguel de Unamuno found that for almost all believers of their day God primarily mattered as the provider of immortality.[12] If God has ceased "to matter" to many Europeans who claim to believe in him, the drift to a this–world–only interpretation of Christianity may well be responsible. And that Christianity has not correspondingly declined in the United States might also be noted, for this may be connected with the continuing strength of belief in immortality in American religion.[13]

What the Christian Hope Entails

Let us now turn to the question of what the Christian hope entails. It has two essential components: the immortality of the soul and the resurrection of the body. Both beliefs are affirmed in the New Testament, in the writings of the early Fathers, in the teaching of the Schoolmen and the Reformers, and in the latest pronouncements of the present Pope.[14] I shall argue below that the two beliefs are essential for any genuinely personal continuance and that both are logically possible in that they may be affirmed without necessarily contradicting other well-established knowledge that we have about the world.

But before I attempt this, I must comment on the suggestion made by many representatives of the "biblical theology" movement that the immortality of the soul should be dismissed as an alien Hellenistic intrusion into the pure Hebrew concept of man as a psychosomatic unity whose future hope depends wholly on the belief in supernatural restitution of his total embodiment. The background to this view is the fact that early Judaism unequivocally identified personhood with physical embodiment, and that this doctrine is in stark contrast with Plato's view that the person is the soul. It is common to hold that this Hebrew understanding of man lies behind the New Testament teaching and explains why the New Testament places so much emphasis on the resurrection of the dead and states that God "alone has immortality" (1 Timothy 4:16). The strongest evidence in support of this view is the fact that all four Gospels present the resurrection of Jesus in fairly straightforward physical terms, and in every case report the emptiness of his tomb as evidence for his actual "up-rising."

But there are a number of problems with this view. First, it is historically the case that the initial sharp contrast between Hebrew and Greek ways of thought did not endure. In later Judaism it is quite easy to show that the soul could be regarded as distinct from the body, and that this change in Jewish thought was not necessarily derived from Greek philosophy but emerged naturally from within Judaism as Jewish thinkers began to follow up and explore the implications of their developing belief in the possibility of a life after death.[15] And when the New Testament is approached without the presupposition that its authors shared the same views as their distant ancestors, it at once becomes apparent that a wide variety of opinion about the nature of man can be discerned in the New Testament, and even in the writings of individual authors. St. Paul in particular is thoroughly inconsistent in his anthropology. Thus, in 2 Corinthians 5, he cannot decide whether he expects his new "spiritual body" to be put on over his existing one or whether the future life will require him "to leave his home in the body" altogether. He asserts both ideas with equal confidence in almost successive verses. And with regard to the resurrection of Jesus, it is noteworthy that many scholars believe that St. Paul knew nothing of the empty-tomb tradition. Certainly his denial that flesh and blood could ever inherit the Kingdom of God (1 Corinthians 15:50) seems hard to reconcile with any kind of belief that Jesus' flesh and blood had already done so! I have argued at length elsewhere for a spiritual understanding of the resurrection of Jesus, so will not repeat myself here, except to stress that there can be little doubt that there are two conflicting traditions within the New Testament material and that one important line of early Christian thought saw the resurrection appearances of Jesus as visionary in form.[16] St. Paul explicitly called his own experience, which he felt to be fully on a par with that of the earliest disciples, "a heavenly vision" (Acts 2:6-19). He had no doubt of its reality. It transformed his whole life to see the risen Lord. Yet he was also sure that it was no resuscitated earthly body that he saw but rather a vision of the glory that lies ahead. It was a physical body that was buried, but a spiritual body that was raised (cf. 1 Corinthians 15:42–44).

The same understanding of Jesus' resurrection is expressed in the first letter of Peter where we read "in the body he [Jesus] was put to death; in the spirit he was brought to life," and because this had happened to Jesus we too have been "born anew to a living hope" and can expect of the dead that "although in the body they received the sentence common to all men, they might in the spirit be alive with the life of God" (1 Peter 3:18, 1:3, 4:6).

Hence it is altogether too simplistic to describe New Testament theology as working solely within the anthropology of ancient Judaism, or to insist that the only understanding of Jesus' resurrection that is possible is one that requires the restoration of the same psychosomatic entity that had existed previously. And when this line of reasoning is extended to the Christian hope in general, yet further problems arise. For if the concept of the soul were indeed to be excluded in favor of the ancient Hebraic identification of personhood with the existing physical embodiment, then it is really not possible to talk in terms of radical transformation. For the whole point of identifying persons with their bodies is lost if "different," "changed," or "spiritual" bodies are to be postulated for our supposed future life.

A truly psychosomatic account of human personhood insists that "man is a physical and psychical whole which consists of a complex of parts, each part being at the same time physiological and psychical in itself."[17] Precisely this view is presented in the Old Testament in which heart, kidneys, bowels, liver, inward parts, flesh, and bones are all explicitly mentioned as shaping and determining our present character and emotions.[18] It was for this very reason that the ancient Hebrews did not at first even consider the possibility of life after death, for they believed man's only possible true life was on this earth and depended wholly on the continuing in being of his personal embodiment. When they began to consider the idea of a future life, so too quite inevitably did they begin to question their former anthropology.

The only notion of a future life compatible with a strictly psychosomatic account of man is one entailing the literal reconstitution of the decomposed or cremated corpse. And when one spells out the implications of this, almost all contemporary Christians acknowledge its impossibility. Hence when Christians today talk of resurrection, what they almost invariably mean is that after death *we* receive new and quite different bodies to serve as vehicles for our self-expression and development in heaven. And the only bond of union between our present and future bodies is that they are "owned" successively by the same personality. This is the view adopted by the Church of England Doctrine Commission in 1938 and by the Catholic Bishops of Holland in their 1965 catechism.[19] This understanding of resurrection raises no insuperable practical difficulties because modern physics allows for the theoretical possibility of plural spaces in no spatial relationship whatever to each other provided that each is subject to entirely different physical laws. Hence we can postulate that the resurrection world (heaven) exists in another space and provides a wholly new kind of environment for our further development and advance. This would tie in with St. Paul's view that heaven transcends all that we can visualize or expect: "things beyond our seeing, things beyond our hearing, things beyond our imagining, all prepared by God for those who love him: (1 Corinthians 2:9).

However, it is not always appreciated by the many writers who embrace this understanding of resurrection that it depends absolutely on the validity of the concept of the soul. It is a necessary part of the hypothesis that the point of contact between the two worlds cannot be physical. If therefore *I* am to exist in this heaven in another space, it follows that what is meant by the word *I* cannot be exhaustively confined to my present embodiment. This is implicitly recognized by many writers who describe what ensures continuity between the two worlds in terms like "the person," "the essential part of what we are," "the vital principle of our being," "the pattern of what we are," or "our moral and intellectual qualities." The joke is that these phrases used by many writers who often claim not to believe in the soul happen to be the meaning that the Concise Oxford Dictionary gives to the word "soul." Hence, though many deny the word they find themselves compelled to affirm everything that the word actually means, for without some notion of a non-material principle of continuity, no wholly-other mode of existence in heaven can be postulated.

The Concept of the Soul

What then is involved in the concept of the soul? I see it first and foremost as a belief that the locus of personal identity for any individual is his own mental life. I *am* the subject of my conscious experiences to a far greater extent than I am my body. Of course, it is through my body that others identify me, and through awareness of their bodies that I identify them. Nevertheless I do not identify my own selfhood with my body, even though it is through the body that I initially learned the language I subsequently apply to my inner mental life.

Consider for example the claim some people make to have dreams in which the subject of the dream experiences has or is another body, answers to another name, and exists in a different historical context from the dreamer. It is significant that the dreamer always identifies himself with the subject of those dream experiences. Bernard Williams disputes this and argues that to dream that one was Napoleon is merely to dream that one was playing the role of Napoleon as an actor might.[20] But this is not true to the reported experiences. When a person reports a dream in which he was Napoleon, he does not mean he had a dream in which he acted being Napoleon; he means he had a dream in which he found himself in a Napoleon-like body and a Napoleon-like situation answering to the name of the French Emperor and having a variety of adventures, appropriate to what he supposed to be that life situation and time. And once we concede that in imagination or dream people do from time to time identify themselves with another name, body, and lifestyle, then it is clear that their present embodiment is not central to their own self-understanding. In support of this, let us note that few seem to find any difficulty at all with plots of fairy tales or science-fiction stories that involve body transfer. If the meaning of *self* were identical with the meaning of *body,* then the plot of such stories would be impossible to follow.

I suggest the reason why talk of body transfer is thought to be intelligible is the fact that personal identity is discerned in two different ways: from without and from within. Most of the time we identify others through their distinctive physical characteristics and behavior patterns, but we do not normally recognize ourselves through observations of ourselves but through our inner feelings. What makes me *me* is not my external appearance to which I may be relatively indifferent, nor my behavioral patterns of which others may be more conscious than I, but rather it is that I am the subject of the thoughts, feelings, memories, and intentions of which I am consciously aware.

Imagine that tomorrow morning I woke up remembering all I

did today and thinking about my plans for tomorrow, then let us suppose that on looking into the mirror I found that the face I proposed to shave was completely and utterly unfamiliar. I would undoubtedly be terrified, bewildered, and utterly distraught, but in the end I would be forced to conclude that something inexplicably terrible had happened to *me*, namely, that *I* had acquired a new and different body. I suggest I would have no choice about reaching this conclusion for what would it be to doubt that one remained the self one was conscious of remaining?

Of course, because the criterion of identity is public, a judicial inquiry would almost certainly not recognize the person with the completely and utterly unfamiliar face as Paul Badham. But that is not the point. I have already stressed that there is a difference between the way we identify others and the way we know ourselves to be the persons we are.

The first element in the concept of the soul is thus a purely logical point concerning the nature of personal experience, namely, that thinking, feeling, and self-awareness constitute the sense of individuality a person has. And I argue that because it is intelligible for the individual person to identify himself as having a different embodiment and a different historical setting in a dream or story, then it is equally intelligible to suppose that he could identify himself with a different embodiment and a different setting in a life after death. Hence, although at this stage in the argument we may think that the notion of the soul getting a new body is profoundly unlikely, it is not, I suggest, unintelligible.

Likewise, it is an interesting fact that people who report out-of-the-body experiences always identify themselves with the alleged out-of-the-body subject, rather than with the unconscious body they think they have left. Whatever explanation we give of such odd events, the way they are reported supports the view that from the point of view of the meaning of selfhood, to the individual, selfhood is invariably identified with the thinking and feeling subject.

But talk of the soul is not just a claim that our self-identity is most properly focused on the subject of our conscious experiences. It goes on to claim that the subject is capable of surviving bodily death. However, the soul can only survive bodily death if it is credible to suppose that it exists before death as a substance that it is at least logically possible to differentiate from the body.

Many suppose that this belief is no longer tenable because of all that modern science has shown us about the intimate relationship that exists between all our thinking, feeling, and willing and some quite specific brain states. However, H. D. Lewis in his *The Elusive Mind* has argued cogently that a neo-Cartesian interactionist dualism can fully accept all that modern physiological study shows concerning the influence of body on mind, and yet at the same time it alone does full justice to the important logical distinction between mental experience and brain event.[21] Moreover, only a dualist account of man can do any kind of justice to certain well-established, though unusual, features of our experiencing.

The first is telepathy, by which I mean the transfer of information from one mind to another mind without the use of the neural pathways of the brain. Concerning its intellectual validity let me simply quote the judgment of Professor Eysenck in 1960: "Unless there is a gigantic conspiracy involving some thirty University departments all over the world and several hundred respected scientists in various fields, many of them originally hostile to the claims of the psychical researchers, the only conclusion an unbiased observer can come to must be that there does exist a small body of people who obtain knowledge existing in other people's minds by means as yet unknown to science."[22] It is certainly striking that virtually all who attend to the evidence seem now convinced that telepathy is a reality. Moreover, with every year that passes the case appears to grow stronger as more instances are reported and earlier reports are vindicated. The relevance of this to our present discussion was best expressed by Keith Campbell: "Parapsychological phenomena, by definition, demonstrate capacities of mind which exceed any capacities of brain. The brain is receptive only to information that arrives by neural pathways and so is confined to perception by way of the senses. . . . If some people are receptive to the contents of the minds of another by some more direct means such as telepathy then those minds are just not brains."[23] That argument seems to me unanswerable, and Keith Campbell left a notable hostage to fortune when he developed it.

Secondly, I turn to the data of that kind of religious experience that purports to be a direct experience of God. I believe that the experience that talks of direct encounter between the soul and God is the living heart of religion. All the greatest theologians of the Eastern orthodox tradition have insisted on the immediacy of the mystic's knowledge of God and say that it is neither mediated nor assisted by the senses. A similar approach may be seen in the

Augustinian-Franciscan solution to the philosophy of religion, which asserts that God is knowable in himself without mediation. The importance of this tradition can scarcely be overestimated. Almost all books on prayer insist on the importance of quieting the senses and of opening up oneself to God. Think of the habit of seeking out a place of complete quiet, of closing the eyes, and putting the hands together—all such activities presuppose that the sense of the presence of God is only distracted if data from the senses continue to pour in upon one's mind. Only when as far as possible one has closed off one's sensory input is one in a state where encounter with God becomes likely. This type of religious understanding depends on a dualist view of man as its necessary condition. For it asserts that God can make the reality of his presence known other than through neural pathways; in other words, that knowledge of God can be understood as communicated to us though some process akin to telepathy direct to the mind and not via sensory stimuli.

My own belief is that this type of religious experience is at the root of most people's deepest religious feelings, and the Thomist way of moving from the world to God represents a second reflective stage in the person's religious development. Of course much religious experience takes the form of considering the beauty of the world, or of worship, or of a sense of duty, and abstracting from these experiences to the notion of a transcendent God—but I suggest that the movement of thought from the world to the transcendent depends upon a preexisting, mystical, and intuitive immediate awareness of God, which can only be a reality if dualism is true.

Finally, I turn to the experiences of people who have been resuscitated in intensive care units, who would undoubtedly have died but for modern medical advances. Although the majority of the resuscitated remember nothing, those who do remember claim to have a very distinctive series of experiences that are reported with near unanimity, from young and old, educated and illiterate, and from every conceivable religious background. For our present purposes, the most important feature of the experience is the claim of these people that, at the moment of apparent death, *they* went out of their bodies and found themselves looking down with interest on the resuscitation attempts. After recovery, they accurately described what was going on while they were unconscious, and their perspective was from a point of view different from that of the body on the operating table. These findings are of absolutely crucial significance for the concept of the soul, for if a single out-of-the-body experience is correctly described as such, then the soul is a reality. If consciousness can, even for a moment at the brink of death, think-observe-and-remember from a different perspective than that of the physical brain, then brain and mind are not identical and consciousness can exist apart from the body. And if consciousness can exist apart from the body, then the soul is a reality, and the most fundamental obstacle across the road to immortality has been removed.

This does not mean that the Christian hope can simply be identified with belief in the soul's survival. As we saw earlier, the Christian hope is much wider than this and looks also for a resurrection of the dead in which our whole being will everlastingly share in a divine life.[24] We, therefore, see the immortality of the soul as part of a richer and fuller hope in which the soul's survival guarantees the continuity of our self-identity between this life and the life of the world to come.

NOTES

1. For full documentation see Anton Van der Walle, *From Darkness to the Dawn* (London: SCM, 1984), p. 120.

2. Nelson's complete concordance to the RSV Bible (London: Nelson, 1963), p. 59.

3. Cited in J. Stevenson, *A New Eusebius* (London: SPCK, 1963), p. 59.

4. Bede, *A History of the English Church* bk. 2, chap. 13.

5. Athanasius, *On the Incarnation,* chap. 54; *Orations,* bk. 1, chap. 39.

6. According to the Catechism of the Anglican *Book of Common Prayer* of 1662.

7. John Hick, *Evil and the God of Love* (New York: Macmillan, 1966), pt. 4.

8. Antony Flew and Alasdair MacIntyre, *New Essays in Philosophical Theology* (London: SCM, 1955), chap. 6.

9. Flew and MacIntyre, *New Essays in Philosophical Theology,* chap. 6; and John Hick, *The Existence of God* (New York: Macmillan, 1964), pp. 257ff.

10. Bruce Reichenbach, *Is Man the Phoenix?* (Lanham, MD: University Press of America, 1983), chap. 8.

11. For a full discussion of this see my *Christian Beliefs about Life after Death* (London: Macmillan, 1976; London: SPCK, 1978; New York: Barnes and Noble, 1977), chap.. 1.

12. William James, *The Varieties of Religious Experience* (London: Fontana, 1963); M. de Unamuno, *The Tragic Sense of Life* (London: Fontana, 1967).

13. Anton Van der Walle, *From Darkness to the Dawn,* p. 11, cites figures showing that 38 percent of English people are believers in immortality, and 37 percent of German Lutherans. By contrast, 70 percent of Americans affirm such belief.

14. Letter of Pope John Paul II, "On certain questions concerning eschatology" (17 May 1979), cited in J. Neuner and J. Dupuis, *The Christian Faith in the Doctrinal Documents of the Catholic Church,* revised edition (London: Collins, 1983), p. 691.

15. James Barr, *Old and New in Interpretation* (London: SCM, 1966), p. 52.

16. Paul Badham, *Life After Death* (London: MCU, 1981); Paul Badham, *Christian Beliefs about Life after Death,* chap. 2; Paul Badham, *Immortality or Extinction?* (London: Macmillan, 1982; London: SPCK, 1984; New York: Barnes and Noble, 1982), chap. 2.

17. Eric C. Rust, *Nature and Man in Biblical Thought* (London: Lutterworth, 1953), p. 104.

18. Eric C. Rust, *Nature and Man in Biblical Thought;* Walter Eichrodt, *Theology of the Old Testament,* vol. 2. (London: SCM, 1967) and A. R. Johnson, *The Vitality of the Individual in the Thought of Ancient Israel* (Cardiff-by-the-Sea, Cal.: Cardiff, 1984).

19. *Doctrine in the Church of England* (London: SPCK, 1962), p. 209; The Bishops of the Netherlands, *A New Catechism,* (London: Burns and Oates, 1967), pp. 479, 474, 473.

20. Bernard Williams, *Problems of the Self* (London: CPU, 1973), pp. 42–45.

21. H. D. Lewis, *The Elusive Mind* (London: Allen and Unwin, 1969).

22. Hans J. Eysenck, *Sense and Nonsense in Psychology* (London: Penguin Books, 1957), p. 133.

23. Keith Campbell, *Body and Mind* (London: Macmillan, 1970), p. 91.

24. Cf. Paragraph 18 of *The Pastoral Constitution of the Church in the Modern World,* Second Vatican Council, (7 December 1965).

5

Eschatology in Recent Catholic Thought

THOMAS McGOWAN

Modern Western society has tended to keep the subject of death on the fringe of human consciousness and polite conversation. As the Victorian age found it necessary to deal with sex pornographically, so the twentieth century has similarly resorted to treating death in a psychologically unhealthy way. Both sex and death have been shunted off into dark corners of existence instead of being faced as valid human experiences. Lately, however, especially in the social sciences and theology, there seem to be efforts to confront death as a reality and to position it more honestly within the total context of life. After all, death is the event in life that confronts a person most starkly with questions of the purpose of life and the significance of the future. If a person does in fact affirm the value of life right now and hope for the future, this must be done openly and realistically in the face of death.

My focus here is Christian, and especially Catholic, theology. The basic question to be faced by the discipline of theology concerns what the gospel of Jesus Christ tells us about death and about the meaning of human life in the face of death. There is a practical aspect to such a study, which tries, for example, to come to some understanding of the feelings and experiences of the dying person, the moral decisions often forced on those in a dying situation, the grief process, and the social rituals connected with dying and death. It is the more theological concerns, however, that will be taken up here. For the past few decades, Christian theology, both Protestant and Catholic, has rediscovered in the doctrine of eschatology a point of entry into the whole theological enterprise. Death forces Christian theology to work on adequate responses to the claims of Christian faith that in Jesus Christ the world is offered new life and hope, that the goals and values of life do somehow transcend death, that life does have meaning.

The Origin of Death

First of all, where does death come from? The answers to this question usually fall into three possible categories: death is natural and as such requires no explanation; death is unnatural and so a violation of what it means to be human; and, finally, death is somehow the very act that indeed makes us human.

The argument that death is an integral part of what constitutes "nature" is perhaps best illustrated in Sigmund Freud's analysis of the death instinct in *Beyond the Pleasure Principle*.[1] Freud's premise is that the essence of reality is a chaos and not the "oceanic feeling" or sense of oneness and community that the infantile ego seeks. The universe is ultimately disordered, unharmonious, and diffuse. Since instinct is for Freud "an urge inherent in organic life to restore an earlier state of things," it leads inevitably to a return to that initial condition of simplicity and separateness.[2] The highly complexified reality called human life falls back to its original inorganic and inanimate state. The conclusion is evident: since everything living dies for internal reasons, death is the most natural of human events.[3] Freud admits that the notion of natural death is quite alien to primitive peoples, who attribute every death to the influence of an enemy or an evil spirit. He further concedes that there is some comfort in believing that death is the result of a "remorseless law of nature" rather than to "a chance which might have been escaped."[4] But he quickly discounts these objections by turning to biology and concluding that the scientific evidence does not contradict the recognition of death instincts and therefore "we are at liberty to continue concerning ourselves with their possibility."[5]

An existentialist thinker like Simone de Beauvoir, however, is not satisfied with such an explanation. She sees life as a series of unanswered questions and death as the stumbling block that makes these questions unanswerable. When writing about the death of her own mother in *A Very Easy Death,* she denies that there is any such thing as a natural death.[6] Since a human person's very presence calls the whole world into question, he or she is not limited even by death. For de Beauvoir death is always an "accident" and an "unjustifiable violation."[7] This theme of violation is even more forcefully played on by Edwin Schneidman: "We must face the fact that death is the one act in which man is forced to engage. The word 'forced' has a special meaning here. It implies that death, like torture, rape, capital punishment, kidnap, lobotomy, and other degradation ceremonies, is a form of coercion and impressment. The threat of being erased, of being reduced to nothingness, can be viewed reasonably only as the most perfidious of forced punishments."[8] And perhaps the best known expression of this existentialist frustration with death is that of Dylan Thomas:

Do not go gentle into that good night.
Old age should burn and rave at close of day;
Rage, rage against the dying of the light.[9]

Death in this view is an extinction that infests life with the germs of absurdity; it is a fact but one that is fortuitous and brutal. Human existence must be wrenched out of the simply natural if it is to have any unique value. But death always lurks as the enemy, always casts doubts on whatever humans accomplish, always seems to win out over life at the end. This is an intolerable situation, which must be railed at if we are to maintain any semblance of humanity in the face of death.

Perhaps the posture of Simone de Beauvoir and Dylan Thomas reflects the existentialist retreat to the individual, who soon discovers that the self, the singular *I,* cannot cope with death alone. As *otherness* or a *you* seems to be necessary if a person is to be redeemed in death by discovering his or her true destiny. Leo Tolstoy's classic story, *The Death of Ivan Ilych,* illustrates very well the third position, that death is the very act that makes us human.[10] Tolstoy emphasizes the necessity of human relations in making death a fulfilling rather than a horrifying experience. He does not dismiss death by appealing facilely to optimistic Christian doctrines of life after death but rather reconciles himself to it by taking to heart the paradoxical saying of Jesus that it is only in losing the self that one can find it. This can be achieved most authentically, says Tolstoy, in the personal act of dying. Ivan Ilych has been caught up in the web of secrecy with which society hides both life and death. It is only through the death-affirming peasant Gerasim that Ivan comes to recognize his own death for the radical event it is. He finally realizes that death is not the intruder who attacks from without but instead the creative act of coming to self by letting go. When he does this, all that has been oppressing him drops away—fear, pain, even death itself—and only the unchanging truth of what it is to be human remains.

Christian theology also has struggled with the problem of the origin of death. The traditional doctrine has been that death is the result of sin and as such is unnatural. Augustine, for example, expressed the view that if Adam had not sinned he would not have died. Writing in *The City of God,* Augustine says: "The first men were so created that if they had not sinned, they would not have experienced any kind of death; but that, having become sinners, they were so punished with death, that whatsoever sprang from their stock should also be punished with the same death."[11] Death comes, therefore, as an expression of God's anger: a curse that fills humans with dread because it is perceived as unnatural. Ever since Augustine there has been an enduring tradition in Christian theology that has insisted that death is an unintended part of God's creation. At no time, however, has this been the only orthodox Christian position. Among contemporary Protestant theologians, for example, Karl Barth affirms both the goodness of God's creation and the finitude of the human person. The goodness of God's creation means that even in death God is with us and for us; finitude means that it is natural for a creature to be subject to death. "Death is a man's step from existence into non-existence," he writes, "as birth is his step from non–existence into existence. In itself, therefore, it is not unnatural but natural for human life to run its course."[12] And another contemporary Protestant theologian, Richard W. Doss, asserts that we die because as bodily organisms we participate in the transitoriness of the material world. "We are born and we die," he bluntly states.[13]

Even Thomas Aquinas hedged a bit on this issue of death as punishment: "Death is in a certain sense according to nature and in a certain sense contrary to nature."[14] The "contrary" to nature aspect of death, according to Josef Pieper, is that it has entered creation because of original sin, while the "according" to nature aspect is that the human race always possessed the *posse mori* or the ability to die.[15] But to have a notional understanding of the universality of death is not necessarily to accept death's inevitability for oneself. As Karl Rahner observes, although "death is the most universal thing, and every man declares it is natural and a matter of course that one dies," nevertheless "there is alive in every man a secret protest."[16] The enigma in this situation is that despite all empirical proofs to the effect that everything that is born eventually dies, we remain unswervingly convinced that death is not simply something "natural."

How can this tension be resolved? If death is really an unnatural event does it not flaw the human condition in a fundamental way? Pieper responds in rather traditional Catholic fashion that death does not mark any essential alienation from a person's created reality. True, there was a primordial transgression that profoundly influenced the human race, but this did not produce a "different" race.[17] God's "gift" to humans, Pieper adds, "would have consisted in the spiritual soul's having so effectively infused the body with its formative power and thus made it alive, that this body-soul unity would not have dissolved against man's will."[18] Death did in fact enter creation through sin, Pieper believes, but not human finitude, the being-able-to-die.

Contemporary Christian theology, I believe, when addressing itself to this question of the etiology of death, certainly intends to define a person not in terms of what is shared with animals and plants but of what is utterly distinctive to humanity. When Christian faith proclaims the universality of death, therefore, it is not stating a self-evident biological fact but rather something proper to the human being and proper to his or her relationship with God. It is only in death that a person is a full, free, spiritual being, because only then can he or she most meaningfully choose to be such. If people never died, if they were doomed to an unending life of temporariness and incompletion, their freedom and their very humanity would be crippled. Why should they plan anything? Why undertake anything? Only those who must die are capable of truly loving life, of running risks, of believing in the future. The great insight of the Christian people when they proclaim mortality is that death is a gift and not a curse; it is the ultimate boundary of human potentialities. Of course, Christian theology also says that death is the consequence of sin. This is not to claim, however, that the first person would not have died biologically. What it seems to say is that while death should have been a pure act of self-affirmation, it has become a thing of suffering and fear. So death is the "result of sin" in the sense that it is falsely seen as destruction from without instead of creation from within.

Death as Final Option

Another doctrine, which recent Christian theology has reexamined, is the belief that death somehow marks the absolute end of a person's moral life and locks him or her into an unalterable state in heaven or hell. Usually this traditional view carries with it the image of death as a stalking antagonist, waiting to pounce on the unwary and hold them forever in bliss or woe. Richard Doss, for

instance, echoing St. Paul, describes death as an "enemy, a catastrophic destructive force which comes upon us, and we are unable
to do anything about it."[19] This specter of being overpowered by
death is of course one aspect of the dying experience, but there is
also what Josef Pieper calls "that astonishing sense of freedom
arising from the very starkness of the confrontation with death."[20]
It is this freedom, which some contemporary theologians, especially
Catholics, are emphasizing in terms of death as the final option.[21]

The idea of a final judgment at death may at first seem to be at
odds with the observations of present-day psychology. Human
beings can grow in insight and wisdom with age and experience.
Their decisions are often preliminary, shortsighted, confused, or
misguided. People change their minds! How can this stop at death?
Are we not still developing when we die and do we not need
further opportunities to grow in other ways and even in other
worlds? But Christian doctrine has always asserted the finality of
death for the judgment of good and evil. Perhaps a resolution of this
apparent conflict lies in the recognition that ultimately some kind of
final decision involving the summation of a life is more humanizing
than not. The responsibility for achieving a unified, completed
human life is frightening, but it is also integrally tied up with our
dignity and worth as human beings. "If our lives were to go on and
on without resolution," writes Anthony Saldarini, "our decisions
would accomplish nothing and be trivial. Whether at the end of
one, two or two thousand lives, we must come to completion."[22]
Any understanding of death and resurrection that implies a simple
resumption of an unfinished life can leave the erroneous impression
that the present life does not really count too much. "To insist on
the reality and finality of death," Monika Hellwig observes, "is to
insist that there is no human maturing, no 'growing up' from
childishness or half-conscious living into adulthood after death. The
image of God in which the human person is created is something to
be achieved in the course of biological life or not at all."[23]

Surely this notion of death as a personal, even personalizing,
event is what Martin Heidegger points to when he defines the
human person as *Sein-zum-Tode,* being-towards-death.[24] This
means that our essence is best understood in the light of death. For
Heidegger, it is this facing of death that forces us to deal with the
question of ultimate meaning. It is the fact that we know we are
going to die that opens us to the possibility of full life and thus is the
essence of distinctively human existence. Death constitutes a funda-

mental threat to us and so engenders anxiety at the realization of our own finitude. If we can deliberately confront and accept our mortality, however, we shall preserve our personal integrity in the face of it. Death is then far more than a biological fact in Heidegger's thought; it is the act that shapes and molds human consciousness. Authentic life is possible only when death is confronted as an internal, subjective, personal reality; inauthentic life is the refusal to take time or the precariousness of existence seriously.[25]

Although death has been traditionally defined as the separation of body and soul, it is now described by some Catholic theologians in terms of "personal self-fulfillment," "transformation," and "final option." Roger Troisfontaines, for example, speaks of death as integral to the "law of human growth," by which he means "man's forever-binding obligation to tear himself away, willingly or reluctantly, from an environment where his equilibrium was more passive, more external, and to enter into a more vast, more complex new situation, where he is bound to fail unless he enters deeper and deeper into his own self and is united ever more intimately to the being he discovers step by step."[26] This progress is seen analogically as a series of births, or more accurately "little deaths," which lead as it were through the passages of a lifetime and eventually through the passage we call death to new life. As Troisfontaines expresses this image: "The womb which was an absolute condition for life during the pre-natal period becomes an obstacle . . . the moment that the human being is about to be born. The same thing happens to the later, ever widening substitutes for the womb, like the mother's lap, home, family, school, group, or country. We have seen that the human being is born, grows and attains higher stages precisely by tearing himself away from previous environments which have become like so many prisons."[27] In old age the person is again preparing to leave an environment no longer capable of supporting his or her growth. The passage takes place in death: here the body, a kind of provisional womb, is abandoned so that personal growth may continue. So it is that death is the end of one phase and the beginning of another.

Karl Rahner, another Catholic theologian writing about death in a nontraditional way, emphasizes that death cannot be merely something that happens to us. If death were merely passive, he argues, it would be religiously indifferent. Rather, death is an active consummation brought about by the person himself or herself. By this he means that the "end of man as a spiritual person is an active consummation from within, a bringing of himself to completion, a growth that preserves the issue of his life; it is total entry into possession of himself, the state of having 'produced' himself, the fullness of the being he has become by all his free acts."[28] For Rahner, the act of dying has the power to bring all this about because it is a uniquely free act. It is true that all the seemingly free commitments we make during life are reversible, but the final act, by which we are to be judged for all eternity, is not just the last act of a series, which God for some odd reason chooses to weigh more heavily than all its predecessors, but an act which sums up all the others.[29]

A third Catholic theologian who speaks to this issue of final option is Ladislaus Boros. He sees death as the act of total self-encounter because it is not made in the midst of the limited freedom that marks our present existence but in the utter freedom that death offers. "Death is man's first completely personal act," he writes, "and is, therefore, by reason of its very being, the centre above all others for the awakening of consciousness, for freedom, for the encounter with God, for the final decision about one's eternal destiny."[30] Death frees the person from all the encumbrances accumulated during life. Everything to which the dying person clings must be taken away. "His things, his possessions, his power, even his friends, people dear to him, his hopes and dreams, all that he has built up and achieved in his life. One day all masks must fall, all roles too must come to an end: all the parts that man plays before the world and before himself."[31] Only then, Boros continues, is it possible to make an absolute decision. It follows that since such a decision realizes once and for all the whole extent of a person's being, it exhausts all possibilities and is absolutely final.[32]

In summary fashion, these theologians are saying that death should be seen more as a person's self-creation than passive destruction. Death gives us the opportunity to perform our first completely personal act. All other human acts are characterized by the essential temporariness of our existence; since they are time-bound they are always liable to revision. Death faces no-time, however, and so possesses the opportunity for complete freedom. It follows from this that once a completely free choice has been made we would never again freely want to alter it. This interpretation of the doctrine of the moral finality of death insists on seeing death as an active consummation from within, a growing up, the achieving of the total self.

Immortality versus Resurrection

Contemporary scholars have raised serious questions about the Christian doctrine of the immortality of the soul. If immortal soul means that a human being has an intrinsic quality by which he or she is incorruptible, then why is resurrection necessary? The argument goes: either immortality of the soul or resurrection of the dead. The traditional position says that physical death is the separation of the soul from the body. A human being is created with a dual nature, a spirit united with a body. At the moment of death, the body begins to decompose but the spirit goes to God. At the resurrection the soul will be reunited with its body or perhaps given a new resurrection body with which to enjoy eternity.

But here the problems begin to arise. The early Christian church took over the Greek understanding of the immortality of the soul and somewhat inconsistently taught bodily resurrection alongside it. In the course of this teaching, death became defined as the separation of body and soul and resurrection as the reclamation of a material body by the enduring soul. The modern psychological and behavioral sciences, however, have criticized such a dualistic interpretation of the human person. These disciplines inform us that the human person must be holistic, a unity of body, mind, and spirit. The words that describe mental characteristics and operations, as John Hick argues, "refer to the empirical individual, the observable human being who is born and grows and acts and feels and dies, and not to the shadowy proceedings of a mysterious 'ghost in the machine'."[33] But this is only to return to the understanding in Hebrew psychology of a man or woman as an individual psychophysical entity. In Hebrew thought, such concepts as body and soul cannot be abstracted from the essential integrity of the human person.

The Platonism adopted by most Christian thinkers in the early church saw the human person as essentially an eternal spirit, which for a time uses the body as a musician uses an instrument. It follows that death does not affect the core of personhood. Clement of Alexandria, for example, insisted on the preexistence and immortality of the soul. He writes: "We existed before the foundation of the world. . . . We are the rational creatures of the Logos of God, on whose account we go all the way back to the beginning."[34] For Clement, death is a liberation from the bonds of the present life; it is not an evil but a good. Tatian, on the other hand, is an exception since he rejected both preexistence and immortality in the name of the sovereignty of God.[35] Irenaeus, too, recognized the new element in resurrection by speaking in terms of a new humanity that is recapitulated in Christ.[36] Thomas Aquinas offered a later corrective to the Platonic view of human nature by using Aristotle to argue that it is not the soul that is the "real man" but the existential configuration of soul and body in the unified person.[37] But the end result of the effort to synthesize Greek and Christian thought was that the Platonic view of the immortality of the soul was declared as dogma by the Fifth Lateran Council (1512–17) and continues as the basic way of thinking about life after death even to the present time.

The implications of the recovered sense of the unity of the person in our own time forces contemporary Christian theology to take seriously the radicalism of death. Richard Doss sees this as a healthy move since immortality approaches death in categories that foster a climate of unreality and denial. "People are taught that death is something which really makes little difference," he says, and this "trivializes death and robs it of its power."[38] Death is not a liberation but "an enemy . . . which can only be overcome and defeated by the power of God."[39] The religious difference between the Platonic belief in the immortality of the soul and the Christian belief in the resurrection of the person, adds John Hick, is that "the latter postulates a special divine act of recreation. This produces a sense of utter dependence upon God in the hour of death, a feeling that is in accordance with the biblical understanding of the human being as having been formed out of 'the dust of the earth.' Hence, in the Jewish and Christian conception, death is something real and fearful. . . . It means sheer unqualified extinction. . . . Only through the sovereign creative love of God can there be a new existence beyond the grave."[40] If a person is truly one, death can not be regarded either as a neutral process or as a deliverance but must be seen as destruction. For those scholars who are challenging the old doctrine of immortality, the contrast is a sharp one between immortality as the natural property of a soul and resurrecton as the specific act of God in raising individuals from the dead. On the one hand, there is "unlimited existence whether or not there be a God," writes Hick, while on the other "man is inherently mortal, made out of the dust of the earth, and can have no life beyond death unless God will to recreate him on the other side by a miracle of divine power."[41]

Oscar Cullman has presented perhaps the sharpest criticism of immortality in favor of resurrection. In a provocative lecture delivered in 1955, he argued that the doctrine of death and resurrection is anchored in the Christ event and is incompatible with the Greek belief in immortality. By contrasting the serene death of Socrates with the terror-filled and painful death of Jesus, he concludes that Jesus is the mediator of salvation precisely because of his death. "He cannot obtain this victory by simply living on as an immortal soul," he argues, "thus fundamentally *not* dying. He can conquer death only by actually dying."[42] If life is to come forth from so genuine a death as that of Jesus, he continues, "a new divine act of creation is necessary. And this act of creation calls back to life not just a part of the man, but the whole man."[43] Only if we apprehend with the first Christians the horror of death can we comprehend the Easter exultation of the primitive Christian community. Belief in immortality of the soul is antithetical to belief in such a revolutionary event as the resurrection.

Karl Rahner also sees the classical definition of the separation of soul and body as inadequate because of its failure to speak of death as a personal and totally human event. He suggests that a better interpretation of death sees the soul as entering into some deeper, all-embracing openness to the universe and to God. Even in the present life, because it is united to a particular body, the soul must have some interaction with the larger material world of which that body is a part. But at death the soul is released from the limitation of being related to one particular human body and becomes related instead to the whole world. This does not imply that the soul is omnipresent to the universe or that the world somehow becomes the soul's body. Instead, by giving up its limited bodily structure the soul becomes open to the whole of creation. In death, says Rahner, the relationship of soul to body is not totally ruptured, rendering the soul "a-cosmic," but rather deepened into a "pan-cosmic" relationship with the universe. The pouring out of self at death leads to a new reality, which might be considered not too different from the union with the "All" or the state of Nirvana as presented in some of the Eastern religions.[44]

What the Christian critics of immortality seem to be saying is that the church's definition of death as separation of body and soul is a theological construct that is not in itself the object of faith but is rather the effort of believing people to speak meaningfully about the eschatological mysteries. Hellenistic philosophy and not biblical religion was the agent that split the human person into two parts and in a sense denied death by claiming immortality for the spirit.

The Greeks viewed death as a kind of escape of the person from the imprisonment of the body. It is not surprising, therefore, that Paul was scoffed at by the Athenians for preaching the resurrection: a doctrine that faces squarely the nonbeing of death and yet hopes for the gift of new creation.[45] The Christian belief in resurrection is different from the philosophical belief in an immortal soul. It is, in fact, a disservice to Christian faith to facilely deny the radicalness of death by overemphasizing the belief in a soul that will never die. What could resurrection possibly mean if death is so glibly brushed aside? Surely resurrection involves more than the mere resuscitation of the body for an eventual reunion with the soul; it must point to something completely new in human destiny.

Perhaps it would be beneficial to restate the "separation of body and soul" formula more in terms of a binding together than of a dividing apart. Traditional norms of behavior insist on preserving the ego as a separate entity to be guarded and preserved even while entering into necessary relationships with other independent egos. Society frequently judges sanity to rest on the capacity to adapt to the external world and to avoid as much as possible any personal direct awareness of the inner world. A person may be judged to be insane when his or her self-consciousness slips into a larger context of consciousness and he or she loses the sense of self-identity. Yet many religious traditions and leaders speak of reality precisely in terms of such a loss of self as the way to discover the true self. Jesus, for instance, offers this provocative claim: "Whoever would save his life will lose it, but whoever loses his life for my sake will find it."[46] Josef Pieper applies this saying directly to the question of personal death: "One loses what one tries to hold. What is required of man in the moment of death, for the first and only time, is to realize this very thing. It is required, but at that moment he is also enabled to do so; he is expected literally, not just 'by intention,' not just 'in good will,' not just symbolically and rhetorically, but in reality to lose his life in order to gain it."[47]

Death and Resurrection in the Bible

It is a startling fact that the early books of the Hebrew Bible contain no promise of life after death for the individual. Even Sheol, the abode of the dead, isn't a form of survival but its denial. The word itself probably signifies *underworld* and indicates that the dead were cut off from life here on earth. What survived in Sheol was not simply nothing but a shadowy, ghostly double of the living.[48] It is one vast tomb where all people, good and evil, are at rest. In fact, the early Hebrew scriptures are quite emphatic that the human person does not survive death. Qoheleth 3:19–20 declares, for example, that "the fate of the sons of men and the fate of beasts is the same; as one dies, so dies the other. They all have the same breath and man has no advantage over the beasts; for all is vanity. All go to one place: all are from the dust, and all turn to dust again."[49]

Instead of individual survival after death, it is Israel itself which will live on. The vision of the valley of dry bones in the book of Ezekiel, for instance, has nothing to do with personal resurrection but with the hope of resuscitating the nation.[50] There is, in fact, only one text in the Hebrew bible that seems to refer to personal resurrection, Daniel 12:2: "And many of those who sleep in the dust of the earth shall awake, some to everlasting life, and some to shame and everlasting contempt." The context of this second century B.C. scripture is the persecution of the Maccabean patriots by Antiochus Epiphanes. Resurrection here seems needed to answer the question of theodicy: will justice win out? Since some Jews had aposticized and were oppressing their fellow Jews while others had suffered martyrdom for their faith, God must act decisively to separate the good from the evil. Since power in this life lies with the sinners, it is required by justice that God raise the dead in order to reward the good and punish the evil.

In the Greek Old Testament (2 Maccabees), set like Daniel in the context of the Maccabean persecution, there are similar references to the resurrection of the just and unjust.[51] And the author of the Wisdom of Solomon, a Hellenistic Jew writing sometime in the first century B.C., is clearly influenced by the Platonic doctrine of the immortality of the soul. Speaking of the souls of the righteous, he says their "hope is full of immortality."[52]

At the time of Jesus, the question of the resurrection of the dead was a point of controversy between two rival factions, the Sadducees and the Pharisees. While the Sadducees continued to adhere to the ancient tradition that Sheol is the final abode of all the dead, the Pharisees accepted the innovative position that there would be a resurrection of the dead.[53] This Jewish hope for resurrection was primarily an eschatological sign, which would identify the dawning of the new age. The Christian belief in the resurrection of Jesus is different in the sense that it proclaimed the risen Christ here and now and went beyond the hope for a mere continuation of mortal life. Jesus' resurrection marked a once-and-for-all liberation from the power of death: "We know that Christ being raised from the dead will never die again; death no longer has dominion over him."[54]

For Paul the hope for the eschatological union with Christ is rooted in the present sacramental union through baptism. He writes: "Do you not know that all of us who have been baptized into Christ Jesus were baptized into his death? We were buried therefore with him by baptism into death, so that as Christ was raised from the dead by the glory of the Father, we too might walk in newness of life. For if we have been united with him in a death like his, we shall certainly be united with him in a resurrection like his."[55]This union, he adds, is a true conformity between the Christian and Christ: Jesus "will change our lowly body to be like his glorious body."[56] Nor must this conformity to Christ await the resurrection of the dead at the end of the world. Rather, the Christian can be joined to Christ at the time of his or her death. Faced with the possibility of his own execution, Paul reflects on whether it would be better to die now and "be with Christ" or to live in order to continue his work for the church.[57] From this we can see that Paul expected the immediate reward of being with Christ after death. The union with Christ, which had begun in baptism and which will be completed in the Parousia, is in no way interrupted by death.

But how are the dead brought to Christ? The Christian response, of course, is through resurrection, but, for Paul, resurrection is not an event separate from the person of Jesus Christ. Indeed, it is Jesus' resurrection that empowers his followers to "walk in newness of life"[58] and to be a "new creation."[59] It is because of Jesus' resurrection that all can hope for life despite death. Jesus is the "firstfruits," says Paul, by which he means that Jesus stands for the whole of humanity.[60] With Christ's resurrection, the resurrection of the dead has already begun.

Paul's conception of resurrection, however, has nothing to do with the resuscitation of corpses. The empty tomb tradition in the Easter accounts of the gospel is probably indebted to the Jewish thinking that a person does not have a body but is a body. To proclaim the resurrection of Jesus while his body lay in the tomb would have seemed like nonsense to many in the early church. Paul refuses to take too physical a view of the resurrection, however, and does not identify the resurrection body with the mortal body.

Resurrection for him concerns God's recreation of the individual, not as the organism that died but as a spiritual body. He says this new being is unlike the old in the same way as a full stalk of wheat differs from the wheat seed that was planted.[61] What Paul succeeds in teaching with this metaphor is that in resurrection not only does something remain of the old but something new comes into being. After all, it is the wheat seed and not some other kind of seed that grows into the mature wheat plant. But it is a new life, not a return or a recovery. Paul's image of the seed that truly dies in the transformation to this new life carries the notion of resurrection not as a going back but as a coming through to a new creation.

The essence of the New Testament proclamation, therefore, seems to be that in the dying and rising of Jesus Christ an event, which gives a totally new understanding of life and death, has occurred. This single salvific event of death–resurrection confirms for the Christian the conviction that it is all right to hope.

Death as Sacrament

The modern secularization of the symbols of death has in many instances deprived the contemporary person of his or her own death and even the right to mourn the dead. Philippe Ariès has traced this development in the history of Western attitudes towards the dying person, mourning processes, and funeral rituals, showing how the old symbols have lost their vitality.[62] In the United States, for example, the art of laying out and disposing of the body has evoked a series of new and quite elaborate practices, including the embalming of the body, its exhibition in a funeral parlor, visitation by friends and relatives, flowers and music, and interment in a park-like cemetery. Although criticized by some as only a form of commercial exploitation, such rituals, admittedly secular in nature, do at least testify to society's refusal to empty death of all meaning and to the human need to solemnize the occasion ritualistically.[63] Christian theology, especially in the Catholic liturgical renewal movement of the past few decades, has endorsed this urge for ritual, not by creating new symbols but by rediscovering the dormant life in the ancient ones.

In Christian life the passage through death to new life, which is proclaimed in the New Testament, is ritualized in sacrament. Death is, in fact, the "basic sacrament," claims Boros, because "as the supreme, most decisive, clearest and most intimate encounter with

Christ of a man's whole life," it "summarizes all the other encounters, concentrating in itself the whole spiritual history of a man."[64] As the basic sacrament it is present and active in the inner structure of each individual sacrament and points forward to life's supreme encounter with Christ in death. Baptism, for instance, signifies the end of an old life and the beginning of a new one in Christ. This has a "paschal character," according to the official interpretation of the rites of the Roman Catholic Church, "since the initiation of Christians is the first sacramental sharing in the death and rising of Christ."[65] Unfortunately, contemporary baptismal practices have tended to shift the emphasis of the symbolism from this death-life cycle to one of washing, but the ancient rubric clearly intended that the catechumen be divested of his or her old identity by being plunged into the water and symbolically dying with Christ.[66] Like Christ, the catechumen would then rise, put on new clothes, take a new name and assume the new dignity of a Christed person. Similarly, the sacrament of the eucharist celebrates in the breaking of the bread and the drinking of the wine, the reconciling power of the death of Christ for the church. The alienated, atomized, fearful people who symbolically die with Christ rise up as a unified community of Christians, the church, the Mystical Body of Christ.

The Christian liturgy, therefore, ritualizes the developmental stages of human life in terms of the death-resurrection mystery of Jesus Christ. The funeral ritual, for instance, marks the transition from life to death to new life. It is instructive to note here how the funeral ritual of the Roman Catholic church has undergone significant changes since the Second Vatican Council in a renewed effort to highlight this paschal symbolism. The old rite of burial emphasized the sadness and despair of death by the use of black vestments and prayers such as the De Profundis (Psalm 129), Miserere Mei (Psalm 50), and Libera Me, Domine: "Deliver me, O Lord, from everlasting death on that day of terror when the heavens and the earth will be shaken as you come to judge the world by fire."[67] The new rite, in contrast, "celebrates the paschal mystery of Christ."[68] The paschal candle, signifying the resurrected Christ and first blessed at Easter, is carried in procession. Instead of a eulogy, the directions read that there should be a homily that "relates Christian death to the paschal mystery of the Lord's victorious death and resurrection and to the hope of eternal life."[69] The church's expectation of resurrection for the dead person lies principally in the paschal significance of the baptism and eucharist that were received during his or her lifetime. White vestments are used, for instance, in remembrance of the baptismal garment, and a prayer is said recalling Paul's teaching that baptism is a sign of an already accomplished resurrection. The prayers suggested for the Mass make clear this connection between the sacraments and the paschal mystery: "Our brother (sister), N., was given the promise of eternal life in baptism: Lord, give him (her) communion with your saints for ever. . . . N. ate the bread of eternal life, the body of Christ; raise him (her) up, Lord, at the last day."[70]

The Christian sacraments offer a ritualized participation in the death and resurrection of Christ in anticipation of the full participation to take place at death. Such ritual participation can alleviate but not destroy entirely the terror of death as the last enemy. The Christian no more than anyone else is secure in the face of death, yet his or her faith is that death is indeed a creative event. The paschal mystery, which is sacramentalized in baptism and eucharist, gives the Christian the hope to leap into this last unknown called death in the belief that he or she will be grasped by Christ.

Conclusion

Earlier I suggested that the basic question to be faced by Christian theology with regard to the eschatological mysteries asks what the gospel tells us about death and about the meaning of human life in the face of death. Even though the answer of faith is the proclamation of the resurrection of Jesus Christ, the theologians must still explain what it means for a Christian confronting death to believe in a consummation in eternal life. In this chapter, I have tried to show that the ancient doctrines that attempted to define Christian belief concerning death and resurrection are in the process of being reinterpreted by contemporary Christian theologians, most notably in the Catholic community. These theologians seem to agree that the gospel message, which is being clarified in this work of renewal, claims at least this much: if one believes in God as revealed in Jesus Christ, then one believes that this world is not the ultimate reality, that life does have meaning, and that God's kingdom is the kingdom of eternal life.

NOTES

1. Sigmund Freud, *Beyond the Pleasure Principle,* trans. James Strachey (New York: Bantam Books,1959).

2. Sigmund Freud, *Beyond the Pleasure Principle,* p. 67.

3. See Freud, p. 70.

4. Freud, p. 80.

5. Freud, p. 87.

6. Simone de Beauvoir, *A Very Easy Death,* trans. Patrick O'Brien (New York: Warner Paperback Library, 1973).

7. de Beauvoir, *A Very Easy Death,* p. 123.

8. Edwin S. Schneidman, *Deaths of Man* (New York: Quadrangle, 1973), pp. 66–67.

9. Dylan Thomas, *The Collected Poems of Dylan Thomas* (New York: New Directions Books, 1957), p. 128. Albert Camus has a similar view: "Because of death human existence has no meaning. All the crimes that men could commit are nothing in comparison with that fundamental crime which is death." From *The Myth of Sisyphus,* quoted in Ignace Lepp, *Death and Its Mysteries,* trans. Bernard Murchland (New York: Macmillan, 1968), p. 132.

10. Leo Tolstoy, *The Death of Ivan Ilych* (New York: The American Library, 1960).

11. Quoted in Richard W. Doss, *The Last Enemy* (New York: Harper and Row, 1974), p. 25.

12. Richard W. Doss, *The Last Enemy,* p. 69.

13. Doss, p. 70. For an exegesis of the Genesis account, see Otto Kaiser and Eduard Lohse, *Death and Life,* trans. John Steely (Nashville, TN.: Abingdon, 1977), p. 22. These writers argue "that there can be no suggestion that in the opinion of the narrator man had been created immortal and had lost the corresponding attribute through the fall."

14. Quoted in Josef Pieper, *Death and Immortality,* trans. Richard and Clara Winston, (New York: Herder and Herder, 1969), p. 64.

15. Josef Pieper, *Death and Immortality,* p. 67.

16. Quoted in Pieper, p. 49. This tension between a notional and a personal acceptance of death is illustrated in Tolstoy's *The Death of Ivan Ilych* when Ivan finds it is impossible to move from a rational, syllogistic understanding of mortality to the recognition of his own dying situation.

17. Pieper, pp. 60–63.

18. Pieper, pp. 70–71.

19. Doss, p. 54.

20. Pieper, pp. 94–95.

21. See Roger Troisfontaines, *I Do Not Die,* trans. Francis E. Albert (New York: Desclee Co., 1963); Karl Rahner, *On The Theology of Death,* trans. Charles Henkey (New York: Herder and Herder, 1965). For a recent attempt at restating the traditional Christian doctrines concerning death and resurrection in the

light of contemporary theological, philosophical, and medical developments, see Hans Kung, *Eternal Life?*, trans. Edward Quinn (New York: Doubleday and Company, 1984).

22. Anthony Saldarini, "The Bible and the Near-Death Experience," in Brennan Hill, *The Near Death Experience: A Christian Approach* (Dubuque, Iowa: Wm. C. Brown Co., 1981), p. 52.

23. Monika K. Hellwig, *What Are They Saying about Death and Christian Hope?* (New York: Paulist Press, 1978), p. 61.

24. Martin Heidegger, *Being and Time* (New York: Harper and Row, 1962), p. 294.

25. For a brief summary of Heidegger's thought on death, see John Hick, *Death and Eternal Life* (New York: Harper and Row, 1976), pp. 97–101; see also Doss, pp. 59–62. Although contemporary Christian theology on death owes much to the philosophy of Heidegger, the idea of death as a decisive act goes back to the Church fathers. John of Damascus, for example, compared a human being's last decision to that of an angel, who in the first moment of existence decided irrevocably for or against God. This implies that a human being at the moment of death can decide in a totally radical and effective way, such as was never possible before, the whole of his or her existence. See Pieper, p. 87.

26. Troisfontaines, p. 133.

27. Troisfontaines, pp. 134–35.

28. Karl Rahner and Herbert Vorgrimler, *Theological Dictionary*, trans. Richard Strachan (New York: Herder and Herder, 1965), p. 117.

29. For a summary of Rahner's thought on death as final option, see Robert J. Ochs, "Death as Act: An Interpretation of Karl Rahner," in Michael J. Taylor, ed., *The Mystery of Suffering and Death* (New York: Alba House, 1973), pp. 119–38.

30. Ladislaus Boros, *The Mystery of Death,* (New York: Crossroad, 1973), p. 165.

31. Ladislaus Boros, "Death: A Theological Reflection," in Taylor, p. 143.

32. See Boros, *The Mystery of Death,* p. 93.

33. John Hick, *Philosophy of Religion* (Englewood Cliffs, N.J.: Prentice-Hall, 1983), p. 124.

34. Quoted in Jeroslave Pelikan, *The Shape of Death* (New York: Abingdon, 1961), p. 37.

35. Jeroslave Pelikan, *The Shape of Death,* p. 14.

36. Pelikan, p. 109.

37. See Pieper, p. 39.

38. Doss, pp. 87–88.

39. Doss, p. 87.

40. Hick, *Philosophy of Religion,* p. 125.

41. Hick, p. 180.

42. Oscar Cullman, "Immortality of the Soul or Resurrection of the Dead: The Witness of the New Testament," in Krister Stendahl, ed., *Immortality and Resurrection* (New York: Macmillan, 1965), p. 18.

43. Cullman, "Immortality of the Soul or Resurrection of the Dead," p. 18.

44. See Rahner, *Theology of Death,* and Rahner and Vorgrimler, pp. 115–18. John Hick, *Death and Eternal Life,* pp. 232–34, offers as criticism of Rahner's theory that it affirms only a natural development and posits no real need for resurrection. On the other hand, I would criticize Cullman's views as making resurrection too discontinuous with nature.

45. Acts 17:22–34.

46. Matthew 16:25.

47. Pieper, p. 103.

48. See Kaiser and Lohse, p. 34.

49. See also Genesis 3:19 and Job 14:7–12.

50. Ezekiel 37.

51. 2 Maccabees 7.

52. The Wisdom of Solomon 3:4.

53. See Lloyd R. Bailey, *Biblical Perspectives on Death,* (Philadelphia: Fortress Press, 1979), pp. 24–25.

54. Romans 6:9.

55. Romans 6:3–5.

56. Philippians 3:21.

57. Philippians 1:21–24.

58. Romans 6:4.

59. 2 Corinthians 5:17.

60. 1 Corinthians 15:20. See Doss, p. 91, for an interpretation of "firstfruits" as meaning a new point in the evolutionary process.

61. 1 Corinthians 15:36–38.

62. See Philippe Ariès, "Death Inside Out," in Peter Steinfels and Robert M. Veach, eds., *Death Inside Out: The Hastings Report* (New York: Simon and Schuster, 1963).

64. Boros, p. 165.

65. "Christian Initiation of Adults," Decree of the Sacred Congregation for Divine Worship, in *The Rites of the Catholic Church* (New York: Pueblo, 1976), p. 22.

66. Although the decree of the Sacred Congregation concerning baptism allows the application of the water by immersion, sprinkling, or pouring, it emphasizes that the washing "is not merely a rite of purification but a sacrament of union with Christ." *The Rites of the Catholic Church,* p. 29.

67. See *Collectio Rituum* (New York: Bonziger Brothers, 1964), pp. 230–40.

68. *The Rites of The Catholic Church,* p. 652.

69. *The Rites of The Catholic Church,* p. 674.

70. *The Rites of The Catholic Church,* p. 710–11.

6

The Teaching of the Quran Concerning Life after Death

SULAYMAN S. NYANG

Since the beginning of human society mankind has wondered about life and death. Much has been said and written about these twin phenomena and the human condition that they symbolize and dramatize. Of the various views advanced by poets, philosophers, and prophets, the greater majority of mankind seems to embrace the belief in a life beyond the grave as taught by the Abrahamic religions.[1]

Writing in the 1970s, of this century, the British historian Arnold Toynbee, in an essay entitled "Man's Concern with Life after Death," captured the general feeling of many people when he stated:

At the present day the belief in a reembodiment of the dead is still officially obligatory for all Zoroastrians, Jews, Christians, Muslims, Hindus, and Buddhists; and these six religions, between them, still command the adherence of a great majority of mankind. The teaching of the first four of these religions is that a human being lives only a single life; that his soul survives his death, disembodied; and that, at some unpredictable future date, every soul will be re-embodied in order to undergo the last Judgment and, according to the verdict, to enjoy physical bliss in Heaven or physical anguish in Hell. The teaching of Hinduism and Buddhism is that a soul (or, a Buddhist would say, a not yet cleared karma-account) is reborn in psychosomatic form not just once but a number of times. According to Buddhist teaching, the series of rebirths can be terminated if, in one of the recurrent bouts of psychosomatic life, the karma account is cleared, for its clearance opens the way for an exit into Nirvana. Hindu teaching does not offer this way of escape. According to Hinduism, rebirth continues at least for the duration of the current epoch (Kalpa)—and the time-scale of Hindu cosmology is as vast as modern astronomy's.[2]

This view of death and immortality is both real and deep-seated. As Toynbee again states, "the concern over the sequels to death is at its maximum in the heart and mind of a believer in Nirvana who strives to make his exit into it, and of a believer in post-mortem judgment and in Heaven and hell who strives to make sure that his post-mortem destiny shall be Heaven."[3]

Of the three major Abrahamic religions, Islam has generally been characterized by scholars as the one that talks most about the hereafter. Writing on the Quranic understanding of resurrection and judgment, Dalton Galloway states:

The resurrection and judgment, as is common knowledge, occupies a large and important place in the Kor'an. Scarcely is there a chapter without reference to the subject, and there are five chapters given almost entirely to the description of the Great Day, one of them (Sura 75) being entitled "The Resurrection." In the Mind of the Prophet there seems to have been as strong a conviction that there is a general resurrection and judgment and hereafter, as that "There is no god except Allah."[4]

This recognition of the Quranic emphasis on life beyond the grave has also been noted by another Western observer of Islam. Writing on Islamic Society in the volume edited by Toynbee and Koestler, M. S. Seale reminds his Western audience that "the term al-'akhira, the 'hereafter,' occurs one hundred and thirteen times in the Quran."[5] Of course, what is a novelty to the Western student of comparative religions is undoubtedly a daily spiritual diet to a practicing Muslim in the heartland of Islam. To the average practicing Muslim, life is a gift from Allah and when the Appointed Time comes, the individual departs from this World (*Dunya*) bound for a rendezvous with his Maker in the hereafter. It is therefore necessary to see the belief in a future life as integrally related to the total Islamic view of life in this Sublunar World including man's role in this world and the significance of his faith in and devotion to Allah.

The Islamic View of Man and the Sublunar World

The Quranic view of man is that he is created out of the best mould but can become the lowest of the low. (Surah 95, lines 4–5).[6] Man, according to the Quran, is unique because, of all creation, only he accepted the responsibility of Allah's vicegerent. This great trust, which the natural elements and the mountains shied away from because of its awesomeness, has put man in a special position in the cosmic scheme of things.[7]

Indeed, in various chapters of the Quran there are striking statements, which, taken together, give a picture of the origins, earthly mission, and destiny of mankind. These Quranic teachings make it categorically clear that man is given life on earth so that he may serve his Creator and be rewarded by Him in the hereafter.

In the creation story of the Holy Quran, we learn that God's decision to create man and woman was for a specific purpose, because He told his angels that, though they had entertained apprehensions about man's responsibility on earth, He knew what they knew not.[8] From this Divine Answer, numerous theological arguments about human destiny have been constructed. Some Muslim thinkers have taken this to mean that, on the scale of spiritual development, there is no limit to human advancement and man may even surpass the angels.

Related to this Quranic statement is the *ayat* (Sign in the Holy Book), which affirms that man was not created for sport.[9] This Divine Pronouncement makes it categorically clear that man's brief sojourn on earth is for a *serious mission*. The Quran constantly reminds man that his road to *al-Janat* (heaven) is likely to be blocked by Satan, that all his deeds on earth are to be accounted for, and that his firm faith in the supreme Being is strengthened by the purity of his thoughts and deeds.

Another teaching of the Quran with regard to man's role in the universe is the understanding that sinfulness corrupts the soul of man and turns him from the *Sirat al-Mustahim* (right path) to the path of Satan and his confederates. In order for man to move closer to the Islamic vision of him, he must live above mere life (above animal existence) and act out in his daily life the teachings of the *Shariah*. It is only through faithful practice of Quranic teachings that man can become a fully-fledged Muslim. And by doing so, man learns to see the more positive side of his being and the great rewards that await him in the hereafter (*al-akhira*).

Again, in talking about sin and the Islamic vision of man, one can add that Islamic thought takes a totally different view of man's destiny from the sister Abrahamic faiths. Whereas Christians of various denominations still believe that the historical manifestation of Jesus Christ was true and that his crucifixion was ontologically and eschatologically significant because it opened the door of salvation to human beings, whose genetic links to Adam and his wife had condemned them *ab initio* to eternal damnation, Muslim theologians make no such claims for their Prophet Muhammad.

Rather, they argue that Muhammad and his prophetic counterparts in history were protected from sin by Allah and the best thing we as individuals living in society can do for the good of our faith and our community, is to follow the example of *al-Imam al-Muslimin* (the Imam of the Muslims).[10] This Islamic imperative is heeded by the Sufis who see the Holy Prophet Muhammad as the *al-Insan al-Kamil* (the Universal Man) and then begin their quest for *Nur Muhammadiyya* (the Light of Muhammad) through vigorous vigils, prayers, and retreats *(halwa)*. Such an exercise in spiritual example-following is also known to orthodox Muslims, whose sophistication and worldly learning convince them not to dabble in Sufism and not to mistake the Divine Message with the *bidas* (innovations) and superstitions of the common people.

From what we have said so far it is clear that the concept of sin is crucial to Islamic ontology, Islamic metaphysics, and Islamic eschatology. When viewed ontologically from a Muslim perspective, sin becomes a unit in the human/spiritual universe. According to the Quranic version of the creation story, the rebellion of *Iblis* (the Archangel) was the first and most significant act of sin in the creation.[11] It was sinful because the perpetrator committed an act of negativity towards his creator at three levels: first of all, by refusing to bow before man as his Creator willed, this former archangel of Allah introduced into *cosmic time* and into the realm of human consciousness what had hitherto been the alien *concept of disobedience*. This is to say, the act of disobedience on the part of Iblis demonstrated at the angelic level what was to be later replicated on the plane of human life and activity by Adam and his wife.

Second, the defiance of Iblis, according to the Quranic story of creation, opens up a new beginning in cosmic time in the sense that Allah identified an enemy from within his inner circle and then meted out the appropriate punishment. Prior to Iblis' defiance the universe was orderly and obedient to all Divine commands. Viewed from this perspective, one can argue that Iblis' defiance was ontologically and eschatologically significant in that his act of rebellion set a poor example to the subsequent history of Adam and his children. Here is one of the serious ironies of cosmic religious history. It was indeed the creation of Adam and his wife that led to the refusal of Iblis "to bow before those who are created out of dust"; yet it was the same Adam who in turn went against the Divine order only to suffer the same expulsion as the archangel who had earlier refused to bow before him.

The third point that needs to be made here about Iblis' rebellion and its implications for the Islamic concept of sin and its vision of man is that the downfall of Iblis from the pinnacle of angelic glory to the pits of the Seven Hells anticipated at the angelic level what was to happen on the human plane. This development linked human history to cosmic history and resulted in Allah's decision to divide up humanity into two categories, namely *men of prophecy* and *men of society*. The differences between these two types is the differential in Divine Mercy and Divine Grace. The former is protected from sin and for this and other reasons could transmit the Divine message without falling into the webs of temptations from Satan and his confederates. The latter, however, does not enjoy such spiritual favors and for this reason needs guidance from the chosen prophets among mankind. It is indeed in this context that Muslim teachers argue that the Holy Prophet Muhammad was sent only as a *Mundhir* (a warner) and a *Huda* (a Guide) to humanity. He was not a savior and could not forgive anyone his or her sins; and even when it comes to intercession for others on the Day of Judgment, he would be able to do so only at the pleasure of Allah. This Islamic view, I would stress here, is another affirmation of the humanity of the Prophet Muhammad and the spiritual and historical limitations of his role as Allah's chosen messenger to the Children of Adam.[12]

Man's Belief in Allah and its Significance for the Hereafter

Having examined the Quranic texts that focus on man's origins and his metaphysical responsibilities, let us now address the question of faith in Allah and its implications and consequences for his destiny. According to the Holy Quran, man cannot and must not be called a believer unless and until he gives proof that Islam has found its way into his heart or mind. The late Shaykh al-Azher, Professor Mahmud Shaltout, reminded his fellow Muslims in the 1950s that, "Islam requires, first of all, a deep belief in it without any doubt or suspicion, as is made clear in many texts of the Quran and in the general agreement of the ulama of Islam. This emphasis on the primacy of belief was the first message of Muhammad to the Arabs, just as it was the message of all apostles and prophets; as the Quran says: "Say (O Muslims): we believe in Allah and that which is revealed unto us and that which was revealed unto Abraham, and Ishmael, and Isaac, and Jacob, and the tribes, and that which Moses and Jesus received, and that which the Prophets received from their

Lord. We make no distinction between any of them, and unto Him we have surrendered" (Surah 11, line 136).[13]

The Muslims who are instructed by the Holy Quran to follow the example of the Holy Prophet Muhammad have decided since the very beginning of the Islamic movement to follow his teachings and his *Sunnah*. This emulation of the Holy Prophet is, in Muslim eyes, the best thing to do here below. For not only does the Prophetic example in the form of the *Shariah* provide the rules and regulations that create proper relations between us and the Creator, such as *Salat* (Prayer), *Suam* (fasting) and the giving of *zakat* (Quranically stipulated charity), but it also guides man in his relations with his brother in Islam or the non-Muslim community. Furthermore, according to Shaykh Shaltout, the Quranic teachings help mankind to organize the structure of the family and encourage reciprocal affection; lead man to an understanding of his place in the universe, encourage research into the nature of man and animals and guide man in the use of the benefits of the natural world.[14]

This Quranic message, it should be stated, also emphasizes the inevitable relationship between belief and faith. This is to say that one cannot be truly a believer without being a practicer of what one believes to be eternal truth. The Quran makes it clear that the result of belief is faith, and it affirms this point in the following *ayat:*

Verily those who say,
"Our Lord is God,"
And remain firm
(on that path)—on them
shall be no fear,
Nor shall they grieve.
Such shall be Companions
of the Garden, dwelling
Therein (for aye): a recompense
For their good deeds.[15]

Since belief and faith are so inextricably linked, Islam has always expected man to externalize his faith in Allah through an expression of solidarity with other Muslims in his social universe. Although each human being is responsible for his own soul at the Day of Judgment, the fact remains that his life here below is not lived in isolation. Rather he is forced to live with other humans in society. It is this existential reality that makes the life of the Muslim one of dual responsibility. This is to say, he is responsible for the spiritual cultivation of the seeds of faith in his own private world of inner consciousness; he is also responsible as a member of the *Ummah* (Muslim Community) or the human society, to collaborate with other believers in the human quest for the planting and cultivating of the seeds of faith in the Most High God among men.

Because of the sociality of man, his faith in Allah cannot be sealed off from the wider community of man. Indeed, belief may be private, but faith must be made public to have effect in human society. This is how the individual accountability of man interferes with the public day of reckoning, which the Quran repeats over and over again.

Though belief in Allah is the roadmap to the hereafter (*al-akhira*), it is faith and good works that serve as the engine and highway to get us there. To keep to our metaphors and analogies, one can again say that in the journey to *al-akhira,* man's temptations are the numerous potholes that are likely to slow down his spiritual vehicle and damage his engine. The service stations and toll booths in this spiritual journey are the religious structures created by men to help one another in this difficult and painful encounter with life and death.

As we can see, belief in Allah is a necessary condition to being a Muslim; but in order to be truly *Islamic,* one must not only have faith in Allah but must concretize his faith through good works and services to the Creator. From these Quranic evidences, one can conclude that man is a special creation delegated to serve as Allah's vicegerent in the sublunar world; that his belief in Allah is the beginning of his journey to the *al-akhira* (hereafter) and that he can enter heaven (*al-Jana*) only after having been brought to book; and that on the day of judgment no man can save another. In the view of the Quran, man's greatest moment of weakness is when the Trumpet is blown and the Lord of the Worlds summons (*kun-fa yakun*)[16] all his creation to give an account of their lives in the space-time worlds he let them live and act out their lives. It is not man alone that is accountable on this day. Jinns and animals too will be there responding to the questions of Allah's angels.

The Quranic View of the Day of Judgment and Man's Immortality

The Islamic view of the Day of Judgment and Immortality is inextricably linked to its view of man and his role on earth. After having explored those aspects of this subject, let us move to the discussion of the Quranic teachings on the Day of Judgment and on the immortality of man beyond the grave.

In order to grasp the Quranic understanding of the Day of Judgment, let us briefly spell out the five key Muslim principles that man must accept and live by if he is to be distinguished from the *Mushrikin* (polytheists) and *Kuffar* (unbelievers). Basic to Islamic thought is the belief in *tawhid* (the unity of Allah). Man cannot think of a life beyond the grave without believing in a High God who created him and all there is in the Universe. The Muslim is constantly reminded by the Quran to look at the workings of Nature so as to recognize the Divine handiwork. He is also asked to apply intuition to appreciate better the Divine message of the Holy Prophet Muhammad that is presented to the people of Mecca and Medina.

In describing the Day of Judgment, the Quran paints a very gloomy life for the unbelievers and hypocrites of this life. We are told that on this day the individual responsibility of each person to accept the revelation of Allah will be the determining factor in the judgment of souls. The son or daughter who failed to accept the teachings of Islam is responsible for his or her deeds here on earth. His belief and behavior can neither benefit nor harm his or her parents. The same thing applies to his or her parents. Neither their belief nor their behavior can affect him or her on the Day of Judgment. This Quranic view of the Day of Judgment is well stated in Surah 31, where Allah states:

O Mankind! keep your
duty to your Lord and
fear a Day when the parent
will not be able to avail
the child aught, nor the
child to avail the parent.[17]

This idea of judging the individual extends to all beings who are ontologically charged with the power of free will. This universal principle of judging all regardless of color, race, gender, tribe, or nationality is echoed throughout the Quran. For example, in Surah 49, Allah reveals:

O Mankind! We created
You from a single (pair)
Of a male and a female,

And made you into
Nations and tribes, that
Ye may know each other
(Not that ye may despise
Each other). Verily
The most honoured of you
In the sight of God
Is (he who is) the most
Righteous of you.
And God has full knowledge
And is well acquainted
(With all things). [18]

In addition to the basic belief in the oneness of Allah, there are the
beliefs in His messengers, in the holy books they brought to mankind, and, of course, in the Day of Judgment and the hereafter. The
five principles in Islam constitute the important pillars on which
one's faith is built. Anyone who denies one of them cannot be
treated as a Muslim. Yet, as Shaykh Mahmud Shaltout pointed out
two decades ago,

it does not follow that he
who does not believe in
any of these facts would be
considered a true believer by
Allah and would therefore suffer
eternal damnation. It simply
means he would not be treated
as a Muslim; he would not
be under any obligation to
worship Allah according to
Muslim rules. He would not
be prevented from doing
things prohibited by Islam—
Such as drinking wine or
eating pork—and on death
he would not be washed
and prayed for by Muslims. [19]

Shaykh Shaltout's interpretation of the Quran led him to conclude that a person is indeed an unbeliever if, after having been
freely convinced of the truth of these beliefs, he decided to reject
them, or any part of them, through obstinacy, pride, love of Satan
or the pomp of power, or the fear of being criticized. [20] The person

who is not so privileged, according to the al-Azhar Shaykh, is not an unbeliever and will not suffer everlasting punishment.

The five principles that we identified above, be it noted, are beliefs whose acceptance creates the opportunities for the individual believer to prepare for his journey to the hereafter. They do not only register the individual's recognition of the original source of his own creation, but they also affirm his faith in the existence of a spiritual bridge linking the here and now and the hereafter. Through such a bridge Divine Messages are conveyed via angels and human beings chosen as Prophets. Without the faith in the oneness of Allah, without faith in His Scriptures and the Prophets, and without faith in angels who traverse both worlds in the service of their Master, man cannot talk about a Day of Judgment. For a Day of Judgment can only be meaningful to humanity when human beings are given a mission and a set of guidelines to follow while they live on earth.

Given these Islamic beliefs one can now say that the Muslim who prepares for the hereafter knows that his life in the Sublunar World is a stage on which he performs his dress rehearsals for the Great Day. To adequately prepare for this Hour of Reckoning, he must live by the five Pillars of Islam on a daily basis. Not only should he make the *Kalimat* (the first article of faith testifying to the unity of Allah and to the Prophethood of the Holy Prophet Muhammad) a living reality in his life and consciousness, but he should also say his five daily prayers, perform the fast, give the zakat, and go to the Holy Cities of Hijaz to perform the Hajj. Through the living concretization of these Islamic beliefs and practices, the Muslim makes his life beyond the grave more and more attractive.

What does the Quran teach about those who believe and do good work? It emphatically states that these are the inheritors of *al-Janat* (Paradise) where they will live forever. The Quran reiterates this certain promise to the believers and doers of good so many times that many a commentator has noted the graphic details with which the Quran portrays the hereafter. In one powerful passage we read that the Angel of Death called Azrad will address those who enter the new World of the Dead. The Quran maintains that those good men who are caused to die by these Angels of Death, will hear the reassuring mark:

Peace be unto you!
Enter the Garden because
of what ye used to do[21]

Those who live in sin and believe not when the Angels of Death seize their souls, will be interrogated by these angels. They will be asked about what they were doing here on earth. And they will reply: "We were oppressed in the land." The Angels, according to the Quran, will retort: "Was not Allah's earth spacious that ye could have migrated therein?" Because their answers will be unsatisfactory and because Allah has indisputable evidence against this class of human beings, He will send them to *al-Jahanem* (hell) where they will dwell till He grants them Mercy.

Related to the Muslim belief in the Day of Judgment and Immortality is the belief that certain angels are charged with the responsibility of recording all human deeds. These record keepers are being emulated today by our security forces in their use of videotapes and bugging devices; but even under the most effective Orwellian State the deeds of man will not be as efficiently and fully recorded as by the Divine Method. The Quran informs us that these registers of human deeds are everywhere and man cannot elude them as he often does policemen in human society:

Lo! there are above
you guardians, generous
and recording, Who know
(all) that ye do[22]

This Quranic revelation is very significant for it touches a very important aspect of the Muslim view of the Day of Judgment and Immortality. As we can see, man is not only created out of the best mold, he is also entrusted with the heavy responsibility of being Allah's caliph (vicegerent). This is to say, he is the custodian of the earth and all that is therein. He is ordered to adore his Creator just as the angels and Jinns are so commanded. But what makes man's mission and sojourn on earth a grave responsibility is that he is not only given an *Appointed Time,* but he is also held accountable for his deeds on earth. To make sure that he obeys, Allah sends a stream of rightly guided Prophets to bring revelations and provide guidance to misguided man straying from the *Sirat al-Mustahim* (the Right Path).

But as I indicated earlier, the Day of Judgment and the hope of eternal life in *al-Janat* are not reserved for mankind alone. In the Quran we read that both man and Jinns are created to adore Allah. Unlike men who enter the realm of Divine Creation wearing *turab* (dust) and using it as the vehicle of self-expression among conscious beings, the Jinns are creatures fashioned out of essential fire. For example, in words echoed over and over again throughout the Holy Book, Allah states:

And the Jinn did we create,
aforetime of essential fire. [23]

The Jinns too are to account for their deeds at the end of time, for as the Quran reveals, some are believers in Allah and some are unbelievers, and unjust. [24] Those among the Jinns who believe will be welcomed to *al-Janat* (Paradise) and those who deny the Divine Message will be sent to *al-Janaham* (hell) as firewood.

The Jinns will be held accountable for another matter: their seduction of mankind. In the Quran, Allah describes the Day of Judgment when both men and Jinns are brought before Him. On that day, Allah will address the Jinns as follows:

O ye assembly of the Jinn!
Many of humankind did ye
seduce. And their adherents
among human kind will say:
Our Lord!
We enjoyed one another, but
now we have arrived at
the appointed term which
Thou appointedst for us.
He will say: Fire is your
home. Abide therein forever,
Save him whom Allah
Willeth (to deliver). Lo! thy
Lord is wise, Aware. [25]

With regard to the angels, the Quran states in many verses that these beings possess all the spiritual virtues and none of the short-comings of human beings. Unlike the Jinns, who the Quran described as whisperers and provocators—evils that are sometimes found in men—the angels live every moment of their existence obeying the Divine command. Charged with a wide range of functions and duties, these spiritual beings run Divine messenger errands to Prophets in the days before the arrival of the final revelation (*al-Quran*). Implicit if not explicit in the Muslim's belief in Muhammad's role as the terminal point of Divine Prophecy, is the complementary belief in the post-Quranic period of human history; no man can claim to be a recipient of a Divine Message that entitles him to be called a Prophet in the Islamic sense.

With regard to the soul, or spirit, on the Day of Judgment and in the hereafter, the Quran does not offer many clues. Addressing this same question, Shaykh Mahmud Shaltout wrote that two Quranic verses from two different sources are the only sources we can go by to understand the nature of the soul in the hereafter. From the creation story, according to him, we learn that the soul is the source of life.[26] This view is reinforced in another verse where Allah identifies the soul with that which leaves the dying men.[27]

Shaykh Shaltout, after having discussed this same problem of the soul, advises that "there is no Quranic text which prohibits searching for such a supernatural spirit, whether or not such researches might be fruitful,"[28] He quoted the Quranic verse that told the Prophet to tell his followers and those who ask about the soul that it is by the command of Allah it exists and knowledge about it is very little.

Conclusions

From the foregoing discussion we can make a number of conclusions about man and his destiny at the end of time. First of all, we can say that man is created for a *purpose* and is *responsible* for all his deeds here on earth. Secondly, the Day of Judgment is a *certainty,* and all Muslims are required to believe in the oneness of Allah (*tawhid*), in all the scriptures sent to Mankind, in all the Prophets, and in the angels.

Thirdly, one can also conclude that the Quranic view of the Day of Judgment is that man, Jinns, and the rest of creation will be brought to book. Man's uniqueness on the Day of Judgment lies in the fact that he will be judged according to the records against him presented by the record-keeping angels, and no one can intercede for him.

Fourthly, we can also conclude that in the Quranic view eternal damnation is for those who refuse to believe and do what Allah has enjoined upon mankind. Last but not least, we can conclude that the Quranic view promises man a life of immortality, although the nature of such a life is beyond our comprehension.

NOTES

1. By Abrahamic religions we mean Judaism, Christianity, and Islam. Of course, there are other minor religious groups, such as the Bahais and Ahmadis, who also trace their spiritual roots to the Prophet Abraham.

2. See Arnold Toynbee and Arthur Koestler, eds., *Life After Death*. (New York: McGraw Hill Book Co., 1976), p. 29.

3. Toynbee and Koestler, eds., *Life After Death*, p. 32.

4. See Dalton Galloway, "The Resurrection and Judgment in the Koran," *The Moslem World*, vol. 17 (1922), p. 348.

5. See Toynbee and Koestler, eds., *Life After Death*, chap. 5, p. 125.

6. *The Holy Quran* as translated by Yusuf Ali.

7. For Quranic references to this human responsibility, see chap. 6, verse 44.

8. For the Quranic Creation story see also the following texts: Surah, 96: line 5; Creation of Adam, 2:30–34; Fall of Adam, 2:35–39, 7:19–25; Adam tempted by Satan, 20:121; Adam and Iblis, 2:34, 7:11–18, 15:31–44, 17:61–65, 18:15, 20:116–23, 37:71–85.

9. See *The Holy Quran*, 21:16–17, translated by Yusuf Ali.

10. For the passages on the sinlessness of Prophets, see 2:151; 21:25–27; 66:6. For a Muslim scholar's analysis of this fact, see Maulana Muhammad Ali, *The Religion of Islam* (Cairo, Egypt: National Publication and Printing House, n.d.) pp. 233ff.

11. For details on Iblis' rebellion, see the following passages of *The Holy Quran* 2:34; 7:11–18; 15:31–44; 17:61–65; 18:50; 22:116–23; 38:71–85.

12. For discussion of the holy prophet Muhammad, see Ameer Ali, *The Spirit of Islam* (London: Methuen, 1965).

13. Mahmud Shaltout, "Islamic Beliefs and Code of Laws," in Kenneth W. Morgan, ed. *Islam The Straight Path* (New York: Ronald Press, 1958), pp. 88–89.

14. Mahmud Shaltout, "Islamic Beliefs and Code of Laws," p. 89.

15. See *Holy Quaran*, 26:13–14.

16. In various chapters of the Holy Quran, we learn that whenever God wishes to act, he says, "be and it is."

17. See *Holy Quran*, 31:33.

18. See *Holy Quran*, 49:13.

19. Mahmud Shaltout, p. 92.

20. Mahmud Shaltout, p. 92.

21. *The Holy Quran*, 32:11, and 16:34.

22. *The Holy Quran*, 82:10–12.

23. *The Holy Quran,* 15:27.
24. *The Holy Quran,* 72:14–15.
25. *The Holy Quran,* 6:129.
26. *The Holy Quran,* 14:28–29.
27. *The Holy Quran,* 16:83–84.
28. Mahmud Shaltout, p. 102.

7

Death and Immortality in Islamic Thought
SALIH TUG

In this chapter, I will try to explain briefly the concepts of mortality and death in Islam. I confess that this subject is one of the most important fields in Islam, requiring some specialization to speak about authoritatively, and I am not of that field. After having made that point I shall proceed to tackle the subject, explaining its main features in general, and then more specifically within the framework of the thought of al-Ghazali, a Muslim thinker of the eleventh century, who is well known today in both the East and the West.

As far as I know there is no independent work by any Muslim thinker dealing solely with the idea of mortality and death. However, based on the verses of the Holy Quran and the Traditions of the Prophet Muhammad, Muslim scholars and mystics have produced explanations within their own works on these subjects.[1]

What remains, therefore, is to collect all of this scattered information in Islamic literature and compile it in a single paper. It would have been beyond the scope of this chapter to describe in detail all the views of the major Muslim thinkers over the centuries on the subject. For this reason I shall focus on al-Ghazali.[2] Using his explanations, I will try to elucidate the idea of death in Islam.[3]

First of all, it must be kept in mind that the subject is entirely metaphysical. It cannot be demonstrated to the direct experience of man. Death occurs once in a man's life, and he goes on to the immortal world without having had the opportunity to describe the experience. The Holy Books of the East and the verses of the Quran, as well as the Sayings (Traditions) of the Prophet (Muhammad), while revealing some information about the eternal life and Holy World, do not say anything directly or in detail about the nature of death. Once again I would emphasize that the subject is a metaphysical and Holy one, and has some features that cannot be explained by the human intellect alone.

This Life as a Preparation For Eternity

It is commonly emphasized by Muslims that death does not bring the life of man to an end; it only opens the door to a higher form of life. Just as from dust man is evolved, from the deeds that he does, the higher man is evolved. Hence we find the Holy Quran referring again and again to man's evolution from a very low origin and proceeding on to life after death.[4]

The acceptance of life after death is, therefore, one of the fundamentals of Islam. It opens up a wide vista of progress before man, a new world of advancement before which the progress made in this life sinks into insignificance.[5] The Quran says:

And whoever desires the hereafter, and strives for it as he ought to strive and [as] he is a believer, their striving shall be recompensed. . . . See how We have made some of them to excel others, and certainly the Hereafter is much superior in respect of degrees and much superior in respect of excellence.[6]

The Quranic verses detail for us the whole process of human evolution as well as the part played by religion in human life. Man arises out of the earth. The earthly matter has passed through several stages of evolution before it finds its sublimation in the human form.

The Quran says:

And certainly We created man of an extract of clay; then made him a small life-germ in a firm resting place, then We made the life-germ a clot; then We made the clot a lump of flesh; then We made the lump of flesh bones; then We clothed the bones with flesh; then We caused it to grow into another creation; so blessed be Allah, the best of the creators.[7]

And also the verse:

Then after that you will most surely die.[8]

So mankind begins by taking the form of the life-germ, which though microscopic in size, is the repository of the physical, intellectual, and moral features of man. The germ grows and becomes man. In an adult human, it is usually the physical aspect that is more thoroughly realized.

But the human frame is only a vehicle by which the soul must develop itself. The soul has to evolve itself by its own effort from the crude form of simple consciousness to a certain stage of spirituality. This evolution can be worked out only through the cultivation of our innate faculties. Man's soul possesses infinite potential for advancement. He has to till the field in the depths of his soul and bring out his latent faculties. But just as the ordinary peasant needs rain to bring forth his crops, so the soul needs rain to bear fruit. That rain comes from Allah in the form of Revelation and is given to humanity through the medium of Prophets. Man should become a receptacle for this spiritual rain if he wishes to reap a good harvest. Without it the field of the human soul becomes sterile and subject to decay.

Our present life is a preparation. It is necessary to bring out our faculties and raise them to a certain stage of evolution during our earthly sojourn. Then alone shall we be fit for progress in the life after death.

Death is thus not annihilation but a gateway for entering into a new life; a life of unlimited progress.[9] But we can enter that life only if we have made ourselves fit for it in our physical lifetime. This may be illustrated by an example: suppose we pluck two seeds from a tree; one ripe, the other immature. We found both under similar conditions but we get no plant from the immature seed although it commenced its life with the same potentialities as the ripe one. Similarly if we have not attained a certain stage of spiritual development in our earthly life, we can not enter the heavenly life.

What Happens after Death

Now, after departing from the physical body, the soul does not enter its life in heaven or hell at once. It remains suspended in the ethereal world, which in Islam is called *Barzakh*. Here its faculties remain in abeyance, though intact, and this state will continue until the hour of resurrection, after which it will be sent to either Heaven or Hell. But the impressions left on the soul by its actions while on earth come to the surface in the state of *Barzakh*. One's character being the crystallization of one's thought, after death "the thoughts that he or she was thinking in this world take their shape . . . happy shapes or shapes of calamities according to what he believed in this world."[10]

Now, the souls that are suffering from spiritual diseases and do not come up to a certain standard will be sent to a quasi "spiritual hospital" called hell. The Quran has much to say on the subject but to go into details here would be a long digression. Suffice it to say that hell will be one of the stages in the process of evolution for the soul that has not utilized the opportunities provided for it in its earthly sojourn. It stunted its faculties becoming diseased and corrupted, but after cure it shall come out of that state and start on its evolutionary journey.[11]

As I have indicated in the beginning, we know very little about the reality of death. Some people of insight give us general information on the conditions of dying people, particularly that people are divided into many classes after death, but what exactly will happen to an individual cannot be determined.

Al-Ghazali himself attaches a great deal of importance to the concluding stage of man's life (al-khatimah). It seems that man will be able to know whether he is "sa'id" (good) or "shaq" (evil) during the agony of death. When a man dies while the love of this world is still dominant in his heart, his condition will be very perilous, since, as al-Ghazali says: "Man dies according to how he lives."[12]

To think that his soul will be snatched away while he is in this stage inspires fear and terror in a man. This is because he knows that the condition of the heart does not change after death. The quality of the heart is changed through the works of the physical organs. When these organs are nullified, the work will be nullified too. He knows equally well that there is no chance of coming to this world again and obtaining what has already been missed. At this realization his grief will be greatly increased.

Only the basic faith in, and love of, God that have been established in the heart and strengthened through good actions can eventually erase from it this state into which it has fallen in the process of dying. This is only one of two degrees that al-Ghazali calls, "Bad Ending" (Su' al-Khatimah).[13]

The other degree, which is greater than the first, is the condition of the heart that is overtaken by either doubt or denial during the agony of death. If the spirit is snatched away while the heart is in one of these, a veil appears between man and God that leads to eternal separation and endless punishment. Thus, the "Bad Ending" is the beginning of a miserable spiritual life, which can be either temporary (first case) or eternal (second case).

Al-Ghazali, whom we may suppose to be inspired by the Quranic verses and some sayings allegoric in character of the Prophet Muhammad, emphasizes that when death approaches and the forelock of the Angel of Death becomes visible to man, he often knows that what he has believed through ignorance is false. This is because the state of death is as the removal of a curtain. Some matters may be disclosed to man while he is in this state, says al-Ghazali.[14] The disclosure that some of what he believed in due to ignorance was false will cause him to deny even the truth in what he believed, or at least to have doubt in it. Now, if his soul is snatched away at this stage before he can stand firm and return to the foundation of faith, he will finish his life with a "Bad Ending" and his soul will leave him when he is in the state of polytheism (*shirk*).

As for the one who dies as a lover of Allah, he will go towards Allah like a servant who yearns to meet his master. This does not mean that he has no fear of the "Bad Ending." As a matter of fact, good men and even prophets have always been perplexed by and fearful of the agony of death and the "Bad Ending," having knowledge of what these are all about.

According to al-Ghazali, the obedient man realizes while dying that he is good before God. His soul will be taken away probably without difficulty. He may see the Angel of Death in its most beautiful form, and it may even be made known to him what sort of place he will be given in heaven.[15] The wretched people too will know something about their place in hell. For them, dying and seeing the Angel of Death will be a great punishment. This is a brief description of the situation of both good and evil men at the time of death in the eyes of the Great Muslim mystic, al-Ghazali, who is mostly inspired by the Quranic verses and sayings of the Prophet Muhammad.

According to a saying of the Prophet Muhammad, "the grave is either a pit of the pits of Hell-Fire or one of the meadows of Heaven." To al-Ghazali, whoever denies this is an innovator who is veiled from the light of God. In the grave of the person who has deserved punishment seventy doors of hell will be opened, although the ignorant man looks into the grave and says that he sees nothing. Such ignorance is due to the love of this world in his heart. It seems that the interrogation of the angels, which in Islam is called *Munkar* and *Nakir*,[16] takes place first and then the punishment begins. This punishment may vary. The evil man tastes many different kinds unless God shows His mercy. As is well known, al-Ghazali finds it useful to repeat in his works almost all the colorful descriptions of the punishments of the grave then in vogue in Islamic eschatological literature. Al-Ghazali believes that punishment in the grave exists; we can not see it because our physical eyes are not created to see what belongs to the metaphysical world.

In his analysis of the "Ending," "the agony of death," "interrogation," "the punishment of the grave," and what happens on "the Day of Judgment," al-Ghazali concentrates all men into two major classes, namely the good (sa'id) and the evil (shaqi).[17] The matter, however, is more complicated than this. In order to understand the real nature of goodness (sa'adah) and evil (shaqavah) in the other world, a close examination of all classes of people in the world to come is necessary and this is far off the topic of my communication.

In conclusion, I quote from the Holy Quran:

Lo, Allah changeth not the condition of a people, until they have changed that which concerneth themselves.[18]

May the Almighty Allah enable us to fulfill our duty to propagate His religion and thus to serve humanity, which is passing through a great spiritual crisis and may our services be accepted by our Merciful Creator.

NOTES

1. John B. Noss, *Man's Religion,* (London: Macmillan, 1963), pp. 528–29.

2. For a more detailed explanation of al-Ghazali on the subject please see the article of M. S. Aydin in *Ilahiyat Fakultesi Dergesi,* vol. 26 (1983).

3. John B. Noss, *Man's Religion,* pp. 547–48.

4. Cf. Holy Quran 56:57–61 and 75:36–40.

5. Muhammad Ali, *Translation of the Holy Quran* (Lahore: 1951), p. 55.

6. Cf. Holy Quran 17:19–21.

7. Cf. Holy Quran 22:5.

8. Cf. Holy Quran 23:15.

9. Muhammad Ali, *Translation of the Holy Qu'ran,* p. 56; also M. S. Aydin in *Ilahiyat Fakultesi Dergesi.*

10. F. R. Ansari, "Beyond Death," *Muslim News* (Cape Town), 7 Sept. 1973, p. 6, col. 3.

11. F. R. Ansari, "Beyond Death." Also compare with the work of the Turkish mystic of the nineteenth century, Ibrahim Hakki *Ma'rifetname* (in Turkish).

12. M. S. Aydin in *Ilahiyat Fakultesi Dergesi.*

13. Aydin, p. 224.

14. Aydin, p. 224.

15. Aydin, p. 225.

16. Aydin, p. 226; also compare it, for a conception of Angelology in Islam, with John B. Noss, *Man's Religion,* p. 530.

17. Compare with John B. Noss, *Man's Religion,* page 548.

18. Cf. Holy Quran 13:11.

8
Death and Immortality in Hinduism
MARIASUSAI DHAVAMONY

The Meaning of Death in Hinduism

In Hinduism there exists not only a reverence for the dead but a constant periodical performance of commemorative obsequies as a positive obligation incumbent on the relatives of the dead. Hindus believe that it is their duty to support and contribute by offerings and homage to the happiness of the dead in the other world to which they are believed to pass after death. Their beliefs on death and afterlife, and their funeral rites reveal a profound meaning of death and immortality. We shall be dealing with the classical sacred texts of Hinduism to elucidate this meaning.

The Vedic Idea of Death Rig Veda 10.14 is a funeral address, partly to Yama, the god of the dead, and partly to the soul of the departed whose body is being consumed on the pyre.[1] It describes Yama as the chief of the blessed dead, who is spoken of as the ruler of the departed and as the gatherer of the people, who gives the dead a resting place and prepares an abode for them. It was he who first discovered the way to the other world after death, and his messengers are two dogs, which guard the way trodden by the dead proceeding to the other world. Rig Veda 10.18 is a funeral prayer. The relatives and friends of the dead man are assembled around the corpse before placing it in the grave. The hymn begins with the rite of adjuring death to depart, and summons those present to devotion. Then the feeling of joy that death has not befallen any of the assembly is expressed and all are urged to enjoy life in the future. A stone laid between those present and the dead symbolizes the separation of the realms of life and death. It expresses the desire that a long life for all be decreed in the other world. The husband's brother or the priest summons the widow to separate herself from the corpse, and he takes the bow out of the hand of the dead man as the symbol of his ability. The hymn closes with the wish that the deceased may find a place in the other world. In other hymns (Rig Veda 10.15–17) it is said that Agni carried the corpse to the other world of the Fathers and the gods. They pray to Agni to preserve the body intact and they burn the goat that is sacrificed as his portion. Savitar conducts the dead on the path to the heavenly world and Pusan protects the dead. Passing along the path trodden by his ancestors, the spirit of the dead man goes to the realm of light and enjoys life in the company of the Fathers with Yama. Before the pyre is lighted, the widow, having lain beside the dead man, arises, and his bow is taken away from his hand. This suggests that in earlier times the widow and the weapons of him were burnt with his body.[2]

The Teaching of the Upanishads on Death The legend of the Naciketas, as narrated in the Katha Upanishad, contains the follow-ing teaching.[3] There are two ways: the way of good and the way of pleasure. The way of pleasure is the way of illusion, of an apparent material wealth, obtainable by the senses, which leads to repeated death. One enters the way of good, i.e., of knowledge of the true reality, through the help of a spiritual teacher. One has to give up the way of pleasure and even the good that seeks heavenly satisfac-tion, if the highest good of all is to be attained. The highest good consists in the vision of the inmost reality by the *adhyatma-yoga*.[4]

When a person dies, the various component parts of his body unite with their corresponding counterparts in nature, while the sum total of his karma remains attached to his self (*atman*). The force of this karma decides the nature of his next birth where he reaps the fruit of what he merits. The whole cycle of rebirth is determined by the law of action, good or bad. Birth and death are in continual succession for a man who is involved in this cycle. Libera-tion consists precisely in escaping, through the spiritual means of knowledge and love of God, from the round of birth and death, and attaining the immortal state of identity with the Absolute (*brahman*) or union through love with a personal God. These alternatives represent the teaching of the nondualist and theist traditions, respec-tively. The Naciketas episode illustrates the attitude to be taken towards death. Death and other human problems belong only to the earthly sphere. Death appears like other human earthly realities equally undesirable. The fire sacrifice is the sure means of gaining access to heavenly immortality. Since Naciketas is interested only in the absolute reality, which is not subject to transmigration, Yama reveals the secret doctrine of the immortal self: "The knowing self is never born; nor does he die at any time. . . . He is unborn, eternal, abiding and primeval. He is not slain when the body is slain."[5]

The Brhadaranyaka Upanishad, after the description of the departure of the self from the bodily frame, contains a discourse on the transmigration of the self in accordance with his good or bad actions; namely, the self of the unliberated passes from one state of existence to another in the round of births and deaths.[6] Death is also considered as the process of absorption into the Real, into the Self. "When a person here is deceasing, his voice goes into his mind; his mind into his breath; his breath into heat; the heat into the highest divinity. That which is the finest essence—this whole world has that as its soul. That is Reality (*satya*). That is the Self (atman). That art thou, Svetaketu."[7] Only ignorance and persistence in the thought of a separate self prevent one from actually being the Self. Death is hence the loosing of the cords of the heart, which bind man to an illusory life and to the thought of a separate self-existence. To the spiritually enlightened man, death is a passage from the unreal to the real, from darkness to light, and from mortality to immortality. It is by death that he detaches his true self from the evils of his current embodiment, and when he dies he leaves all suffering behind. But the unenlightened person becomes involved in the cycle of rebirth.

Hindu Funeral Rites in the Law Books According to the Law Books, the dead man is washed and annointed; the hair and the beard are cut off and the nails are closely trimmed.[8] He is freshly clothed, garlanded, and carried, either in men's arms or on a cart, to the cremation ground. The procession, carrying fires at the head, consists of relatives and mourners with loosened hair. The footprints of the party are wiped out by means of a bundle of twigs tied to the corpse, so as to prevent the spirit of the dead returning to haunt the living. During the procession verses are repeated, which urge the dead to join the ancestral spirits and Yama, to leave sin behind, to avoid the dogs of Yama; some other formulas drive evil spirits away from the dead. The body is then laid on a funeral pyre, situated in the midst of three fires. The widow is placed beside him, but she is soon asked to rise again with the words: "Arise, O woman, to the world of the living; departed is the life of him with whom thou liest; to marriage here hast thou attained with him as husband who graspeth thy hand." Here the husband's brother or some other (a pupil or aged servant) is meant to take the widow into his care. If the dead is a *kshatrya,* the bow is taken from his hand; in the case of a brahman, the instruments of the sacrifice are placed on the pyre. A cow or a goat is burnt with the corpse to satisfy the dogs of Yama. The pyre is then lighted, and Agni is invoked to take the dead safely to the ancestors. Other prayers and offerings are addressed to Yama, the Angirasas, and Sarasvati. The meaning of the ceremony is clear from the words of the prayer: "From him thou art born; may he in return be born from thee."

Then follow the departure of the mourners who do not turn round; the relatives perform purificatory rites (*asaucha*). Namely, they bathe and offer libations of water for the dead, and change their clothes, sleep on the ground, and refrain from eating flesh, etc. The fire formerly tended by the dead man is now taken out of the house otherwise than through the door. On the night after death a cake is offered to the dead, and a libation of water is poured out; a vessel with milk and water is also placed in the open air, and the dead man is called upon to bathe in it. The third or tenth day is that of collecting the bones of the dead. The remains of the dead are taken before sunrise far from the village to a place free from thorny plants. The bones are placed in the ground, covered with stones and earth. Water and milk are poured in the place. Then the performers go away, not turning back, purify themselves, and offer a *sraddha* to the dead.

The *sraddha* is complementary to the funeral rites for the purpose of transforming the dead, a vague and harmful spirit, into a "father," a strong and friendly ancestor. This rite takes place usually on the day of the new moon after midday. It consists of offerings of balls of food (*pinda*). The brahmans carefully chosen (usually three) represent the Fathers, i.e., the direct ancestors. The master of the house gives them food and gifts and honors them like Fathers.

Funeral rites close the concluding chapter of a Hindu's earthly life. During his life he consecrates his earthly life by performing diverse rites at the various stages of his growth (*samskaras*). At his leaving from this world, his survivors consecrate his death for his future happiness in his next life. A Hindu text says, "It is well-known that through the sacraments after the birth one conquers this earth; through the sacraments after the death the heaven."

The Mahabharata on Death Vyasa says to Yudhisthira: "Death has been ordained by the Creator himself for all creatures. When their hour comes, creatures are destroyed duly. The death of creatures arises from the creatures themselves. Creatures kill themselves. Death doth not kill anyone, armed with her bludgeon.

Therefore they that are wise, truly knowing death to be inevitable, because ordained by Brahma himself, never grieve for creatures that are dead." Death is thought of *as a necessity* for creation to continue. Man's fate is solely due to his karma. Man is killed as a result of his *own karma* in the past. We are all subject to the influence of our respective karmas. Karma is an aid to salvation even as sons are, and karma also is an indicator of virtue and vice in man.[9]

As regards the nature of death, the great Epic teaches that the dissolution of the elements at death does not mean dissolution of the indwelling self (*jiva*), which never dies, although it is inevitable. There is no destruction of the living creature or of what is given or of our other acts. The creature that dies only goes to another form. The body alone dissolves away. That which is called death is only the dissolution of the body. The soul, wrapped in diverse forms, migrates from one form to another, unseen and unnoticed by others. Death means the flight from the body of something that is different from the body. "Creatures obtain weal or woe as the fruit of their own acts. They that are wise, observant of virtue, and desirous of doing good unto all living creatures, they, acquainted with the real nature of the appearance of creatures in this world, attain at last to the highest end."[10]

The Bhagavad-gita on Death Since the spiritual self of man is eternal and immortal, it cannot be born or die and is above the process of becoming. But the self, in as far as it is associated with the bodily conditions (psychosomatic mechanism), is embodied, and as such is said to be born and dying over and over again until it is ultimately released from the cycle of rebirth.[11] "For the death of all that is born is certain, as also is certain the birth of all that dies; so in a matter that no one can prevent, you should not grieve. The beginnings of contingent beings are unmanifest; their middle course (their empirical life) is manifest; their ends are again unmanifest: what cause then for mourning here."[12] Krishna speaks of two paths that are open to the soul at death: "Fire, light, day, (the moon's) light (fortnight), the six months of the (sun's) northern course, dying in these, knowers of Brahman go to Brahman. Smoke, night, (the moon's) dark (fortnight), the six months of the (sun's) southern course, (dying) in these, the yogi wins the light of the moon, and back he comes again."[13] When men die at a time in the year that befits their own self-made destiny, they pass to the worlds of Brahman by way of the gods (*devayana*) or to the moon by way of the Fathers (*pitriyana*) in accordance with the merit or demerit of their deeds, and knowledge and loving devotion. Krishna instructs Arjuna on the supreme importance of one's last thoughts at the hour of death, for they in fact will determine one's future existence. The dead man's thought should be fixed on God, the highest person, or on the Imperishable; this alone will release him from rebirth:

Whoso at the last hour, leaving his body, remembers me and passes on, come to my being; there is no doubt about this. Whatever state a man may remember when at the end he abandons his body, to that state he goes, for ever does that state make him grow into itself. . . .

For if you fix your mind and soul on me, you will no doubt come to me. With thought integrated by spiritual exercise and constant striving, and seeking no other resort, let a man meditate on the divine exalted Person; he then goes to that Person.

With mind unwavering at the time of passing on, integrated by love of God and by the spiritual exercise, forcing the breath between the eyebrows duly, this man will go to that divine exalted Person. . . . Repeating Om, the Brahman, the One imperishable (or "in one syllable") let him keep me in mind: then when he departs, leaving aside his body he will tread the highest way."[14]

Every man becomes what he worships. The worshippers of gods go to them; those who worship the Fathers will go to them. The worship itself depends on the nature of the actions one performs and of the faith one shows in worship. Those who worship Krishna with loving devotion, being fully integrated and possessing of knowledge, will go to Krishna and participate in his mode of being. When the moment of death approaches, a man is haunted by the thought of that object alone on which his mind has dwelt most deeply in the course of his life. Hence one should think of Krishna again and again in life; performing his duties in a disinterested spirit, he shall meditate on Krishna, keeping his mind and understanding on Him; then at the hour of death he will attain Him, his mind ever fixed on Him alone.

The Puranic Idea of Death The Puranas propose and insist on love of God (*bhakti*) as the only way to solve the problem of living and dying.[15] The cycle of rebirth is an endless process, without beginning and end, and only a few liberated persons could escape from the fetters of time, which is cyclic. Although time is the ultimate destroyer, it is the quality of the actions of a man's past life that determines the quality and status of his present life; and so the process of rebirth goes on, death after death. We have the legend of the king Nrga to illustrate this truth.

Yama, the god of death, appears gracious and gentle to a man of good actions, and terrible and fearsome to the unrighteous man. Yama as righteousness (*dharma*) is a fair and impartial judge. The general Puranic teaching is that the man who has no loving devotion to the supreme God will be caught up in the cycle of rebirth, which is governed by the law of karma and impartiality ruled by Yama, the god of death. When a man dies, Yama's attendants claim the soul of the dead. It is precisely the love of God (*bhakti*) that can release the soul from the inexorable fetters of Yama, i.e., from the cycle of rebirth, and enable the soul to attain to the abode of the supreme God, Vishnu or Siva. Time, as the symbol of the destructive life process, is subject to Almighty God who can by his grace free the soul from the cycle of rebirths.

The *bhaktas* take a positive attitude toward death; they are deeply convinced that they will reach God's eternal abode (Vishnu's vaikuntha or Siva's kailasa) through their love (*bhakti*), without passing through the cycle of rebirth and the fetters of Yama and his attendants. The legend of Devaraja illustrates the remarkable power of the even accidental love of God. There are also legends that illustrate the contrary; namely, that some who were devotees but failed in loving devotion to God at the last moment had to undergo suffering and misery. All this intends to teach that liberation from fetters is effected only by God's grace. Without love of God, in the *bhakti* religions continual births and rebirths follow for the man who has no faith in God and relies on himself. Death is a terror for him. Sought after by the messengers of Yama, those who lack love of God are caught up in the round of births and deaths. In the nondualist trend of Hinduism, death is a mere passage for the liberated man in life (*jivanmukta*) to leave the body and be totally identified with the Absolute (Brahman).

Gandhi's Reflections on Death As a sort of conclusion of the discourse on death and its meaning, I prefer to cite some passages from Gandhi's writings. "It is not always a fact that the pain of death is greater for men than the pain of living. It is we ourselves who have made of death a fearful thing."[16] "People die only to be born again. Sorrow therefore is entirely uncalled for."[17] "It is nature's kindness that we do not remember past births. Where is the good either of knowing in detail the numberless births we have gone through? Life would be a burden if we carried such a tremendous load of memories. A wise man deliberately forgets many things, even as a lawyer forgets the cases and their details as soon as they are disposed of."[18] "It is well if we live and it is equally well if we die. . . . Somehow or other we refuse to welcome death as we welcome birth. We refuse to believe in the evidence of our senses, that we could not possibly have any attachment for the body without the soul, and we have no evidence whatsoever that the soul perishes with the body."[19] "The idea that death is not a fearful event has been cherished by me for many a year, so that I recover soon enough from the shock of the deaths even of near and dear ones."[20] "Both birth and death are great mysteries. If death is not a prelude to another life, the intermediate period is a cruel mockery. We must learn the art of never grieving over death, no matter when and to whom it comes. I suppose that we shall do so when we have really learnt to be utterly indifferent to our own deaths, and the indifference will come when we are every moment conscious of having done the task to which we are called."[21] "It is better to leave a body one has outgrown. To wish to see dearest ones as long as possible in the flesh is a selfish desire, and it comes out of weakness or want of faith in the survival of the soul after the dissolution of the body. . . . True love consists in transferring itself from the body to the dweller within and then necessarily realizing the oneness of all life inhabiting numberless bodies."[22]

Hindu Eschatology

Eschatology ("the doctrine of last things") concerns the final destiny of the individual and also the future of the universe. The term is used in the history of religions, since all religions in some form or another contain teachings about the goal of human life and human history as well as about the universe itself, and the origins of things. The Hindu eschatology can be called eternalistic, for it considers time as the endless cycle of births and deaths and seeks to escape from the cycle of rebirths. The "last thing" consists in the deliverance of the individual from the unreal realm of the empirical and temporal to the timeless realm of the spirit.

Cosmic Eschatology The theory of *kalpas* (cosmic eras) was not known during the Vedic period.[23] In later literature, especially in the Epic and the Puranas, we find it fully developed. Each of these *kalpas* is conceived as measuring the duration of one single world, from creation to dissolution; it is equivalent to one day in the life of

Brahma. This in turn consists of a thousand great ages (*mahayuga*), each of which contains four ages (*yuga*): *krta, treta, dvapara,* and *kali yuga.* Righteousness (*dharma*) is full in the *krta* period; it is three-fourths in the *treta* period; *dvapara* is the period of half virtue and half vice; during the *kali* age man and the world are at their lowest and worst; i.e., only one-fourth of virtue is to be found. The development curve of actual humanity as well as that of the past and of the future is a retrogressive evolution, leading to an intermediate dissolution (fire followed by flood); at the end of time comes the great dissolution, which coincides with the end of the life of Brahma. The world will be reabsorbed into Brahma by involution and remain in that state until the hatching of a new cosmic age. As the Bhagavad-gita observes: "For whenever righteousness declines and unrighteousness uprises, then I (Krishna) create myself (incarnate), to guard the good, and to destroy the wicked, and to confirm the right. I come into being in this age and in that."[24] This statement of Krishna applies also to other *avatars* in different ages whenever *dharma* declines and *adharma* is in the ascendency. God is born in the families of virtuous men, assumes human body, and exterminates all evils caused by asuras and evil spirits.

Creation of the universe takes place and lasts during Brahma's day; at its close the universe is dissolved for the same length of time (Brahma's night). The way of representing history in the Hindu context resembles an organic process. Time and history is cyclic, rhythmical; this conception allows for the periodical annihilation of both time and history. We can say that the mentality reflected in this conception of time and history is that which bases its attitude towards the world not on sense impressions and rational inference, according to which time is linear and continuous and inorganic, and history is scientific, but on metaphysical intuition into the impermanence and cyclical renewal of Nature and of empirical reality in general.

The universe according to the Hindu conception is called the "cosmic egg," which contains in its upper half seven celestial stories, the topmost of which is the dwelling place of Brahma. The bottom half contains seven subterranean stories, which are the home of the Nagas and other fabulous beings; hell is situated in the lowest part, the place of punishment. The earth is situated between the two spheres at the center of which is Mount Meru, the world's pivot. Around Meru are located the four "island continents" (*dvipa*). We can summarize the general account of the cosmogony as follows:

There are two kinds of creation: primary and secondary. The first explains how the universe proceeds from *prakrti* (eternal prime matter) and the second in what manner the forms of things are developed from the elementary substances previously evolved, or how they reappear after their temporary destruction. Both these creations are periodical, but the termination of the first occurs only at the end of Brahma's life, when all the gods and all the forms are annihilated and all the elements are merged into primary substance. The latter takes place at the end of every *kalpa* or Brahma's day. It affects only the forms of inferior creatures and lower worlds, leaving the substance of the universe entire and the sages and gods unharmed.

The process is conceived by Vaishnavas thus: The day of Brahma dawns and God awakes. During the night of Brahma, Vishnu lies, unconscious and recumbent, on the cosmic serpent Sesha, and as dawn approaches a lotus blooms miraculously from his navel, and from the lotus springs the creator-god *Brahma,* while Siva, the destroyer or rather the agent of reabsorption springs from his head. From these beginnings the universe evolves. According to Vaishnavism again, there is periodic intervention of Vishnu, in the form of an *avatar,* to restore order and righteousness in the universe, to punish the unrighteous, to reward the righteous, and to show men the way of liberation and union with God.

Although time is subordinated to Brahma and Siva in various aspects of creation and dissolution respectively, the Hindu aspiration is precisely to transcend time and its cyclic round of rebirths. Time itself has no ultimate meaning and purpose except to bind man to misery and suffering. Hence the religious quest of the Hindus, in various spiritual paths that help them get out of this time-bound cycle of existence, is to reach the state of eternal and blissful existence either through a union with a personal God in perpetual love and dependence (theist current) or through the complete absorption with the Absolute (Brahman) in total identity without distinction (nondualist trend).

Individual Eschatology Mostly the ninth and the tenth books of the Rig Veda contain references to a life after death. Rig Veda 10.14 deals with death and the future life. The spirit of the dead man passes by the path trodden by the Fathers, and goes to the realm of light and meets with the Fathers who revel with Yama in the highest heaven. Yama, the first man, has been the pathfinder for successive generations after him and has searched out a way to the "world of the just" for those who die afterwards. The spirit of the dead man, freed from all needs, passes through the air to new life. Led by Pusan, the spirit crosses the stream and passes by Yama's watchful dogs to the world of the spirits. The righteous dead pass over water to get to paradise. The dead also pass over a bridge. The term *asu* (spirit, breath) expresses physical reality, while *manas* (mind) expresses the seat of thought and emotion in the Rig Veda. Human life depends on the presence of *asu* and *manas*. In life after death *asu* and *manas* are united as they are on earth; this indicates that all the functions of the mental life remain intact. The body also has a part in the afterlife. Hence the full personality of the departed is believed to remain after death. Though men obtain immortality only after death, the corpse plays a part in the future life for the body shares in the existence of the other world. The dead are said to obtain immortality not by their own inherent capacity but by the gifts of the gods. Agni is said to exalt a mortal to immortality and to be the guardian of immortality.[25] People pray to Agni, Mitra, and Varuna for immortality. But the meaning of immortality is not the same in every case. It may mean a long life here on earth, or a continued life of a man in his offspring, or immortality after death. Hence the death from which a devotee prays to be delivered often means abrupt death or premature death. He yearns for a long terrestrial life.

The Fathers are the ancestors who have passed through death and attained to life in the third heaven. These are the seers who made the paths by which the recent dead go to join them. Yama, who later on is considered as judge of the dead, presides over the Fathers. The paradise in the Rig Veda is a place of bliss and happiness.[26] The good revel in the company of Yama and partake of the funeral offerings. If the righteous go to heaven, the wicked are said to go to an abode that can be termed hell. If it is not a place of punishment for the wicked in the Rig Veda, still the evil spirits are sent by the gods to a place of bottomless darkness. Every sinner creates his own hell, i.e., creates for himself this deep pit through his own evil deeds from which no exit is possible.[27] Hell is darkness, and demons are spirits of darkness. But no torture of the sinner is indicated.

In the Brahmanas, immortality is gained by those who rightly understand and perform sacrifice, while those who are deficient in this respect die before their time and go to the next world where they are weighed in a balance and receive good or evil according to their deeds.[28] The pious man is promised the highest reward in the next world with his entire body. Here certainly personal immortality is involved. The doctrine of the Brahmanas is that after death all are born again in the next world where they are recompensed according to their deeds, the good being rewarded and the wicked punished. But the Brahmanas are not explicit with respect to the duration of the reward or punishment in life after death. It is perhaps in this context that we can trace the beginning of the doctrine of rebirth in different lives after death. The Satapatha Brahmana also says that the good proceed either by the path leading to the Fathers or by paths leading to the gods.

One of the most significant doctrines of the Upanishads is the development of the idea of rebirth as a consequence of one's action. In the Brhadaranyaka Upanishad, a distinction is made between the way of the gods and the way of the Fathers. The way of the gods is that of those who have faith, the way of this spiritual elite. A spiritual person conducts them to the world of Brahman; from this there is no return. The way of the Fathers is that of those who have duly offered sacrifices, shown generosity in almsgiving, and performed sacrifices. This is the way of the righteous men who have only followed the ordinances of traditional religion.[29]

In the Upanishads, three classes of souls are distinguished. Those that rely on faith in the eternity of the atman are released from the cycle of rebirth. Those who perform Vedic duties of sacrifices, almsgiving, and austerity return to the world in human form after being in the world of the Fathers. Those who do not know both these ways are condemned to the life of an insect or a reptile.[30] For the first time in the history of Brahmanism, the doctrine of transmigration is taught as a result of the law of action (*karma*). The law of action is a universal law of immanent retribution according to which every good act meets with reward and every evil act meets with punishment, either in this life or in the next. Such a law demands that a man be reborn to reap the fruit of his action. The soul's reward in heaven or punishment in hell is only temporary, for once the retribution is over, it reverts to earthly life. The final liberation from this cycle of rebirth is effected through higher wisdom.

In the Mahabharata, two beliefs, namely, karma doctrine and that of heaven and hell, sometimes stand separate: in some texts reference is made to an abode in Indra's heaven without any allusion to rebirth, in other texts reference is made to a high or lower birth here after without mention of heaven or hell.[31] Commonly the two beliefs are combined by proposing that rebirth follows the penalty of hell or reward of heaven. Final liberation consists in being released from the bondage of the cycle of rebirth. This state is described in different ways. The soul becomes Brahman, infinity, or deathlessness, or the one Self of all things, without pairs of opposites. It is a state where one does not grieve or die, where one is not born or reborn. It is a state where they rejoice in the well-being of all creatures. In the ultimate state of liberation (*moksa*) where souls become Brahman or enter into God in union, it is not clear that anything of their personality remains, after their empirical self has been destroyed. The Bhagavad-gita has provided the most concentrated expression of the destiny of man. The liberated man attains the state of Brahman. Casting off all selfish desires, renouncing the claims of "mine" and "I," and the practice of the discipline of "sameness," man will come to realize the unvarying presence of the eternal Being in all contingent beings. This is the meaning of Brahma-nirvana spoken of in the Gita.[32] True, liberation means the realization of freedom from the bonds of rebirth, and of Brahman, eternal, changeless, and blissful. But God is above the state of nirvana and therefore of Brahman.

Thus ever disciplining himself, the man of discipline, with controlled mind, will approach that peace that culminated in nirvana, and subsists in me.[33]

This is not the final end of man, for Krishna says that nirvana which is Brahman subsists in him (God). Hence liberation implies not only the realization of Brahman but the realization of God's mode of being and acting, of participation in God's mode of existence and activity.

With self by yoga integrated, he sees the self in all beings standing, all beings in the self: the same he sees in everything. Who sees me in all, and sees all in me, for him I am not lost, nor is he lost to me.[34]

Both the liberated self and God may be said to pervade all things, but the omnipresence of the liberated man is dependent on God himself, on his omnipresence. The realization is the prelude, subject to God's grace, to participate in the being of God himself who is above Brahman. According to the Bhagavad-gita, the supreme goal consists in the supreme love of God (*bhakti*) beyond the realization of one's transcendent self as Brahman. Moksa is going to "the

Supreme Spirit"; it is going to Krishna; it is a dwelling in Krishna, entering into his substance.

If one's mind be disciplined in the discipline of constant striving, straying to no other object, so by meditating on the divine supreme Spirit, he goes to him.[35]

Let your mind dwell on me alone, stir up your soul to enter into me; thenceforth in every truth in me you will find your home.[36]

Liberation then as the supreme goal of man in its positive aspect means the felt participation of the soul in the total being of God. It is only through participation in the divine nature that man is made fit for deification. By love of God (*bhakti*), the liberated man realizes God's nature, so to say, from inside, i.e., he knows God as he is in himself.

By love he comes to know me as I really am, how great I am, and who; and once he knows me as I am, he enters (me) forthwith.[37]

This God-realizing love leads man to the total possession of God's love and his being. Krishna, the *avatar* of God, discloses his final and most secret message of his own love for his *bhakta* and takes possession of him in union of love. This theist view of the final destiny of man is interpreted differently by the nondualist trend within the Hindu fold.

Conclusion

With respect to the common Hindu teaching on the final liberation of man, the attainment of immortality takes on two potent currents of spiritual experience and doctrinal formulation. Moksa for the nondualist (*advaitin*) does not mean that the self merges into Brahman as a river merges into the sea, but that the self realizes itself as it eternally exists; i.e., in perfect identity with the Absolute. Hence liberation is not a state to be newly attained but is the very nature of the Self become conscious of its identity with the All-One. On the contrary, *moksa* for the theists means no more than the transcendence of time and space, and only after such transcendence is the personal relationship with God in love and surrender keenly experienced, and it this experience which gives the soul ultimate bliss. In the state of liberation, the individual self only acquires some characteristics similar to those of God, but does not and cannot become identical with God because of the radical difference between the two.

═══ NOTES ═══

1. Yama is the deified Lord of the dead; originally he is considered to have been the first to die and to have shown to others who died after him the path to the abode of the departed.

2. From the Rig Veda 10.14–18 it is evident that the Vedic Indians adopted the method of cremation usually for the disposal of the body, though burial of the corpse was also practiced.

3. Katha Upanishad, chap. 1–3; cf. also Taittiriya Brahmana 3.2.8.

4. Adhyatma-yoga is the discipline by which one contemplates one's deeper self; it is the practice of meditation, a quiet, sustained effort to apprehend the truth of the self.

5. Katha Upanishad 2.18.

6. See Brhadaranyaka Upanishad 4.3.35–36; 4.3.38; 4.4.1–2.

7. Chandogya Upanishad 6.8.6.

8. See Apastamba Dharma Sutra 2.6.15; *Sacred Books of the East,* vol. 2, pp.137ff; Gautama Dharma Sastra, chap. 15; *Sacred Books of the East,* vol. 2, pp. 255ff; Asvalayana Grhya Sutra, chap. 4.2–8; *Sacred Books of the East,* vol. 29, pp. 237ff; Vishnu Smrti, chap. 29 ff; *Sacred Books of the East,* vol. 7, pp. 75ff.

9. The Mahabharata 7.52–54; cf. also 12.256ff.

10. The Mahabharata 11.3; 12.185ff and 218.

11. The Bhagavad-gita 2.12–13.

12. The Bhagavad-gita 2.27–28.

13. The Bhagavad-gita 8.24–25.

14. The Bhagavad-gita 8.2–13.

15. See Bhagavata Purana 10.64; 1.13.46–50; 5.26.38. Siva Purana, Uma Samhita 7.9–25.

16. *The Diary of Mahadev Desai,* p. 110.

17. *The Diary of Mahadev Desai,* p. 21.

18. M. K. Gandhi, *Letters to a Disciple,* p. 172.

19. M. K. Gandhi, p. 148.

20. M. K. Gandhi, pp. 167–68.

21. M. K. Gandhi, p. 172.

22. M. K. Gandhi, p. 89.

23. The Mahabharata 3.148; 12.231; 12.341; 12.232; Vishnu Purana 1.3; 3.2 & 3; 4.24; Bhagavata Purana 3.11.

24. The Bhagavad-gita 4.7–8.

25. Rig Veda 1.31.7; 5.4.10; 5.63.2.

26. Rig Veda 9.113.7–11.

27. Rig Veda 2.29.6; 7.104.3; 4.5.5.

28. Satapatha Brahmana 11.2.7.33; 6.2.2.27; 10.6.3.1; 10.5.4.15–16; 1.9.3.10.

29. Brhadaranyaka Upanishad 6.2.15–16; Chandogya Upanishad 5.10.

30. Chandogya Upanishad 4.15.5–6; 5.10.1–8.

31. The Mahabharata 18.2; 12.21; 12.310.

32. The Bhagavad-gita 5.24–25.

33. The Bhagavad-gita 6.15.

34. The Bhagavad-gita 6.29–30.

35. The Bhagavad-gita 8.8.

36. The Bhagavad-gita 12.8.

37. The Bhagavad-gita 18.55.

9

The Advaita View of Death and Immortality
R. BALASUBRAMANIAN

Issues Involved in the Problem of Death and Immortality

For the purpose of discussing the problem of death and immortality, we may specifically raise the following questions: (1) Does "death" mean the total extinction of man without any remainder whatsoever? If the answer to this question is in the negative, then (2) What is it that survives death—is it something material like the visible external body of a person, or something nonmaterial, or a complex entity that is both material and nonmaterial? Whatever be the answer to this question, one may again ask: (3) Is that something that survives death perishable or not like the visible external body? (4) If there is something that is imperishable or immortal in man, what is it?

The question about the survival of death is not a new one. It was raised and answered in the Upanishads. The *Katha* Upanishad introduces the problem of death through the story of Naciketas. Auddalaki Aruni, in an angry mood, offered his son, Naciketas, as a gift to Yama, the God of Death. Since Naciketas remained without food for three days in the abode of Yama when Yama was on a tour, the latter offered him three boons. The first boon that Naciketas requested was that his father should recognize and talk to him free from anger when he returned to his home. As the second boon, he wanted instruction about the Fire, "which leads to heaven and which is the support of the world." Yama readily granted both of these boons. The third one related to the mystery of death. Naciketas said: "The doubt that arises consequent on the death of a man is this: some say, 'It [(i.e., the Self)] exists;' and others say, 'It does not exist.' I would like to know this, being instructed by you. Of the three boons, this one is the third."[1] Though Yama requested Naciketas not to inquire about death and promised to grant him anything else that he would care for—wealth, women, long life, or a vast kingdom—the latter declined all of them as ephemeral and insisted on knowing the truth about death. Yama finally agreed and said: "The Self is not born, nor does it ever die. After having been, it does not cease to be; nor the reverse. Unborn, eternal, unchangeable, and primeval, it is not slain when the body is slain."[2]

The problem of death and immortality can be discussed only by an analysis of the nature and destiny of man. I shall discuss this problem from the Hindu point of view with special reference to the Advaita Vedanta, which develops its immanent metaphysics by an inquiry into the nature of man to find out what is "real" or "immortal" in him. The problem of death and immortality cannot be dealt with as an isolated issue unconnected with metaphysics. The solution to this problem, whatever it may be, presupposes a philosophy of man.

Composition of Man

Though Advaita holds the view that ultimate reality is one and nondual, it develops its metaphysics by making a distinction between the Self and the not-Self for the purpose of analysis. According to Advaita, the Self alone is real and immortal; and everything else that we know and experience—the objects of the external world, our own body, senses and mind—is unreal and mortal. Everything other than the Self is brought under the convenient label of "not-Self." The Upanishadic term for the Self is Atman. What is called Atman is no other than Brahman. A text of the Mandukya Upanishad says: "This Self is Brahman."[3] Though two different words, "Atman" and "Brahman," are used, the entity denoted by them is the same. This dichotomy between the Self and the not-Self, which runs through the metaphysics of Advaita, must be kept in the background for a clear understanding of the problem of death and immortality.

As a system committed to immanent metaphysics, the Advaita focuses its attention on man and his experience for discovering reality. There is a detailed analysis of the nature of man in Chapter II of the Taittiriya Upanishad.[4] Following this analysis, Advaita holds that man, who is caught up in empirical existence, is a complex entity consisting of spirit and matter, or Self and not-Self. The spirit or Self in man is associated with matter or not-Self during empirical existence. The components of matter, with which the Self is associated, are the gross body (*thula-sarira*), the subtle body (*suksma-sarira*), and the causal body (*karana-sarira*). Using the terminology of sheath (*kosa*), the Upanishad says that the Self is covered by five sheaths in the same way as a sword is covered by a sheath. These five sheaths that cover the Self are arranged one inside the other telescopically. The outermost sheath is called *annamaya-kosa,* the sheath of food; and inside it are the sheath of vitality (*pranamaya-kosa*), the sheath of the mind (*manomaya-kosa*), the sheath of the intellect (*vijnanamaya-kosa*), and the sheath of bliss (*anandamaya-kosa*), the last one being the innermost one. These five sheaths are apportioned to the three bodies, and so there is correlation between the sheaths and the bodies. The sheath of food constitutes the gross body, which is external and visible. The sheaths of vitality, mind, and intellect constitute the subtle body, which is not visible in the same way that the gross body is visible. The sheath of bliss constitutes the causal body.

It is not necessary here to go into further details regarding the composition of gross and subtle bodies.[5] However, a brief reference may be made to the part played by them in the life of man. The gross body is the instrument through which the enjoyment of gross objects becomes possible. The cognitive, affective, and conative aspects of life are connected with the work of the subtle body. We ascertain the nature of an object as such-and-such; and this is the work of the intellect (*buddhi*). Doubt, desire, memory, and other features are associated with the mind (*manas*). The volitional aspect, which manifests itself in the form of action, is connected with the vital nature of man. It means that the *inner life* of man comprising intellectual, aesthetic, and moral aspects is taken care of by the subtle body. Also, the subtle body is the link between one birth and another. This point will be discussed later. Owing to its association with the subtle and gross bodies, the Self becomes the subject of knowledge, the agent of action, and the enjoyer of the fruits of action.

Avidya, which means ignorance, is the cause of man's bondage. It is, therefore, the causal body of man. What is to be noted here is that, since the Self in man is associated with material bodies or sheaths, it is spoken of as "embodied." So long as it is embodied, it is in bondage and not free. The Self in its embodied condition is called "empirical self" or "*jiva.*" Inasmuch as the material component with which it is associated in the empirical life serves to individualize it, it is also called "individual self." Advaita uses the expressions, "empirical self" and "individual self," to refer to man. Man as such is both spirit and matter, or Self and body; he is neither disembodied Self nor selfless matter. Coming under the spell of ignorance, he engages himself in various kinds of activities—scripture-ordained as well as secular—in his day-to-day life by identifying himself not only with things and persons external to him, but also with his body, senses, and mind, without knowing his real nature.[6]

The Real and the Unreal in Man

It is appropriate at this stage to consider the nature of the two factors, the Self and the not-Self, which constitute the being of man. Advaita does not accord to them equal ontological status. It holds on the authority of scripture supported by reasoning that, while the Self is real and immortal, the not-Self, comprising the three bodies (or the five sheaths), is unreal and mortal. There are many scriptural texts that declare that the Self—what the Upanishads call atman or Brahman—is real, eternal, immortal. For example, a text of the *Katha* Upanishad says: "*Purusa* who keeps awake . . . is pure. That is Brahman and that alone is immortal."[7] The Chandogya Upanishad says: "That is real. That is the Self."[8] After explaining how Brahman, which is one's own Self, is in all things Yajnavalkya in the Brhadaranyaka observes that "everything else but this is perishable."[9] It means that the material component, viz, the gross, subtle, and causal bodies, associated with the Self of man, is unreal and mortal. That the visible, gross, external body is mortal is easily understood. Assuming for the sake of argument that there are two other bodies—subtle and causal—besides the all-too-familiar external body in the constitution of man, how do we establish that they too are unreal and perishable? One may also want to know the reasons not only for our belief in the existence of the Self, but also for saying that it is real and immortal. In other words, we require a criterion for deciding whether something is real or not.

Criterion of the Real and the Unreal

Everyone has native knowledge of his own Self. It is the Self that is referred to when a person knows himself as "I". As Sankara puts it, "The inward Self is well known to exist on account of its immediacy."[10] Since it is immediate, it does not remain unknown. The Self is consciousness and so it is self-luminous. It is not an object of knowledge in the sense in which a table or a chair is an object of knowledge. Being the subjective factor in all cognitions, it is known whenever anything is known. It does not require any proof, for it is presupposed in all proof. What is presupposed in every act of cognition, in every proof, is as good as proved. When the Advaitin says that the Self is self-luminous (svaprakasa), it is for the purpose of conveying the idea that, while the Self reveals other things, it itself is not revealed by anything else. Nevertheless, it is always known because of its immediacy. It is altogether a different question whether one who knows the Self knows it as it is, for while the Upanishad describes it as real, knowledge, infinite, and bliss, we claim to know it differently.[11]

According to Advaita, that is real that remains the same all the time.[12] On the contrary, whatever is subject to change is not real. If we apply this criterion, it will be found that, while the Self, which is consciousness, is real, the material adjunct of the Self is not real. The criterion of the real and the unreal that has been formulated here requires some explanation.

Objects such as a pot, which are effects, are subject to change. As effects they have a beginning. Though they exist for some time, they have an end. The general principle is that anything that has a beginning has an end, or that whatever is an effect is impermanent and therefore unreal. Even while they exist, they may undergo changes as a result of loss of properties and parts. What is true of material objects such as a pot is true of all the three bodies that a man possesses during his empirical life. It is well known that the gross body, which is visible and external, has a beginning and an end, and that it undergoes other changes such as growth and decline. Though the subtle body accompanies the Self from one birth to another throughout the empirical career of the Self, it has a beginning, being a product of avidya (otherwise called maya), and also an end, because whatever has a beginning must have an end.[13] The same is true of avidya, which is the causal body of man. Though it is not possible to account for its beginning with reference to something else as its cause—and it is for this reason that it is said to be anadi in the Hindu tradition—it must have a beginning.[14] Being material, it undergoes modification like any other material object. Also, it has an end.

Advaita holds that avidya is removable by knowledge. When a person attains the right knowledge of the Self, that is to say, when a person attains Self-realization, avidya ceases to be; and with the extinction of avidya all that it has produced starting from the subtle body ceases to exist. So long as ignorance continues, man is mortal; and he goes through the cycle of birth and death. The causal nexus that leads to man's bondage or transmigratory existence starts from ignorance; and because of ignorance, desire and aversion arise; and these in their turn lead to deeds, both good and bad; and because of deeds there is birth, which is the cause of suffering. Since ignorance through its causal chain binds a person and makes him mortal, Sankara observes that "death is constituted by ignorance, desire, and deeds."[15] When ignorance is removed through the saving knowledge of the Self, the Upanishad says, "Then a mortal becomes immortal and one attains Brahman here."[16] The point to be emphasized here is that the three bodies of man, which serve as the material adjunct of the Self, do not remain the same; and so they are not real. To say that they are not real is to say that they are mortal. Collectively they symbolize death.

The position is entirely different in the case of the Self. Being of the nature of consciousness, the Self is one and homogeneous, partless, and without attributes. It has neither a beginning nor an end, consequently it is free from other changes such as growth and decline. It is ever present in our experience and remains the same. It will be appropriate in this context to refer to an oft-quoted text from the *Bhagavad-gita* that reads: "The Self is not born, nor does it ever die. After having been, it does not cease to be; nor the reverse. Unborn, eternal, unchangeable, and primeval, it is not slain when the body is slain."[17]

An existent object other than the Self is subject to sixfold change (*sadbhava-vikara*), viz., birth, existence, growth, transformation, decline, and death; and such an entity is necessarily material and composite. But these changes are not possible in the Self. The Self is not produced from and by anything. Having been nonexistent, it does not come into existence; and having existed, it does not cease to be. Since it has neither beginning nor end, it is eternal. It makes no sense to speak of the existence of the Self, which has neither beginning nor end. The Self has no growth by the accretion of parts to it; and its nature is such that nothing can be added to it. That is why it is said to be primeval or ancient (*puranah*). There is nothing new in it. Nor can it decline due to the loss of parts or attributes, for it is partless and attributeless. It is for this reason that it is spoken of as unchangeable (*sasvatah*).

After explaining the meaning of the text from the Bhagavad-gita quoted above, Sankara sums up the central idea conveyed by it. He says: "This verse teaches the absence in the Self of the sixfold *bhava-vikaras*, i.e., changes to which all objects in the world are subject. The passage, on the whole, means that the Self is devoid of all sorts of change." If the Self is not subject to change, it means that it remains the same. It is, therefore, real and immortal. The Self constitutes the real nature of man. It is the real in man who, in empirical existence, is bound by the three bodies, which are mutable, unreal, and mortal. To know the ever-existent Self, which is real and remains as the Self, is to be immortal. Though the Self, which is real and immortal, is ever-existent, still we speak as if immortality is *attained* here in this life itself by one who overcomes death symbolized by ignorance and its products. Keeping this in view, the Upanishad declares that "a mortal becomes immortal and one attains Brahman here (in this life)."[18]

In another way also the criterion of the real has been formulated in Advaita. That is the real, which is not subject to sublation (*badha*) at anytime. On the contrary, that which is subject to sublation is not real. Consider the case of a person who mistakes a rope for a snake. He claims to see a snake and says, "This is a snake." When he realizes a little later the mistake he has committed, he says, "This is not a snake, but a rope." The snake, which was the object of his earlier cognition, gets sublated by the subsequent cognition. On the strength of the subsequent cognition, he declares that the snake seen by him earlier is not real. The point to be noted here is that the rope-snake gets sublated because it is not real, whereas there is no sublation for a real snake of our normal waking consciousness.[19] It is not necessary to go into the epistemological issues involved in the perception of a rope-snake. Nor should we consider how real the rope-snake is.[20] Ordinarily we do make a distinction between the rope-snake and the real snake. While we dismiss the former as illusory, as an appearance, as unreal, we consider the latter as real.

The same explanation holds good in the case of our experience of dream-objects. A dream-object is declared unreal because it suffers sublation in the waking state. The dream-lion, like the rope-snake, appears to be real at the time that it is perceived. But it loses its "reality," as the rope-snake does, during subsequent experience. Though existent at one time, they are absent or nonexistent subsequently; and so they are not real. In the light of the illustrations given above, we have to consider whether the Self or the body fulfills the criterion of the real by a thorough analysis of man's experience. Scripture itself shows the technique of analysis of our experience. Though we find this method of analysis in more than one Upanishad, what is set forth in the Mandukya Upanishad has become a *locus classicus*.

Man has not only waking (*jagrat*), but also dream (*svapna*) and deep sleep (*susupti*) experience. All these three states of experience are extremely important for understanding the nature of the Self and the material adjunct associated with it. The Self, the mind, the senses, and the gross external body—all these function and play their part when we know the external world during our waking state. But in the state of dream the senses and body do not function; and they are not required for dream experience. The world of our waking experience is absent in dream experience. The dream objects, whether they look normal or queer, are entirely different from the objects of our waking experience. The same is the case with our gross body. Though it is present in our waking experience, it is absent in our dream experience; and so dream experience may be characterized as "out-of-body-experience." A little reflection is enough to convince us that the body with which we transact so much of business in our dream is altogether different from the gross body of our waking state. It means that the gross body, as well as the external world of our waking experience, suffers sublation when we move from the waking to the dream state.

It is true that the sublation in both the cases is only temporary, for when a person returns to the waking state from dream he knows his gross body to be identical with the one he had before his dream experience; and the external world of the waking state, which gets sublated in a dream comes back once again when the dream state is followed by the waking state. It must be borne in mind that sublation, whether temporary or permanent, is sublation. What is sublated is unreal, though the sublation is temporary. Let us suppose for the sake of argument that a person perceives a rope-snake, subsequently realizes the mistake he has committed, and once again perceives the rope-snake in the same situation as earlier. In spite of the sublation of the rope-snake being temporary, he will maintain that the rope-snake seen by him is unreal because it has suffered sublation, be it once or more than once.

In the dream state the Self and the subtle body function. When a person is in the state of sleep, his subtle body which has been functioning in the other two states ceases to function, because it gets resolved into its cause, viz., *avidya*. Just as a pot relapses into its causal condition, viz., clay, and becomes nonexistent, even so the subtle body becomes nonexistent when it gets back to its cause and loses its identity. In the state of sleep, nothing is known; and no activity is transacted. The absence of knowledge and activity in deep sleep proves the nonexistence of the subtle body. The experience of sleep may be characterized as "out-of-body-experience" in the sense that it is an experience in which both the gross and the subtle body are absent. If they were present, they would have been active; and a state in which the subtle body as well as the gross body is active will not be sleep.

Inasmuch as the subtle body suffers sublation in the state of sleep, it is not real. The Self is present as the witness to the absence of knowledge and activity in deep sleep. But for its presence in that state, recollection (*smrti*) of one's own experience of sleep will be impossible. A person who wakes up from sleep and recollects his experiences says that he did not know anything at that time, that he slept soundly without any disturbance, and so on. The person who slept is now awake. It means that the person who is awake is identical with the one who slept. Though the subtle body of the person was absent in the state of sleep, his Self was present as a witness to the absence of knowledge and activity at that time. It is the same Self that helps him to recollect his deep sleep experience.

Avidya, which is the causal body, persists in the state of deep sleep as the adjunct of the Self. Though it does not function in a full-fledged way as it does in the other two states, the fact is that it exists at that time along with the Self. It is because of its continuance that a person who is in the state of sleep comes back to the states of waking and dream. But *avidya* does not continue forever. If it continues forever, there will be no liberation for man. Liberation presupposes and requires the termination of *avidya,* the source of bondage. Knowledge is the antidote to ignorance. Advaita maintains that *avidya,* which is the root cause of man's bondage, can be removed by the knowledge of the Self. When a person attains the right knowledge of the Self, there is sublation of *avidya* forever. Such a person who is free from *avidya* is called the liberated-in-life (*jivanmukta*). Since *avidya* has been removed forever, he has no more birth and death. He becomes immortal, deathless. Thus, while there is sublation for all the three bodies, there is no sublation for the self. It is the Self, which persists all the time, in all states of experience; and so it is real and immortal. The material adjunct comprising the three bodies is unreal and mortal.

The Disembodied Self

What emerges from the foregoing analysis is that the Self per se is bodiless. Man who is the individual Self is, no doubt, a complex being consisting of the Self and the body. He lives and carries on the business of life in this world neither as the Self nor as the body, but as an embodied being. The Self, which is consciousness, cannot by itself be engaged in any kind of action. In itself it is neither the subject of knowledge, nor the agent of an action, nor the enjoyer of the fruits of action. Like the Self, the body has its own disability. Being material, it cannot by itself know anything. Nor can it initiate any action on its own. The Self can be involved in some action or other only with the help of an instrument such as the mind, the senses, and the body. In the same way, the mind–sense–body complex can function only when it is inspired by the conscious Self. Man's life as it is reveals much more than an interaction or interrelation between the Self and the body. It shows what Sankara calls "reciprocal superimposition" (*itaretara adhyasa*) between the Self and the body. By reciprocal superimposition, Sankara means that the nature of the Self is superimposed on the mind–sense–body complex and that the nature of the latter is superimposed on the former.

A brief explanation will help us to understand Sankara's view. The Self is sentient and is capable of revealing things. The mind, on the other hand, which is material (*jada*), cannot know anything. Owing to a false identification of the Self and the mind, the nature of the Self is transferred to the mind with the result that the mind is credited with the power of comprehension. The gross, visible body has birth and death; but the Self, as stated earlier, has neither birth nor death. Due to ignorance, the characteristics of the gross body are illicitly transferred to the Self with the result that the Self is thought of as having birth and death. So the fact is that man, because of this identification, functions as one integrated being, though the two components in his being are of divergent nature.

From the fact that man functions as an integrated being, one should not draw the conclusion that the Self and the body are inseparably related in such a way that the one cannot exist without the other. It is absurd to speak of the relation between them as inseparable. If the relation between them is inseparable, the destruction of the gross, visible body will imply the destruction of the Self. But this is not true. We have already shown, both on the authority of scripture and by means of reasoning, that the Self is real and immortal. The other difficulty will be that, since the Self is real and immortal, we will be compelled to say on account of the alleged inseparable relation that the body also is real and immortal. This is equally absurd. This is the reductio ad absurdum of the view that holds that the Self and the body are inseparably related.

The Nyaya school speaks of two kinds of relation, viz., *samavaya* and *samyoga*. The first one called samavaya (inherent relation) holds good, according to the Nyaya school, between a substance and its quality, between whole and parts, between cause and effect, and so on. It is not possible to think of a *samavaya* relation between the Self and the body as they are not related as substance and quality, whole and parts, and so on. The second variety of relation called *samyoga* (conjunction) holds good between two entities such as the table and the ground. It is an external, temporary relation. The Self, which is consciousness, is not an entity to be related with the body by means of conjunction.

According to the Advaita, there cannot be any real relation between two entities that possess different ontological status. The Self is real, but the body is unreal; and so they do not have the same ontological status. There is a real relation between clay and pot, because the relata here have the same ontological reality. On the other hand, there is no real relation between the rope and the rope-snake, because while the former is empirically real, i.e., *vyavaharika*, the latter is illusory or false, i.e., *pratibhasika*. We cannot deny that the rope-snake is related to the rope, but at the same time we cannot say that there is a *real relation* between them. In fact, it is difficult to figure out what the relation is in this case. According to the Advaita, the relation in this case is a *false* one. The term that is used in Advaita to convey this false relation between the real rope and the illusory rope-snake is *tadatmya*. What holds good between the rope and the rope-snake also holds good between the Self and the body. The relation between the Self, which is real, and the body, which is not real, is a *false* one. The relation between the immortal and the mortal cannot be anything but false. As in the other case, here also the false relation is spoken of as a *tadatmya* relation. Thus, the Self and the body do not have an inseparable, eternal, necessary relation. It means that the body is external to the Self. There is nothing in the nature of the Self that requires it to be related to the body. At the same time, the false relation that obtains between the Self and the body during its embodied existence will not affect the Self, because by its very nature it is immutable (*kutastha*). The Self per se is bodiless.

The Upanishads do speak of the Self as bodiless. For example, describing the Self a text of the Svetasvatara Upanishad says: "Without foot or hand, yet swift and grasping, it sees without the eye, it hears without the ear. It knows whatever is to be known; of it there is none who knows. They call it the primeval, the supreme Person."[21] Another Upanishad says that the Self is "Without family, without caste, without sight and hearing, without hands or feet. . . ."[22]

Apart from the scriptural authority, we have evidence for this in our own experience. Earlier reference was made to the three states of man's experience: waking, dream, and deep sleep. In dream experience the Self exists without the gross, visible body; and during deep sleep experience it exists without the subtle body. *Avidya,* which is the causal body, ceases to be when a person attains liberation through the right knowledge of the Self. It will be appropriate in this connection to refer to the behavior of the enlightened man, who is called a *jivanmukta,* the liberated-in-life. The *Bhagavad-gita* speaks of him as a *sthitaprajna,* one who is steady in knowledge. It gives a detailed description of him: his condition when he is in the state of *samadhi,* his speech and behavior when he comes out of the state of *samadhi,* and his condition when he comes into contact with objects, good and bad.[23]

The liberated man is one who is free from the sense of "I" and "mine," which is the differentia of bondage. He is in the state of peace, which is bliss par excellence. "Being free from all desires, he moves about without attachment, without selfishness, and without vanity."[24] He is awake, whereas an ignorant one is asleep. What he sees, others do not see; and what others see, he does not see. In the language of the Bhagavad-gita, what is day to the sage is night to others; and what is day to others is night to him.[25] Such a person, though tenanting a body, is indeed bodiless, free from all the three bodies. From his perspective, the body is no more, though others may see him as possessing a body and bound by it. After explaining when a mortal becomes immortal in this body itself, the Brhadaranyaka Upanishad refers to the condition of the body of the liberated man.[26] It says: "When all the desires that dwell in his mind (heart) are gone, then he, having been mortal, becomes immortal, and attains Brahman in this very body. Just as the lifeless slough of a snake is cast off and lies in the ant-hill, so does this body lie. Then the Self becomes disembodied and immortal. . . ." The body discarded as not-Self by the liberated man lies dead.

Immortality in the Present Life

Though the theistic schools of Hinduism admit that the Self that is in bondage is eternal, most of them hold that it can regain its immortality not in this life here, but only hereafter, at the end of this life, provided it prepares itself in the present life seeking the grace of God for the attainment of the goal. Liberation, according to Vaisnavism, is union with God and enjoyment of perfect freedom and bliss in the celestial world. The individual self that is in bondage can hope for liberation only in the future life, if its preparation is adequate and if the grace of the Lord is vouchsafed to it.

Though the Nyaya-Vaisesika school describes liberation as a state beyond pleasure and pain, it also maintains, like Vaisnavism, that liberation can be attained only after death. According to Sankhya, which is not theistic, *Purusa* or the Self is in bondage because of its association with *prakrti,* and it attains liberation, which is called "final aloofness" (*kaivalya*), only after death. *Sankhya* does admit *jivanmukti,* which is a condition in which the Self, though associated with the body, is not bound by it. But its conception of *jivanmukti* is basically different from the Advaita conception of *jivanmukti.* According to Sankhya, while ignorance of the essential nature of *Purusa* is the cause of bondage, *prakrti* provides the material of bondage. The difficulty with the Sankhya conception of *jivanmukti* is that it is not total and final liberation. Knowledge can destroy ignorance, but not *prakrti* and its products. Inasmuch as the body, which is a product of *prakrti* is real, and cannot, therefore, be sublated by knowledge, *jivanmukti* as expounded in Sankhya is not total liberation.

The position is entirely different in Advaita. Since Advaita holds that ignorance is both the cause and stuff of bondage, the removal of ignorance by knowledge results in liberation that is total and final. For the Advaitin, there is no qualitative difference between *jivanmukti* and *videhamukti*. Liberation is one and the same, whether it is spoken of as *jivanmukti* or *videhamukti*. The Saiva Siddhanta conception of *jivanmukti* is also open to the same objection as the body, which is a product of *maya,* is real and is, therefore, unsublatable by knowledge. Thus, according to all these systems, the Self, though immortal by nature, cannot regain its immortality in full measure in the present life itself, whatever be the spiritual discipline it undergoes in order to make itself fit for the consummation.

According to Advaita, immortality can be attained in the present life itself. It is not a promise of the future, but an assured end within the reach of all here and now. The Advaita doctrine of liberation is, therefore, unique. Advaita justifies this doctrine on three grounds.

First of all, it takes into consideration the nature of the Self. What is real or immortal in man is the Self, which by its very nature is bodiless. Though we cannot say how long it has been in embodiment, there is evidence to show that embodiment (*sasariratva*) is not natural to it. Its association with the body is adventitious. Nor can it be polluted by the material adjunct. With a view to showing how the Self remains pure, free, and unaffected by the external factors such as the mind, the senses, and the body, Suresvara says: "I am not the ego. Nothing is mine. I am bereft of the not-Self always. Like darkness ascribed to the sun, they are all superimposed on me. Even their negation is a superimposition on me."[27] Even *avidya-maya*, which is the cause of the transmigratory existence of the Self, does not and cannot affect the Self. If the Self were to be affected by it, then it must be admitted that the Self is subject to change or modification. Since anything that is mutable is perishable, the Self too, if mutable, is perishable. But the Self is eternal. Its eternality is tenable and intelligible only if it is bodiless.

Secondly, Advaita arrives at the view that liberation can be attained in the present life itself on account of the nature of bondage and its cause. Bondage is a fall from the state of perfection. All schools of Hinduism admit the fact of bondage. They are also agreed that bondage is caused by ignorance, though there is a difference of opinion in the explanation of the nature of ignorance. It is one thing to say that there is bondage and that it is a *fact*. It does not follow from this that bondage is *real*. While other schools of Hinduism hold that bondage is real, Advaita maintains that it is not real. What is real is eternal; and what is eternal will not cease to be. So if bondage is real, it cannot be removed.

To say that bondage is not real is not to reduce it to an airy nothing. It is as much a fact as the empirical world is a fact, and nothing more and nothing less. Reference has already been made to the causal nexus starting from *avidya*, which binds the empirical self. According to Sankara, to think of what is really bodiless as embodied is due to *avidya*. It must be borne in mind that the presence of the body itself is not bondage. On the contrary, identification with it is bondage. And this false identification is due to *avidya* or *maya*. The explanation of the causal nexus given in Advaita, as Sankara points out, is the same as the one given in the Nyaya school.[28] Unlike other schools, Advaita maintains that the Self alone is real and that everything else is perishable. it means that *avidya-maya* too, though existent, is not real.

Thirdly, Advaita insists that the remedy that one suggests to cure a disease must be appropriate; and this consideration leads Advaita to the doctrine of liberation-in-life. If ignorance is the cause of bondage, then it can be removed only by knowledge. Sources from which we can obtain the saving knowledge are available here. Since the possibility of attaining this knowledge in the present life itself cannot be ruled out, Advaita maintains that immortality can be attained in this life itself. To quote Sankara, "Since the embodiment of the Self is caused by wrong conception, it is established that the person who has attained the true knowledge is free from his body even while still alive."[29] It may be pointed out that the assurance that immortality can be attained in this life itself provides a new dimension to, and deepens the significance of, this life.

Death of the Gross Body and Transmigration

Hinduism does not accept the theory of one life. The present life is determined by the past and determines the future. It is not the first life. Nor will it be the last, unless release is attained here itself. It is not necessary here to consider the Hindu doctrine of *karma,* which is closely connected with the theory of reincarnation. Hinduism supports the theory of transmigration on the ground that certain innate predilections in man such as the readiness to suck the mother's milk found in a new-born baby and the innate fear of death normally exhibited by all of us are inexplicable, unless they are traced to previous life. The fact that we are not able to explain satisfactorily the observed inequalities of various kinds among us, is another important reason for the belief in the theory of transmigration. There is no need to go into a detailed consideration of these issues here. In the context of the theory of transmigration the Upanishad says: "As it [(i.e., the Self)] does and acts, so it becomes. By doing good, it becomes good; and by doing evil, it becomes evil. It becomes virtuous through good acts and vicious through evil acts."[30]

No one can answer the question *when* the transmigratory existence of the Self started. Hinduism holds the view that the *jiva* is *anadi,* i.e., without a beginning. It means that the explanation of the beginning of life through time is not possible. Nevertheless, the question *why* there is transmigration can be answered. The Upanishad says that "the man who desires transmigrates."[31] What the Upanishad means here is that ignorance, which is the cause of desire is the root cause of transmigration; and so one who is ignorant transmigrates. To the question *how* transmigration takes place, the answer is that the subtle body with which the Self is associated serves as the link between one life and another. We have already stated that the *inner life* of man is dependent on the subtle body. Whatever a person desires, whatever he resolves following his desires, and whatever he does following his resolve—all these are stored up in the form of impressions in the subtle body. When there is death of the gross external body, the subtle body, which is the physical vesture of the Self, departs to form a new life carrying the impressions left over by "knowledge, work, and past experience."[32] The Upanishad says that the Self, which is associated with the subtle body, has, at the time of departure from the gross body, "particular consciousness and goes to the body which is related to that consciousness."[33] The future life is decided even at the time of the departure of the empirical self from the present life. The Upanishad elucidates this point through an illustration of great significance. It says: "Just as a leech supported on a straw goes to the end of it, takes hold of another support and contracts itself, so does the self throw this (gross) body aside—make it senseless—take hold of another support and contract itself."[34]

It will now be possible for us to answer the question, "What is it that survives death?" If we take the word "death" in the most comprehensive sense as standing for the entire body–complex, then the Self alone survives death, because it is immortal. This point does not require any further elaboration. A person who realizes the Self, who remains as the Self, is one who has overcome ignorance and desires. The Upanishad says: "The man who does not desire (never transmigrates). Of him who is without desires, who is free from desires, the objects of whose desire have been attained and to whom all objects of desire are but the Self—the organs do not depart. Being but Brahman, he is merged in Brahman."[35] Not only the gross body, but the subtle body consisting of the mind, the organs, and the vital airs, and the causal body as well, cease to exist after Brahman-realization.

If the word "death" is understood in a restricted sense to mean the death of the gross, visible, external body, then what survives death is a complex entity comprising the Self and the subtle body. The latter is an annexation to the Self until the attainment of liberation. We have already stated that everyone has native knowledge of the Self and that the existence of the Self does not require any proof. The subtle body is not visible like the gross, external body. It is no argument to say that just because it is not visible to the naked eye or even to the sophisticated instruments of the scientist it does not exist. Things do and may exist, even though they are not visible to us. It may be relevant in this connection to mention that, according to the Nyaya school, the existence of the mind can be proved only through inference, even though Advaita holds that the mind is directly known since it is revealed by the Self (saksi-bhasya). Even our sense organs cannot be known directly, and their existence has to be inferred. We have to admit the existence of the subtle body as the material vesture that accompanies the Self from one life to another until self-realization, which is liberation. If material continuity is what is required from one life to another for the purpose of establishing identity, we do have this provided by the subtle body as the link between one life and another. Just as there is bodily continuity persisting through the changes from infancy to old age, even so there is bodily continuity from one life to another through the medium of the subtle body so that one attains a life that one has deserved.

NOTES

1. Katha Upanishad, 1.1.20.

2. Katha Upanishad, 1.2.18. This verse also occurs in the Bhagavad-gita, 2.20.

3. Mandukya Upanishad 2: "ayamatma brahma."

4. The analysis of the components that make up man is known as pancakosa-vicara, i.e., inquiry into the five sheaths.

5. The subtle body consists of seventeen factors—buddhi, manas, five organs of knowledge, five organs of action, and five vital airs. If citta and ahankara are

reckoned separately in addition to *buddhi* and *manas,* then there will be nineteen factors.

6. Consider, for example, expressions such as "my house," "my kith and kin." The degree of identification with external objects and persons may vary from object to object and person to person. What requies consideration here is whether the Self per se has any relation with an external object or person. According to Advaita, such identification with external objects and persons is due to *avidya;* and it will not be difficult even for an ordinary man to realize the mistake he commits in this type of identification. The problem becomes complicated when it is a question of identification with one's body, senses, and the mind. For example, "stoutness," "blindness," and "happiness," are the characteristics, respectively, of the body, the visual sense, and the mind. They are not the attributes of the Self. But in our day-to-day life we do not discriminate the Self from the mind-sense-body complex, but identify it with the material complex. Consider, for example, statements such as, "I am stout," "I am blind," and "I am happy." In all these cases, the "I" stands for the Self; and the characteristics of the body, the visual sense, and the mind are superimposed on the Self. We transact our business of life by means of such false identification. Sankara, in the introductory portion of his commentary on the Brahma-sutra, refers to this identification as *adhyasa.*

7. Katha Upanishad, 2.2.8.

8. Chandogya Upanishad, 6.8.7.

9. Brhadaranyaka Upanishad, 3.4.2.

10. See Sankara's introductory portion of his commentary on the Brahma sutra. Sankara says: *"na tavadayam ekantena avisayah, asmatpratyaya-visayatvat, aparoksatvacca pratyagatma-prasiddheh."*
Also see his commentary on the Bhagavad-gita, 2.18. In the course of an answer to an objection he says: *"na hi atma nama kasyacit aprasiddho bhavati."*

11. Taittiriya Upanishad, 2.1.1: *"satyam jnanam anantam brahma."* Brhadaranyaka Upanishad, 3.9.28: *"vijnanam anandam brahma."*

12. Sankara in his commentary on the Taittiriya Upanishad, formulates the criterion as follows: *"satyamiti yadrupena yanniscitam tadrupam na vyabhicarati, tat satyam."*

13. Adevaitins very often identify *maya* and *avidya,* since their essential nature is the same. Both *maya* and *avidya* are material *(jada),* made up of three *gunas-sattva, rajas,* and *tamas (trigunatmika),* and so on. This, however, does not mean that Advaitins do not make any distinction between them.

14. Unlike other objects, which require a cause for their origination, *maya-avidya* does not come into existence from a cause, because there is nothing else to be the cause of it. Brahman, which is the locus of *maya-avidya,* is not its cause. *Maya-avidya* is said to be self-caused in the Nrsimhapurvatapinyupanishad, 9.3: *"maya ca avidya ca svayameva bhavati."*

15. See Sankara's commentary on the Katha Upanishad, 2.3.14: *". . . avidya-kama-karma-laksanasya mrtyorvinasat."*

16. Katha Upanishad, 2.3.14.

The Advaita View of Death and Immortality

17. Bhagavad-gita 2.20. The English translation of the text is based on Sankara's commentary.

18. Katha Upanishad, 2.3.14.

19. Unlike the rope-snake, the real snake (like the real rope) is part of the empirical realm (*vyavaharika*); and it is sublated only when the entire empirical realm gets sublated at the time of Self-realization. It is, therefore, empirically real.

20. Advaita speaks of three levels of reality—*pratibhasika, vyavaharika,* and *paramarthika.* Objects such as rope-snake and dream-lion are *pratibhasika* (apparently real). Table and chair, tree and mountain, which are objects of our normal waking consciousness, are *vyavaharika* (empirically real). Only Brahman-Atman is *paramarthika* (absolutely real).

21. Svetasvatara Upanishad, 3.19.

22. Mundaka Upanishad, 1.1.6.

23. Bhagavad-gita, 2.54–71.

24. Bhagavad-gita, 2.71

25. Bhagavad-gita, 2.69.

26. Brhadaranyaka Upanishad, 4.4.7.

27. Naiskarmyasiddhi, 2.117.

28. See Sankara's commentary on the Brahma-sutra, 1.1.4. Sankara quotes the Nyaya-sutra, 1.1.2 which reads: *"duhkhajanma-pravrtti-dosa-mithyajnananam uttarottarapaye tadanantarapayat apavargah."*

29. See his commentary on the Brahma-sutra, 1.1.4: *"mithya-pratyayanimittatvat sasariratvasya siddham jivato'pi viduso asariratvam."*

30. Brhadaranyaka Upanishad, 4.4.5.

31. Brhadaranyaka Upanishad, 4.4.6.

32. Brhadaranyaka Upanishad, 4.4.2.

33. Brhadaranyaka Upanishad. See Sankara's commentary on this text.

34. Brhadaranyaka Upanishad, 4.4.3.

35. Brhadaranyaka Upanishad, 4.4.6.

10

Life, Death, and the Deathless in Theravada Buddhism

SAENG CHANDRA-NGARM

Introduction

Man loves life and fears death more than anything else. Life to him is most precious and good, though, in reality, it is bedecked with weaknesses, struggling, and suffering. Death is feared because it seems to be the complete extinction of precious life. The history of human civilization has told us how great cultures of the world tried to preserve life and avoid death. The methods of preserving life range from searching for and producing life-preserving materials to elaborate techniques of mental development. The techniques are believed to be so effective that even recently a Tibetan holy man has been claimed to have lived for 1,200 years.[1]

When all efforts to immortalize physical life had failed, man began to contrive the idea of resurrection: the arising and the eternal living of an individual after the departed soul has returned and joined the dead body. From this conception arose the effort to preserve the dead body in the best possible condition called mummification. The burial of dead bodies awaiting resurrection on the Judgment Day and Eternal Life thereafter is but the outgrowth of Egyptian mummification.

The Hindus have gone another step by rejecting the idea of an immortal body but retaining an immortal soul (atman). The body to the Hindus is always despicable and should be disposed of by fire immediately after death. The immortal soul will migrate to a new body and then the reincarnation process will go on and on until it merges in, and becomes identical with, the Universal Soul (paramatman). The Buddhists deny both the immortal body and the immortal soul, but believe in the life-process, which flows on and on until it expires at nirvana.

The Constituents of the Universe

Before tackling the problem of life, we should know something about the constitution of the universe as alluded to in the Buddhist texts. It seems that the universe is composed of seven primary elements (*dhatu*):

1. Matter in solid state (*pathavi*)
2. Matter in liquid state (*apo*)
3. Matter in gaseous state (*vayo*)
4. Matter in the form of heat energy (*tejo*)
5. Mental element (*vinnanadhatu*)
6. Space element (*akasadhatu*)
7. Nirvanic element (*nibbanadhatu*).[2]

Of the seven elements the first four are material elements (*rupadhatu*). In reality they are only the four states or forms of the same stuff called *matter* in physics. Matter exists eternally under its own laws (*dhammaniyama*). It changes its forms as necessitated by appropriate conditions. All physical phenomena around us are but different forms of matter and they are all temporary. They are in the state of instant becoming or flowing (*annica*). The earth is now in the solid form but there will be a time when it will be in a hot gaseous state. The Buddhist texts have given a vivid description of how the whole solar system (*cakkavala*) gradually becomes a mass of fire.[3]

The mental element seems to be a separate energy in itself. In the hierarchy of beings (*satta*) who populate the universe, there is even a class of beings whose life is composed of mental element only. They are called *arupabraham* and live in a nonmaterial world (*arupaloka*). The other clue that implies the existence of mental energy is found in one of the four higher, nonmaterial meditations (*arupajhana*) in which the meditator concentrates on the unbounded consciousness (*vinnanancayatana*).

Mental energy combined with fine-material produces a class of beings called fine-material beings (*rupabraham*) who live in the fine-material world (*rupaloka*). Some of these fine-material beings are "made of mind, feeding on rapture, self-luminous, traversing the air."[4] They were the only inhabitants of the solar system when the system was in the gaseous state. When our planet was beginning to materialize, these beings were combined with gross matter and became the prototype of mankind.[5]

The mental element is only a type of energy among others even though it may be finer. It is "impersonal" and becomes "personal" only when it is combined with matter and becomes a being (*satta*). The mental element is, therefore, the core of the life stream. It is something referred to as *citta* (mind) in the texts. Consciousness (*vinnana*), perception (*sanna*), feeling (*vedana*) and thought for information (*samkhara*) seem to be only activities of the mind.

The nirvanic element is a separate element existing by itself eternally. More details about this will be given later.

The space element is nothing but empty space that engulfs everything including nirvanic element. Space and nirvana are similar in many respects, such as eternality, uncreatedness, omnipresence, etc.

What is Man?

Having surveyed briefly the composition of the universe, we should now turn to look at the nature of man. Man is a class of beings among the eight classes of beings who populate the universe. They are given here in their hierarchical order from the highest to the lowest:

1. Mental beings (*arupa brahma*)
2. Fine-material beings (*rupa brahma*)
3. Heavenly beings (*devas*)
4. Human beings (*manussa*)
5. Animal beings (*tiracchana*)
6. Spirit beings (*asurakaya*)
7. Ghostly beings (*petas*)
8. Purgatory beings (*niraya sattas*)

It will be seen that humans occupy about the middle of the hierarchy. Just below humans are animal beings who share the same habitat with humans and are similar to them in many physical features. The only difference is that the animal's mind is markedly underdeveloped.[6]

The Constituents of Humans

Man as a psychophysical being belonging to the human class is made up of two main components: matter (*rupa*) and mind (*nama*). The material component manifests itself in the four states of solid, liquid, gas, and heat. When these four states exist in correct proportion and function in harmony, the physical life will go on normally. Traditional medicine of the Orient usually attributes illness to the imbalance of the four states. The mental component consists of four main mental activities: consciousness, perception, feeling, and thought formations (*samkhara*).[7] These five constituents of life are called the five aggregates (*khanda* or *skanda*), which are mistaken for 'Self' by unenlightened people.

How the Life-Process Functions

Human life is a process that flows on and on in time and space. The period from birth to death and the period from death to birth are only two phases of the same process. The former can be called "the waxing period" and the latter "the waning period." The length of each phase varies in accordance with the life span of each class of beings and also with the intervention of innate karmic force in the life-stream itself. The waxing phase of a human, for example, is about a hundred years long, and that of a *deva* may be several million years long. The life stream flows on in conformity to the law of causality. The root cause of the life-process is Ignorance (*avijja*) or the absence of Intuitive Insight (*nana*) into the real nature of life. Normally we tend to see things as they appear and not as they really are. We are, therefore, deluded by appearance and convention. Delusion, in its turn, inspires volition and volition stimulates act (*kamma*). Every volitional act, either mental, verbal, or bodily produces an amount of karmic force or disposition (*samkhara*) in the mind. Karmic disposition acts to preserve life-stream by generating a unit of mental energy (*vinnana*) at the moment of death.

Death marks the beginning of the waning phase of the life-process. The five aggregates disintegrate and the life-stream becomes invisible. The unit of mental energy produced at death is called in later texts the connecting psyche (*patisandhi vinnana*).[8] This mental unit leaves the dead body and travels to a new body in the mother's womb if it is to be reborn in the human class of beings. It serves as the seed of life (*vinnanabijam*) that carries all the properties of the previous life over to the new one. This is perfectly analogous to the plant seed that links two trees together. The Buddha is quite straightforward when he converses with his personal attendant, Ananda, thus, "I have said that cognition (*vinnana*) is the cause of name-and-form (initial form of life in the womb, the embryo). Now in what way that is so, Ananda, is to be understood after this manner. Were cognition not to descend into the mother's womb, would name-and-form become constituted therein?"

"It would not, lord."

"Were cognition, after having descended into the mother's womb, to become extinct, would name-and-form come to birth in this state of being?"

"It would not, lord."

"Were cognition to be extirpated from one yet young, youth or maiden would name-and-form attain to growth, development, expansion?"

"It would not, lord."

"Wherefore, Ananda, just that is the ground, the basis, the genesis, the cause of name-and-form, to wit, cognition."[9]

In another textual source, "the connecting psyche" is mentioned as a mysterious being called *gandhabba*. The Buddha says, "Monks, it is on the conjunction of three things that there is conception. If there is here a coitus of the parents, but it is not the mother's season and the *gandhabba* is not present for so long there is not conception. If there is here a coitus of the parents and it is the mother's season, but the *gandhabba* is not present for so long there is not conception. But if, monks, there is here a coitus of the parents and it is the mother's season and the *gandhabba* is present, it is on the conjunction of these three things that there is conception."[10]

Hermann Beckh (1875-1937) interprets *gandhabba* as a mysterious being equipped with six senses and capable of interacting with the environment. It is this *gandhabba* that enters the womb and brings forth conception.[11]

Beckh's interpretation sounds very commendable for it enables us to understand clearly the logical sequence of each link of the Dependent Origination (*paticcasamuppada*). The idea of *gandhabba* as a disembodied being is also supported by near-death or after-death experiences reported by those who come back from clinical death.[12]

Linking psyche definitely enters the womb of the mother and joins with the embryo (*namarupa*) therein. A new human life then begins to develop. The fully-developed embryo or fetus is equipped with the six sense-doors (*salayatana*). From the six sense-doors, contact (*phassa*) occurs, from contact feeling (*vedana*), from feeling craving or desire (*tanha*), from desire clinging (*upadana*), and from clinging becoming (*bhava*). These five psychophysical activities in the womb are very faint because of the still-underdeveloped six senses. In due time the full-grown fetus is discharged from the womb and the conventional or external birth takes place. After that the five psychophysical activities can function in their full capacities. From the very moment of birth, old age begins and the waxing phase of life ends when conventional death occurs.

What is Death?

Death is defined in the text thus: "And what, Bhikkhus, is dying? Dying is the fall (out of any state), the dropping out of it, the dissolution, the disappearance, the death, the dying, the accomplishment of the life-term, the breaking up of the groups (*khandhas*), the laying down of the body of this or that being in this or that class of beings. This is called dying."[13]

Death is only the end of the waxing phase of the life-stream, and not of the life-stream itself. Linking psyche will always be produced to start a new waxing phase as long as karmic dispositions (*samkhara*) and Ignorance (*avijja*) remain. When the waxing phase has run its alloted term, the life-stream subsides into the state of linking psyche and then the waning, invisible phase of life begins. No one lives forever since the life-stream is an integrated phenomenon and every integrated thing must disintegrate (*upadavayadhammino*). That is why the Buddha calls death "the accomplishment of the life-stream."

Death can also be described as the change of the class of beings. When a man dies, his linking psyche will be attracted to be reborn in any of the eight classes of beings in accordance with his karmic dispositions. A linking psyche charged with positive karmic force (*punnabhisamkhara*) will be drawn to a higher world of higher beings. The one with negative karmic force (*apunnabhisankhara*) is drawn to be reborn in a lower realm. A man can, therefore, be reborn in any species of animals. The Buddha says:

Then I, Sariputta, with my mind comprehend the mind of some person thus: as that person fares along and as he is going along and has entered on that way, so will he arise, at the breaking up of the body after dying, in an animal birth. After a time I see with purified deva vision, surpassing that of men, that, at the breaking up of the body after dying, he has arisen in an animal birth and is experiencing feelings that are painful, sharp, severe. Sariputta, it is as if there were a cesspool deeper than a man's height, full of filth; then a man might come along overcome and overpowered by the hot weather heat, exhausted, parched and thirsty, heading direct for that cesspool itself by one sole way. A man with vision, having seen him, might say, 'As that good man is faring along, and as he is going along and has entered on that way, so will he come to that cesspool itself. After a time he may see him, fallen into the cesspool and experiencing feelings that are painful, sharp, severe. . . .'[14]

A Buddhist who has realized the nature of the life-stream has no fear of death. He knows that death is only the change of status and location. Some who have accumulated more than enough good karma even welcome death, which, to them, is something like promotion to a higher and better position.

Life-Process, a Semi-Eternal Phenomenon

The faring on of the life-stream (samsara) can be regarded as semi-eternal for it is tremendously long. Its beginning and end are unknown (anamatagga) and unknowable. George Grimm has vividly described the endless wandering in this manner, "Thus every being is eternally wandering to and fro within samsara through the five realms, finding itself reborn by the incessant change for the five groups constituting its personality, now as a man, now as a spectre, now as an animal, now as a devil, now and then as a god."[15]

The Buddha himself has even more clearly demonstrated the point with the following analogy:

Suppose, O monks, a man should cut off the grasses and herbs, twigs and leaves of this entire continent of India, should collect them and heap up one handful of them after the other, saying: 'This is my mother, this is the mother of my mother' and so on—there would be no end of the mothers of the mother of this man. But he would reach the very last bit, the end of all the grasses and herbs of this continent of India—and why? Without beginning or end, monks, is this round of rebirths. There cannot be discerned the first beginning of beings, who sunk in ignorance and bound by thirst, are incessently transmigrating, and again and again run to a new birth. . . .[16]

Life-process cannot be fully eternal because it can be terminated by means of following the Noble Eightfold Path, which begins with right view of life (sammadithi), i.e., the realization of the truth of suffering as the result of repeated rebirths. In order to help his disciples to grasp this basic truth, the Buddha has instructed them thus:

What do you think, O monks, which may be more, the flood of tears you have shed on this long way, running again and again to new birth and new death, united with the disliked, separated from the liked, complaining and weeping, or the water of the four great oceans?

Through a long time you have experienced the death of the mother . . . the father . . . the son . . . the daughter . . . brother and sister. Through a long time you were oppressed by sickness . . . you have shed on this long way truly more tears than water is contained within the four great oceans. . . . Through a long time you have shed, sentenced to death as murderers . . . caught as robbers . . . detected as adulterers . . . more blood in being executed than there is water contained within the four great oceans. . . . Through a long time you have as cows and calves truly shed more blood in being decapitated than there is water contained within the four great oceans. . . . Through a long time you have as buffaloes and buffalo-calves . . . as sheep and lambs . . . as he-goats and she-goats . . . as deers and stags . . . as swine and pigs . . . as hens and doves and geese . . . truly shed more blood in being butchered than there is water contained within the four great oceans.

And thus, O monks, through a long time you have experienced suffering pain and misery, and enlarged the burying ground; truly long enough to be disgusted with all productions, long enough to turn away from them.[17]

For those who cling to life and yearn for everlasting life, there is no need to fear extinction, life-process will not extinguish at death as understood by the materialist. As long as there is Ignorance, desire and clinging, the life-stream will continue to flow automatically. The best way to preserve life is to do nothing but to live and lead a normal life as average people do. The only precaution to take is to guard against the tendency to realize the truth of suffering in life.

The End of the Life-Process

There will be a time when an individual will learn the most precious lesson of life, that is, repeated rebirths are suffering (*Dukkha Jati puna-ppunam*). The knowledge of suffering will stimulate the learner to do something to liberate himself from the cycle of births and deaths. Having Right View (*sammaditthi*) and right determination, the aspirant will set right his speech (*sammavaca*), his action (*sammakammanta*) and his livelihood (*sammajiva*); he will try to rid his mind of everything that will breed and strengthen ignorance, desire, and attachment. This mental exercise is called Right Effort (*sammavayama*). When the psychophysical base is well prepared, the aspirant will develop his mindfulness by trying to be aware of all external activities and of all internal or mental activities (*sammasati*). He will then focus his well-developed mindfulness on one particular object (*sammasamadhi*) until it becomes "composed, quite purified, quite clarified, without blemish, without defilement, grown soft and workable, fixed, immovable."[18]

The purified mind will then be directed to watch an apparent activity of the life process itself. Breathing is the most recommendable object to concentrate on since its dynamic nature is very helpful in understanding the basic truths of the life-process. This step is aimed at developing Intuitive Insight (*vipassana*). The idea is to watch passively without investigating and reasoning. An experienced meditator suggests, "And thus through apparently remaining in quite a passive state, mind gradually is becoming more perfect and stronger than by performing outward active work."

"This so called passive state requires the utmost effort and restraint of all sense-impulse in order to neutralize their activities. This 'Passive activity' may be called 'poverty in spirit'—for in such a state a man has no more desire to speculate, to know, or to possess."[19] Even a secular scientist like Aldous Huxley comprehends this principle when he writes, "There is a transcendent spontaneity of life, a creative reality which reveals itself as immanent only when the perceiver's mind is in a state of alert passivity, of choiceless awareness."[20]

At the appropriate moment Right Insight (*sammanana*) will shine forth; the three fundamental truths of impermanence (*anicca*), suffering (*dukkha*) and Egolessness (*anatta*) are realized in their entirety. After that a sense of disgust (*nibbida*) will arise and dispassion (*viraga*) automatically follows suit. At last final deliverance (*vimutti*) from *samsara* is experienced and realized. The stereotype description of the final episode in the scriptures runs like this: ". . . The mind is freed from the canker of sense pleasure (*kamasava*), from the canker of becoming (*bhavasava*), and from the canker of Ignorance (*avijja*)." He comprehends: "Destroyed is birth, brought to a close is the Brahma-faring, done is what was to be done, there is no more being such or such."[21]

Nirvana—the Deathless

When Intuitive Insight has arisen and Ignorance together with its concomitants has vanished, what is left is a liberated mind characterized by the four noble qualities: enlightenment, purity, peace, and compassion. In common parlance, the person has become an *arahant,* the Worthy One, the one who has experienced in this very life, an empirical nirvana.

Ontologically speaking, however, it is not as easy as it sounds to understand the real nature of "nirvanic mind." I would like to propose an idea here for further consideration: an *arahant* is a person whose mental element (*citta*-mind) has been transformed into nirvanic element by means of the Noble Eightfold Path and Intuitive Insight. I agree with Rune Johansson when he writes,

In modern Books about Buddhist philosophy we are generally told that human personality consists of the Khandas, personality factors: *rupa,* "body," *sanna,* "ideation," *vedana,* "feeling," *samkhara,* "activity," and *vinnana,* "consciousness." This is not quite true, since the most important is *citta,* generally translated "mind." *Citta* is the core of personality, the center of purposiveness, activity, continuity, functional self. It is mainly conscious but not restricted to the momentary conscious contents and processes. On the contrary, it includes all the layers of consciousness, even the unconscious; by it the continuity and identity are safeguarded. It has a distinctly individual form. Its original state is characterized by the defilements (*upakilesa*)[22], the emotional imperfections and the obsessions (*asava*).[23] The whole gamut of Buddhist methods therefore aims at purifying the *citta.* If this purification is complete, *nibbana* [nirvana] is attained.[24]

The Cosmic Nirvana

Now what happens when an *arahant* dies? To this question no definite answers are given in the Buddhist texts. The Buddha has opted to be silent on the subject on the ground that it is useless to discuss "something that one never experiences even in dream." This naturally leads to several interpretations. The one most popular is what is classified as nihilism: it maintains that an *arahant* after his/her death passes into complete extinction. The second interpretation is eternalism. It holds that after his/her death, the *arahant's* purified mind exists forever as an individual in a transcendental realm somewhere in the company of other purified minds.

Both views are termed "extreme" and condemned by the Buddha as "wrong view" (*micchaditthi*). Nihilism is untenable because no primary elements in the universe are completely extinct. Eternalism contradicts the doctrine of Egolessness (*anatta*) of all things including nirvana.

The third view is the middle way between the two. It proposes that when an *arahant* dies, her/his physical body disintegrates and its physical constituents return to the world of matter. His/her *citta* or mental element, which has been transformed into nirvanic element (*nibbabadhatu*), merges and becomes identical with the cosmic nirvana or nirvanic element.

The third interpretation is acceptable because it avoids the two extremes and is supported by textual evidence. The Buddha categorically recognizes the existence of the cosmic nirvana when he says, "There is that sphere wherein is neither earth nor water nor fire nor air; wherein is neither the sphere of infinite space nor of infinite consciousness nor of nothingness nor of neither-ideation-nor-non-ideation; where there is neither this world nor the world beyond nor both together nor moon and sun; this I say is free from coming and going, from duration and decay; there is no beginning and no establishment, no result and no cause; this indeed is the end of suffering.[25]

The following passage renders strong support to the existence of the cosmic nirvana, "Monks, there is a not-born, not-become, not-made, not-compounded (condition). Monks, if that not-born, not-become, not-made, not compounded (condition) were not, no escape from the born, become, made, compounded (condition) had been known here. But, monks, since there is a not-born, not-become, not-made, not-compounded (condition), therefore an escape from the born, become, made, compounded (condition) is known."[26]

From the Buddha's own words given above, we can come to the conclusion that there are two sides of existence: the compounded side (*samkhata*) and the uncompounded side (*asamkhata*) or cosmic nirvana and it is possible for an individual to "escape" from one side to the other. And the escape is nothing but the unification of purified *citta* with the cosmic nirvana. This simple interpretation is supported by the following scriptural passage: "[just as the ocean does not shrink or overflow] . . . even so though many monks pass finally away in that condition of *nibbana* [nirvana] without any attachment left, yet there is neither shrinkage nor overflow in that condition of *nibbana* [nirvana] seen thereby."[27]

This view may sound strikingly similiar to the Vedanta idea of

Atman merging with *paramatman,* the Universal Soul, and many orthodox Buddhists may raise voices against it. All arguments to shed more light on this difficult point are welcome by the author.

Conclusion

The universe is composed of matter (*rupa*) in its four manifestations (solid, liquid, gas, and heat). Matter exists eternally. Only its four forms are temporary. Mental element is also eternally prevalent. Matter combined with mental element becomes "being" (*satta*). There are eight main classes of *satta* in the universe.

A being exists in the form of a stream or process. This life-stream flows on and on as long as its root-causes (Ignorance, desire, attachment, and karmic disposition) remain. The life-process may reappear in any of the eight types of beings according to its karmic force. The life-stream can be termed "semi-eternal" since its beginning is not known and its end unforeseeable.

With the power of Intuitive Insight (*nana*) developed by the Noble Eightfold Path, the root causes of the life-stream are destroyed, the mind is transformed into nirvanic element, and the person is called an *arahant*. When the life-process of the *arahant* ceases at death his/her purified or "nirvanized" mind merges and becomes identical with the Cosmic nirvana, which exists by itself eternally as an immortal element.

NOTES

1. Paul Brunton, *A Search in Secret India,* 4th reprint Indian edition (Bombay: B.I. Publications, 1980), p. 198.

2. M II 31 gives the list of the first six elements. The nirvanic element, widely mentioned in other places, is added here by myself.

3. A V 64–63.

4. *Aggannasutta* D. 3. 82

5. *Aggannasutta* D. 3. 83. p. 83.

6. For details see Randy Kloetzli, *Buddhist Cosmology* (Delhi: Motilal Banarsidass, 1983).

7. *Samkhara* has several interpretations given by different authorities. Narada Mahathera of Sri Lanka, following the Abhidhamma line of interpretation, has identified *samkhara* with the 50 mental states (*cetasika*) and singled out

volition (*cetana*) as the most important factor, *A Manual of Abhidhamma* (Kandy: Buddhist Publication Society, 1975); A. Berriedale Keith renders *samkhara* as "dispositions," *Buddhist Philosophy* (London: Oxford University Press, 1923); T. W. Rhys Davids has "conformations or confections" as *samkhara* in *The History and Literature of Buddhism* (Calcutta: Susil Gupta Private Ltd., 1962).

8. In the Abhidhamma interpretation, the *patisandhivinnana* is the first flash of consciousness that arises in the embryo immediately after the last thought-moment (*cuti citta*) has disappeared at death. Between the last thought-moment of the previous life and the first thought-moment of the present life, there is nothing to serve as link. This does not sound logical because the distance in space between the two lives is, in some cases, tremendously long. There must be something to bridge the two if they are independent.

9. *Mahanidanasuttanta*, D II 62–64.

10. *Mahanidanasuttanta*, M I 321–22.

11. A. Berriedale Keith, *Buddhist Philosophy* (London: Oxford University Press, 1923), p. 60.

12. Michael B. Sabom, *Recollections of Death* (London: Gorgi Books, 1982).

13. *Mahastipatthanasutta*, D II 338.

14. *Mahanidanasuttanta*, M I 99–100.

15. George Grimm, *The Doctrine of the Buddha*, 2nd Indian ed. (Delhi: Molitas Banarsidass, 1982), p. 99.

16. Tinakatthasutta, S II 118–19.

17. Tinakatthasutta S. 2. 126–27.

18. This is the typical description of the mind in deep meditation prevalent throughout the texts.

19. Venerable Vappo Thera in "The Mahabodhi," *The Journal of the Mahabodhi Society of India*, vol. 87, no. 1–3, Jan.–March 1979, p. 5.

20. Quoted by John E. Coleman, *The Quiet Mind* (London: Rider & Co., 1967), pp. 75–76.

21. *Culahatthipadopamasutta*, M I 228.

22. M. I. 36.

23. D. I. 84.

24. Rune Johansson, *The Psychology of Nirvana* (London: George Allen and Unwin Ltd., 1969), p. 30.

25. *Nibbanasutta* I, U 80.

26. *Nibbanasutta* III, U 81.

27. *Uposathasutta*, U 55.

11

Buddhism, Karma, and Immortality

BRUCE R. REICHENBACH

Buddhist literature follows in the Vedic tradition of avowing belief in life after death; what is not so clear is the sense in which this belief, as a form of immortality, is to be understood. For example, on the one hand, immortality is likened to the vital energy which, flowing from time immemorial, is passed on from one organism to the next—from the fruit tree to its seed, on to another tree.[1] On the other hand, all kinds of evidences from parapsychology are adduced to justify the belief that the person survives as a discarnate, nonsubstantial spirit and returns to human existence.[2] Between these two views there lies an enormous difference; whereas the first substitutes a nonindividual, continuing vitality for any persistence of the person, the second presupposes such persistence.

This means that we cannot simply plunge headlong into the topic of the Buddhist view of human immortality; before we can begin to discuss whether there actually is life after death, we first must discern what Buddhists mean by life after death. And such a discussion requires prior consideration of the view of the human person that is presupposed. With their treatment of the nature of the human person, then, let us begin.

Buddhism and Metaphysics

Yet even so, we cannot commence so easily, for how can a question about the nature of the human person be raised when there lurks in Buddhism an alleged metaphysical agnosticism? The Buddha taught that it does not fit the case to say that the saint exists after death, that it does not fit the case to say that the saint does not exist after death, that it does not fit the case to say that the saint both does exist and does not exist after death, and that it does not fit the case to say that the saint neither does exist nor does not exist after death.[3]

His point was that to advance theories concerning the existence or nonexistence of persons after death involves one in the broader speculation concerning the nature of the human person, and worrying over the nature of the human person distracts from the primary concern of freeing the individual from misery. "Vaccha, the theory that the saint neither exists nor does not exist after death, is a jungle, a wilderness, a puppet show, a writhing, and a fetter, and is coupled with misery, ruin, dispair, and agony, and does not tend to aversion, absence of passion, cessation, quiescence, knowledge, supreme wisdom, and Nirvana."[4]

Granted that the Buddha, as a religious teacher, eschewed becoming embroiled in distracting metaphysical controversies, yet metaphysical questions cannot be so easily avoided. Practical ethics cannot be separated from broader questions of ontology, especially about the nature of human persons. Even in the Buddha's own teaching this is true. For one thing, the Buddha advanced the doctrine of no-self.[5] True, it is advanced with practical concerns foremost in mind. In recognizing the insubstantiality and transitoriness of all things, one can recognize that all is evil, so that the individual who meditates on the no-self, its transitoriness and evil, is free from all desire for the physical and substantial, and thus becomes passionless and understands that his rebirth is exhausted.[6] Yet the theory that there is no-self or that the *skandhas* are not the self is a metaphysical theory about the self, even if only about the phenomenal. Secondly, in addressing himself to the question of how to attain freedom from rebirth, the Buddha invoked the doctrines of karma and rebirth. But both doctrines are metaphysical as well as moral; both make reference to the workings of "reality," again even if only phenomenal (which itself reflects a metaphysical distinction between phenomena and noumena). Thirdly, in the passage noted above, the Buddha follows his refusal to take a position on the existence or nonexistence of the saint after death with the assertion that though the *tathagata* is free from all theories, he does know the nature of the five *skandhas*.[7] But the very presentation and elaboration of the *skandha*-theory raises metaphysical questions: What are the *skandhas*? How are they related to the self? Is there any reason to accept the *skandha* doctrine?

In short, in spite of the Buddha's refusal to discuss metaphysical questions, such questions must be raised, for certain views of the self and the world are implicit in his discussions of the self as related to the *skandhas,* karma, rebirth, and liberation. Such has been recognized by Buddhists themselves; how else can one explain the *pudgala* controversies over the status and nature of the agent of thought and action?[8] Let us then turn to the question of the nature of the self.

The Buddhist Concept of the Self

From its very outset, Buddhism has attempted to avoid substantialist thinking. Reality is composed of "an unceasing flow of simple ultimates, called *"dharmas,"* which can be defined as (1) multiple, (2) momentary, (3) impersonal, (4) mutually conditioned events."[9] *Dharmas* are ultimate reality ("truly real events"), which, as events or processes, are neither substances nor dependent in the sense of attributes on substances. With respect to human persons, this means that there is no substantial self that underlies either human experience or human existence. Persons and things are nothing more than the "conglomeration of elementary dharmic events," an aggregate of certain physical and psychological events.[10]

What are the components of the aggregate that we term the self? They are five, called *skandhas*. First, there is what is broadly termed the physical. One must be careful here not to consider the physical element in terms of permanent parts of the body or even the body itself. What are referred to here are transitory nonmental events or processes. Secondly, there are feelings; thirdly, perceptions. Fourthly, there are mental dispositions or tendencies, which are the bearers of karma or the tendencies caused by karmic acts. Finally, there is consciousness, also a bearer of karma, which consists of three types of events: (1) mental activity (called pure awareness) considered more or less abstractly; (2) mental activity (called thought) considered concretely; (3) mental activity (called mind) considered in terms of function: receiving sense data, organizing and unifying that data, recalling, making judgments and reasoning, and discriminating the "internal" from the "external."[11]

Yet even here there is a misunderstanding, for the self is not the *skandhas* individually nor their union. Indeed, the unity that is experienced or ascribed to these sets of *skandhas* is apparent only. Just as the "pole, axle, wheels, chariot-body, banner-staff, yoke, reins, and goad unitedly [are not] the chariot," so the five *skandhas* unitedly are not the self. When we identify the self with a given set of *skandhas,* we are creating a fiction based on mistaking two similar sets of *skandhas* as the same or identical. If we would pay closer attention, we would see that no two events are identical. As "the word 'chariot' is but a way of counting, term, appellation, convenient designation, and name of pole, axle, wheels, chariot-body, and banner-staff," so a person's name or "living being" or "self" is merely a "way of counting, term, appellation, or convenient designation."[12] It is a mode of expression by which we can function in the common-sense world. But at heart it is a fiction; there is no self.

To this doctrine of no-self must be added the doctrine of momentariness. The Buddha contended that all was impermanent: whatever is an arising thing, that is a ceasing thing. Practically, this meant that all persons are subject to old-age, sickness, and ultimately death. There is nothing that can acclaim its own immortality or lastingness. As Buddhism developed, however, the doctrine of impermanence developed into the doctrine of momentariness: everything is an event, constantly succeeded by other events. All is flux; even the event itself is in flux. Thus each dharma arises, persists briefly (how long is a matter of internal dispute), and ceases.[13]

This view of the self has serious implications for such basic Buddhist doctrines as the law of karma, rebirth, and liberation. For example, if there is no self, then espousal of rebirth seems nonsense, for it makes no sense to say that the same person would be reborn. That is, there can be no difference between birth and rebirth; we merely choose to call a newborn the reborn. Rebirth, like the doctrine of the self, is a fiction. Similarly with the doctrines of karma and liberation; without a self there can be no subsequent person who experiences the effects of the karma *he* has sown, nor is the liberated person the individual who exhausted his karma. These doctrines too are fictions.

Buddhists, however, draw back from these implications, for such would all but destroy their religious and philosophical perspective. What would remain if both the causation of karma and human liberation were fictions created by us? Their response is that though there is no substantial self, there are identifiable sets of *skandhas,* and though there is no identity between consecutive sets of *skandhas,* neither is there complete difference and discontinuity. The self is both collective (a collection of a certain set of *skandhas*) and recollective (a continuation of successive sets of *skandhas* provided by memory and dispositions).[14]

The Role of Karma

Two substantial questions arise with this characterization. First, in what sense is the self collective? At any given time there are innumerable *skandhas* in existence. The world is a plethora of events. What is it that collects a certain set of events together, bundles them as it were, so that they form the collective feature of human persons? What constitutes the bundling element? What is it that makes a feeling a member of one set rather than another? Or to put it differently, one finds Buddhist writers referring to the person as a psychophysical unit or unity.[15] What is the principle of unity; what is it that makes any given set of dispositions, perceptions, mental acts, feelings, and physical events such that it can be termed a person or at least differentiated from another set?

The Buddhist answer is that there is a causal nexus of conditions that allow us to say that one perception goes with one feeling rather than another. Though there are many feelings and many perceptions occurring at any given time, there is a stronger causal relation between certain perceptions and feelings than between others, or at least we perceive there to be such. Further, it is this causal nexus that explains the unity of the whole. It is karma, "which has brought the five *skandhas* into the present state of co-ordination. . . . As long as the force of karma is thus successively generated, there are the five *skandhas* constantly coming into existence and working co-ordinately as a person."[16] This causal relation between successive *skandhas*, which is such that when this appears, that follows, constitutes an uninterrupted series.

If this is so, then whether the unity or bundling is a fact about the real world or whether it is merely a subjective imposition (a terming on our part) depends on the view of karma held. If karma is an objective causal relation between events, then the unity is more than the result of mere naming. There actually is something, i.e., the causal action of karma, which bundles the *skandhas* into a set. Consequently, there is not complete difference between successive sets of *skandhas*. On the other hand, if karma is merely the subjective presence of causal continuity, the unity is conventional and fictional at best. Karma may psychologically compel or provide impetus for us to collect various *skandhas* together, but it provides no objective basis for such ascription. In short, the question of the real identity of the person hinges on the question of the ontological status of karma.

Unfortunately, it is at this point that Buddhist accounts of the human person lose their consistency. We are frequently given both stories. On the one hand, we are told that there is no real unity between the *skandhas*; the unity found there is merely ascribed to it.[17] The bundling role of karma is subjective only, functioning to (mis)lead us to ascribe unity where there is none. This accounts for the claim that the *skandhas* neither individually nor as a unit are the self. On the other hand, we are assured that the action of karma really causes the human situation. "It is through a difference in their karma that men are not all alike."[18] Karma is an objective feature of the world. This accounts for the claim that there is not complete difference between sets of *skandhas*. As we shall see shortly, this ambiguity has significant implications for the doctrine of immortality.

Secondly, how do dispositions and memory provide continuity to persons or *skandhas*? The Buddhist response is that successive *skandhas* are continuous because one set of momentary dharmas causes subsequent dharmas. Since Buddhists deny that causation involves production, the continuity is not the result of one cause *producing* successive effects. Neither is there anything transmitted in the causal relation. Rather, since the relation between cause and effect is one of functional dependence, it must be that the respective effects are caused in the sense that they arise on condition that certain events are present. As such, it is the causal series of dispositions and consciousnesses that constitute the continuity.

The argument here is that I am the same person who was born forty years ago, not in the sense that something about me has remained constant, for everything about me has undergone change, but in the sense that one can trace a series of causally related events from birth to the present. Again, the functioning of karma proves central, for karma working causally conditions dispositions and consciousness in subsequent sets of *skandhas*, and this causal sequence provides the continuity sufficient to allow us to ascribe both personal continuity and moral responsibility to subsequent persons based upon prior acts, despite the fact that there is no persistent agent.[19]

But what of the recollective feature? This is provided for by memories, which are likewise caused since they are part of consciousness. However, though the recollective functions importantly in this life to provide the individual awareness of his identity, it is not a necessary condition of his identity per se. That it is not necessary can be seen from the fact that though it might so happen that the reborn recalls previous lives, this is not the norm. Its rare occurrence often signals true liberation and spiritual insight. In short, both dispositions and memory derive their existence from the action of karma.[20] Thus, in the case of rebirth, the weight of continuity in terms of necessary and sufficient conditions falls entirely upon karma.

What then can we conclude about the Buddhist view of the human person? The answer is that there is no substantial self or person. What does exist are momentary events of various discrete sorts. When we perceive these discrete events occurring at a particular time and place, we bundle those discrete elements or events and label or term that bundle a particular person or thing. Here, however, we get two stories. On the one hand, a name is nothing but a label for any given set of *skandhas*, a label, which, when either dispensed with or at the very least recognized for what it is, namely, an arbitrary convention, frees the individual from desires relating to the self and consequently brings the realization that rebirth is exhausted. Yet, on the other hand, naming is not entirely arbitrary, for, granted that the doctrine of karma has empirical content, i.e., that karma is objective, the name reflects the dispositions and consciousness that have arisen upon the prior causal conditions and that provide both the bundling and continuity. Whether these "two hands" are consistent is problematic at best. In any case, the doctrine of karma functions as the central motif for both views.

Application to Immortality

It is now time to return to our original issue, the question of the meaning and possibility of life after death. We have already noted the Buddhist contention that there is rebirth; the Four Noble Truths and the Eightfold Path have as their objective the cessation of the misery encountered in countless rebirths. Yet in what sense can this rebirth be understood, for the Buddha affirms that to say that a person is reborn would not fit the case, and to say that a person is not reborn would not fit the case?[21] At the very least it is obvious by now that the same person in the sense of a persistent or substantial self cannot be reborn. In this sense it does not fit the case to say he is reborn. But then in what sense can one speak about the rebirth of the person? In what sense does it not fit the case to say he is not reborn?

D. T. Suzuki writes, "Constant rebirth or reincarnation means no more nor less than the immortality of karma."[22] That is, there is no rebirth of the individual human person; what continues and is reborn is the karmic effects of the individual.

Suzuki notes that there are several forms of transmission of karma. One mode of transmission is genealogical or biological. Karma here is transmitted to successive generations through the record left by the person, which influences how his decendants will respond to circumstances and be treated by others. A good record will bring "the respect they are enjoying and the possibility of inspiration" to further the ancestor's deeds, while a black record will put a curse on the family "as long as its vitality is kept up, no matter how innocent they themselves are."[23] Another form of transmission of karma he terms historical, what I have elsewhere termed immortality as remembrance.[24] Our immortality is realized in the living presence of oneself in the things, persons, or events that continue after one has died. The craftsman, the artisan, the writer, the general, the politician, the religious reformer—all have put something of themselves into what they have made or written or the events they have brought about or influenced. Persons survive through the lasting memory that others will have of them because of what they have done or made: "buildings, literary works, productions of art, implements, and instruments. In fact, almost any object, human or natural, which, however insignificant in itself, is associated with the memory of a great man, bears his karma, and transmits it to posterity."[25] In both instances though the transmission of the karma is objective, its significance is subjective.[26]

Though immortality in this sense is interesting, one must wonder whether it does justice both to the doctrine of rebirth espoused by Buddhism and to its doctrine of the law of karma. The latter requires something more than immortality of influence. The law of karma is an application of justice: that which I reap I have sown. Insofar as justice is involved, I do not reap what another has sown, nor do the consequences of my actions solely devolve upon others. Since I bear the responsibility for the actions committed, justice demands that I bear the consequences. Thus, some kind of postmortem personal existence is necessary to implement the law of karma. Simply passing on influences to future existents or leaving one's spirit in human creations is not sufficient to procure karmic justice.

Suzuki replies to this criticism by rejecting this "individualistic view of karma" as inconsistent with the theory of no-self and the *dharmakaya.* "According to the orthodox theory, karma simply means the conservation or immortality of the inner force of deeds regardless of their author's physical identity. Deeds once committed, good or evil, leave permanent effects on the general system of sentient beings, of which the actor is merely a component part."[27]

That Suzuki's view of justice is adequate or represents orthodox Buddhism is open to question. Space prevents discussion of its adequacy; this will be taken up in a forthcoming book on karma. As to its orthodoxy, this introduces a major difference between Theravada and Mahayana thought. For one thing, while transfer of merit is referred to several times in the Pali canon, the predominant theme is that the individual must work out his own salvation.[28] This runs contrary to the Mahayana concept of the meritorious activity of the Bodhisattvas. Also generally absent from the Pali texts is any concept of group karma. Where this occurs, "it is only in the sense of the confluence of the individual karmic reward and punishment of those involved in a given situation. . . ."[29]

Quite apart from questions of orthodoxy, however, in both Mahayana and Theravada Buddhism, there is a significantly individualistic concept of rebirth, according to which the effects of one person are concentrated in a subsequent existent. That is, there is more than mere birth; otherwise there would not be the round of existence.[30] Rebirth differs from birth in that the person who died lives again in some form connected with the deceased person; in birth there is no such connectedness or identity. It is this actual rebirth that cannot be accounted for by a theory of immortality as remembrance or as subjective.

If Suzuki's analysis is inadequate, it is not because he identified immortality with the immortality of karma, but because of his subjectivist and universalist view of karma. The doctrine of karma is presented as a fundamental postulate that has empirical content. Thus karma, treated objectively, provides the grounds for both unity among contiguous sets of *skandhas* and causal continuity beween the various *skandhic* events: this being, that occurs. Further, rebirth involves the individual. Though the same individual does not exist from moment to moment, let alone from rebirth to rebirth, the individual does not not-exist either; the individual undergoes rebirth in the sense that the events of this moment cause subsequent events and this causation is, in part, the moral causation of karma.

Buddhism, then, does assert the rebirth of the person. However, this rebirth is not transmigration; there is nothing, including consciousness, that passes from one set of *dharmas* to another. How then does it take place? Ultimately, Buddhists contend, it is a mystery, inexplicable to human understanding. Though the religious devotee might stop at this point, the philosopher must press on, for leaving it at this is intellectually unsatisfactory. Some Buddhist thinkers concur and have provided an answer in terms of an analogy. Consider the case of one lamp lighting another.[31] The light does not pass over from one lamp to the other, for it remains in the first; however, there is causal continuity between the two lamps. Similarly, though nothing passes over between death and rebirth, for all that exists are *dharmas* or events, yet there is a causation so instantaneous that there is a continuity of *skandhas* through the causal process.

But this analogy fails. Whereas between the original light and the derived light there is spatiotemporal continuity, between death and rebirth no point of contact exists.[32] Even though the rebirth is instantaneous, it occurs in another place. How then can the one condition the other? How can the reborn be functionally dependent on the just deceased?

Dropping the argument by analogy, one might put it more straightforwardly. The Buddhist wants to contend that if karma can account for personal continuity and identity during our present existence, why cannot it likewise suffice to provide the requisite continuity and identity between existences? Since there exist only discrete events in causal relation with each other, there is, in effect, rebirth at every moment. Thus rebirth following death is no different than "rebirth" between contiguous sets of *skandhas*.[33]

But this is not the case. The continuum of events in this life, the successive states of consciousness, have a certain locus. There is a certain continuity of body, of accumulated experience, of memory and dispositions. But between the death of a person and his rebirth, the continuum has been interrupted. The timing of the rebirth—its instantaneousness—is insufficient to establish this fact, for even though there is temporal continuity provided thereby, spatial contiguity and continuity of memory and experiences are absent. That which is the same about this life is not the same between lives.[34] In short, the karmic activity that explains unity and continuity in the present life is insufficient to explain the continuity between lives presupposed by a doctrine of rebirth.

Furthermore, is this conception of rebirth—the causation of the karmic tendencies in some continuous sequence—sufficient to accord with the concept of justice that the law of karma invokes? If there is no self to transmigrate, and if the person who is reborn is not the same person who now exists, "then is one not freed from one's evil deeds?"[35]

The Buddhist response to this is in the form of an analogy.

Your majesty, it is as if a man were to ascend to the top story of a house with a light, and eat there; and the light in burning were to set fire to the thatch; and the thatch in burning were to set fire to the house; and the house in burning were to set fire to the village; and the people of the village were to seize him, and say, "Why, O man, did you set fire to the village?" and he were to say, "I did not set fire to the village. The fire of the lamp by whose light I ate was a different one from the one which set fire to the village" and they, quarreling, were to come to you. Whose cause, your majesty, would you sustain?

"That of the people of the village, *bhante.*"

"And why?"

"Because, in spite of what the man might say, the latter fire sprang from the former."

"In exactly the same way, your majesty, although the name and form which is born into the next existence is different from the name and form which is to end at death, nevertheless, it is sprung from it. Therefore is one not freed from one's evil deeds."[36]

But again this argument from analogy will not suffice. Suppose that the man borrowed his light from a neighbor before his carelessness burned down the village. Could the village then prosecute the neighbor for setting fire to the village? Why not, given the reasoning above, for the arsonist's fire sprang from or was caused by his neighbor's fire in exactly the same way that the fire which devastated the village sprang from or was caused by his fire? Yet it would be unjust to prosecute the lender of the fire. What this suggests is that, contrary to the Buddhist claim, mere causal continuity is not sufficient to account for moral responsibility. But the Buddhist doctrine of rebirth places its entire justification for karmic accountability on the causal relation. Consequently, it follows that there is a fundamental incompatability between the Buddhist account of rebirth and the account of justice invoked by the law of karma: mere continuity of karma is not sufficient to provide grounds for ascriptions of moral responsibility.

Liberation and Immortality

Before we conclude, something must be said about the implications of this view for final liberation. The karma of the liberated saint is exhausted, while the acts, which he now performs, have no fruits. Lacking karma, there is no ground for the unity of sets of *skandhas* nor for continuity between death and rebirth, and as such there is no reason to ascribe rebirth to the saint; he is free from the cycle of rebirths. Furthermore, according to the Buddhist doctrine of causation, if the cause is removed, so is the effect. And since where there is no cause there is no existence, without the causal conditions of karma there is no existence.[37] Thus, for the finally liberated one in Paranirvana, there is no longer any karma and consequently no unity, continuity, or existence. What this means, in effect, is that though the Buddhist believes in rebirth or life after death, he does not believe that this process necessarily continues indefinitely.[38]

Given that Buddhists do not subscribe to immortality in the sense of unending rebirths, have Buddhists given up belief in immortality in any other sense? The answer to this question depends, in part, upon their view of Paranirvana. We have already noted that the Buddha, in responding to the question of a wandering ascetic named Vaccha concerning the state of the liberated saint, said that it would not fit the case to say he is reborn, neither would it fit the case to say that he would not be reborn. Just as one cannot say where the extinguished flame has gone because the question is illicit, so one cannot say what has happened to the saint.

Two interpretations of this are suggested. Some have argued that the Buddha simply refuses to commit himself to anything for which there is no empirical evidence. For Paranirvana there is no such evidence. Hence, concerning its metaphysical status one must be agnostic.[39] In fact, discourse concerning its metaphysical status is irrelevant; what is significant is that when the saint attains Nirvana he has ended his cravings and hence broken the chain of dependent origination. Paranirvana has a distinctly soteriological role. Concerning immortality in any sense stronger than rebirth one must be silent.

Others have attempted to provide some ontological structure for this soteriological concept. Nirvana exists in contrast to *samsara,* to everything that characterizes our present conditioned existence. Its character as an unconditioned, permanent, unending, changeless, transcendental reality means that it stands beyond all predication and can only be approached via negativa. It is a reality that neither does exist nor does not exist, but transcends existence; which neither is caused nor uncaused, but transcends causation; and so on with respect to whatever predicates one chooses.[40] With respect to immortality in an enduring sense, this means that one cannot say anything about the individual who attains paranirvana, neither that he is immortal nor not-immortal nor that he is nor is not. "The saint who has been released from what is styled form is deep, immeasurable, unfathomable, like the mighty ocean."[41] Human language breaks down at this point.

Where does this leave us with respect to the question of immortality? Since karma provides for the individual both collectivity and continuity, and since Nirvana transcends karma, it is hard to see what sense can be made of the claim that on attaining paranirvana at final liberation the individual has transmuted to a transcendental reality. If Nirvana is truly transcendent to all categories, then it is transcendent to categories having to do both with individual and corporate existence and with immortality. In the transmutation the entire conception of the individual has changed.

In short, two things conspire to cast a cloud over nirvanic immortality: the karmic and hence conditioned nature of the self and the unpredicable, unconditioned nature of nirvana. The Buddhist who affirms the reality of nirvana and some sort of transmutation affirms that there is more than the cycle of rebirths, but in both denying that nirvana is predictable and asserting that it transcends karma, he denies any means of incorporating it within any meaningful metaphysical perspective, which would enable us to speak of human immortality.

Conclusion

To conclude, we have argued that there is an ambiguity in the Buddhist account of the human person. On the one hand, personal identity is merely ascribed; selfhood is a fiction. We are easily misled into thinking that there is personal identity and continuity when in fact there is nothing but a series of events. This perspective entails that rebirth is a fiction, as are the doctrines of karma and liberation. On the other hand, the doctrine of karma is held to have empirical content; karma and liberation are experienced realities. This perspective entails that the person is reborn. We have seen that it falls to karma to provide the objective ground for the personal identity and continuity found in rebirth. But the Buddhist has difficulty explaining how on the doctrine of no-self karma can account for rebirth and, since causal continuity is not a sufficient condition for ascribing moral responsibility, how the reborn can be held morally accountable for the actions of the prior-born.

We have likewise seen that tension exists in its account of immortality at the time of final liberation. Here the tension lies between the conditioned self and unconditioned paranirvana. Since karma provides the collectivity and continuity of the individual, while paranirvana transcends karma, some account of the transmutation of the individual into the nirvanic state is necessary in order to lend intelligibility to any claim of enduring immortality.[42]

NOTES

1. D. T. Suzuki, *Outlines of Mahayana Buddhism* (New York: Schocken Books, 1963), pp. 204–5. Cassius Pereira ("An Elucidation of Kamma," *The Buddhist Review* 9 (1917), p. 61) speaks of this continuing vitality in the traditional language of "current-of-being."

2. K. N. Jayatillake, "The Case for the Buddhist Theory of Survival and Karma," *MahaBodhi* (Colombo) 77 (1969), pp. 334–40, 371–76; 78 (1970), pp. 2–6, 350–55.

3. Majjhima-Nikaya (sutta 63), in Henry Clarke Warren, *Buddhism in Translations* (New York: Atheneum, 1973), p. 117.

4. Majjhima-Nikaya (sutta 72), in Warren, p. 125.

5. For example, "The correct view in light of the highest knowledge is as follows: 'This is not mine; this am I not; this is not my self.'" Samyutta-Nikaya (22.85), in Warren p. 140. The exact meaning of the Buddha's silence about (in most contexts) or refusal to identify the self is somewhat in doubt. For example, some have attempted to show that the Buddha believed in a soul or self, but remained silent about it because it was nonempirical and discussion concerning it did not lead to edification. See T. W. Rhys Davids, *The Birth of Indian Psychology and its Development in Buddhism* (London: Luzac & Co., 1936), pp. 206–14. More recently David Kalupahana writes that what the Buddha denied was that the five aggregates are not the permanent and eternal self; he did not actually deny a 'self' that is over and above, or not identical with, the aggregates. "His silence on these questions was interpreted as implying that there *is* a reality, a transcendental 'self', but that it does not come within the sphere of logical reasoning." *Buddhist Philosophy: A Historical Analysis* (Honolulu: University of Hawaii Press, 1976), pp. 40–41. See also G. S. P. Misra, "The Buddhist Theory of Karma and Some Related Problems,"

The Vishva-Bharati Journal of Philosophy 8, no. 2 (1972), p. 41. What the Buddha actually believed about the self remains a historical problem; whatever the case, our thesis that some metaphysical point of view underlies his assertions and denials is sustained.

6. Samyutta-Nikaya (xxii, 85), in Warren, p. 140. See also Maha-Nidana-Sutta (256.21), in Warren, p. 137: ". . . A priest no longer holds the view that the Ego has no sensation, no longer holds the view that the Ego has sensation, [or] possesses the faculty of sensation; he ceases to attach himself to anything in the world, and being free from attachment, he is never agitated . . . and attains to Nirvana in his own person; and he knows that rebirth is exhausted. . . ."

7. Majjhima-Nikaya (sutta 72), in Warren, p. 125.

8. Edward Conze, *Buddhist Thought in India* (Ann Arbor, MI: University of Michigan Press, 1967), p. 121–33.

9. Conze, p. 97.

10. Conze, p. 97.

11. Conze, p. 112.

12. *Milindapanha* (25.1), in Warren, pp. 132–33.

13. "Strictly speaking, the duration of the life of a living being is exceedingly brief, lasting only while a thought lasts." Visuddhi-Magga (viii), in Warren, p. 150. For a brief account of this conflict, see Y. Karunadasa, "The Buddhist Doctrine of Impermanence," *MahaBodhi* 77 (1969), pp. 217–18.

14. Each "successive phase has within it all the potentialities of its predecessors, which manifest themselves when conditions are favorable." Mysore Hiriyanna, *Outlines of Indian Philosophy* (London: George Allen and Unwin, 1932), p. 145.

15. Jayatillake, pp. 372–73.

16. Suzuki, p. 213.

17. ". . . The words 'living entity' and 'Ego' are but a mode of expression for the presence of the five attachment groups, but when we come to examine the elements of being one by one, we discover that in the absolute sense there is no living entity there to form a basis for such figments as 'I am', or 'I'; in other words, that in the absolute sense there is only name and form." *Visuddhi-Magga* (18), in Warren, pp. 133–34.

18. *Milindapanha* (65.11), in Warren, p. 215.

19. "For when, in any existence, one arrives at the gate of death . . . and the body dries up by degrees and the eye-sight and other senses fail, . . . then consciousness residing in that last refuge, the heart, continues to exist by virtue of karma, otherwise called the predispositions. This karma, however, still retains something of what it depends on, and consists of such former deeds as were weighty, much practised, and are now close at hand, or else this karma creates a reflex of itself or of the new mode of life now being entered upon, and it is with this as its object that consciousness continues to exist." *Visuddhi-Magga* (17), in Warren, p. 238.

20. *Visuddhi-Magga* (xvii), in Warren, p. 238.

21. *Majjhima-Nikaya* (sutta 72), in Warren, p. 125.

22. Suzuki, p. 213.

23. Suzuki, p. 206.

24. Bruce R. Reichenbach, *Is Man the Phoenix? A Study of Immortality* (Washington, D.C.: University Press of America, 1982), pp. 9–13.

25. Suzuki, p. 208.

26. Suzuki, p. 209.

27. Suzuki, p. 192–93.

28. James P. McDermott, "Karma and Rebirth in Early Buddhism," in Wendy D. O'Flaherty, ed., *Karma and Rebirth in Classical Indian Traditions* (Berkeley, CA.: University of California Press, 1980), pp. 190–92.

29. McDermott, p. 175. See also James P. McDermott, "Is There Group Karma in Theravada Buddhism?" *Numen* 23 (1976), pp. 67–80.

30. "Your majesty, to be born here and die here, to die here and be born elsewhere, to be born there and die there, to die there and be born else-where,—this, your majesty, is the round of existence." *Milindapanha* (77.8), in Warren, p. 232.

31. *Milindapanha* (71.16), in Warren, p. 234.

32. H. H. Rowley, *Submission in Suffering* (Cardiff: University of Wales Press, 1951), p. 29.

33. Hiriyanna, p. 153.

34. Paul J. Griffiths, "Notes Towards a Critique of Buddhist Karmic Theory," *Religious Studies* 18 (Sept. 1982), pp. 283–84; Rowley, p. 30.

35. *Milindapanha* (46.5), in Warren, p. 234–35.

36. *Milindapanha* (46.5), in Warren, p. 235.

37. It might be thought that this is merely repeating the heresy attributed to the priest Yamaka in the *Samyutta-Nikaya* (xxii. 85.1; cf. Warren, pp. 138–46). But careful attention to this text shows that the heresy of Yamaka was not in thinking that the saint does not exist after death, but rather that the saint goes from being a saint, i.e., from having a self or identity of being a person who is a saint, to not-existing. Sariputta's response is that even during his lifetime there was no self or person who was a saint. The *skandhas* neither are nor are not the person; the *skandhas* are themselves transitory, even during this existence. So what we call a saint was nothing but an ascription to certain transitory *skandhas,* and that in liberation even the transitory has ceased and disappeared.

38. Of course, if one follows Suzuki, the saint might live on in terms of the subjective influence that he has bequeathed by his deeds. That is, immortality by remembrance is still possible and often actual. But so understood the human person does not possess immortality in the strict sense of never ceasing to be. Only the impact of his karma lives on indefinitely in others.

39. David Kalupahana, *Buddhist Philosophy: A Historical Analysis* (Honolulu: University of Hawaii Press, 1976), pp. 78–88.

40. For a discussion of the debates on whether it exists or not, or has or is a cause, see Conze, pp. 159–63.

41. *Majjhima-Nikaya,* (sutta 72) in Warren, p. 127. Kalupahana, p. 83, argues that this simply means that there is no way of knowing what happens to the saint after death. It supports agnosticism rather than transcendentalism.

42. It is important to note that my argument does not depend on the question of the adequacy of the Buddhist conception of the human person. Objections based thereon are often criticized as mere Westernizations that fail to comprehend the Buddhist perspective. Though I think this criticism can be and often is unjustly used, I have attempted to avoid any such appearance by trying to see what the doctrine of immortality means within its own context, and from there proceeding to measure its internal consistency with other presupposed, central doctrines. It is on this basis that we have measured the adequacy of the Buddhist conception of immortality.

============================ **12** ============================

A Naturalistic Case for
Extinction
LINDA BADHAM

==

Introduction

It is a popularly held view that science and religion are antithetical.
And this view is supported by the sociological fact that leading
scholars and scientists are significantly less likely to be Christian
than other groups in society.[1] Yet even so, there are a number of
very eminent scientists, and particularly physicists, who claim that
there is no real conflict between their scientific and religious beliefs.[2]
And many Christian apologists have drawn comfort from such
claims in an age where the tide of secularism threatens to engulf the
ancient citadel of Christian belief.[3] However, I have my doubts as
to whether or not Christianity is secure from attack by science in
general on some of its most crucial tenets. And, in particular, what I
want to argue in this chapter is that the implications of modern
science are far more damaging to doctrines of life after death than
many Christian writers have supposed.

Resurrection of the Body (This Flesh)

Although many might think that belief in the resurrection of this
flesh at the end of time is now unthinkable, it has to be recognized
that this is the form that orthodox Christian belief took from at
least the second century onwards. Thus the Apostles' Creed affirms
belief in the resurrection of the flesh[4]; the Nicene Creed looks for
the "upstanding of the dead bodies"[5]; and the Christian Fathers
were utterly explicit that the resurrection was definitely a physical
reconstitution.[6] Moreover, such belief is still Catholic orthodoxy: a
recent *Catholic Catechism for Adults* declares that each one of us will
rise one day "the same person he was, in the same flesh made living
by the same spirit."[7] And Wolfhart Pannenberg, one of the most
influential continental Protestant theologians of our day, also af-

firms belief in the traditional doctrine.[8] Hence it seems reasonable to suppose that this form of resurrection belief is still held among Christians. Yet a minimal knowledge of modern science seems sufficient to undermine it completely.

First, there is the problem that 'this flesh' is only temporarily mine. I am not like a machine or artifact, which keeps its atoms and molecules intact throughout its existence, save for those lost by damage or replaced during repair. Rather, I am a biological system in dynamic equilibrium (more or less) with my environment, in that I exchange matter with that environment continually. As J. D. Bernal writes, "It is probable that none of us have more than a few atoms with which we started life, and that even as adults we probably change most of the material of our bodies in a matter of a few months."[9] Thus it might prove an extremely difficult business to resurrect 'this' flesh at the end of time, for the atoms that will constitute me at the moment of death will return to the environment and will doubtless become part of innumerable other individuals. Augustine discussed the case of cannibals having to restore the flesh they had "borrowed" as an exception.[10] But in the light of our current knowledge, shared atoms would seem the rule rather than the exception.

Morever, there is the further problem that even if the exact atoms that constituted me at death could all be reassembled without leaving some other people bereft of vital parts, then the reconstituted body would promptly expire again. For whatever caused the systems failure in my body, which led to my death originally, would presumably still obtain if the body exactly as it was prior to death were remade. But perhaps we can overcome this problem with a fairly simple proviso: the resurrection body should be identical to the body that died, malfunctions apart. After all, it might be said, we have no difficulty in accepting our television set returned in good working order from the repair shop after a breakdown as one and the same television set that we took to be repaired, even though some or even several of its components have been replaced. But people are not television sets. What counts as malfunction? Increasing age usually brings some diminution in physical and mental powers. Are all these to be mended too? How much change can a body take and still be the same person? Nor is it possible to suggest that the resurrection environment might be such as to reverse the effects of aging and disease. For this move implies such a great change in the properties of the matter that is 'this flesh' as to make it dubious whether 'this' flesh really had been resurrected. The more one actually fills out the vague notion of the resurrection of the same flesh that perished, the more problems arise.

And even if the problem of reconstituting each one of us to the same (healthy) flesh he was (or might have been) could be overcome, there would remain the question of where we could all be resurrected. There is a space problem. If the countless millions of human beings who have ever lived and may live in the future were all to be resurrected on this earth, then the overcrowding would be acute. Now there are at least two theological maneuvers that we could make to circumvent this embarrassment. If we want to retain resurrection on this earth, then we might say that only the chosen will be resurrected and thereby limit the numbers. But that solution raises insuperable problems about the morality of a God who would behave in such a way.[11] Alternatively, it might be argued that the resurrection will be to a new life in heaven and not to eternal life on earth. But in that case it has to be noted that resurrected bodies would need a biological environment markedly similar to the one we now live in. This leads to the implication that heaven would have to be a planet, or series of planets, all suitable for human life. The further one pushes this picture, the more bizarre and religiously unsatisfying it becomes.[12]

In sum, then, a little knowledge of the biochemistry of living organisms together with a brief consideration of the physicochemical conditions that such organisms require if they are to live, ought to have rendered the traditional notion of literal bodily resurrection unthinkable.

Resurrection of the Body (Transformed)

It might be argued, as John Polkinghorne claims, that all this is irrelevant: "We know that there is nothing significant about the material which at any one time constitutes our body. . . . It is the pattern they [the atoms] form which persists and evolves. We are liberated, therefore, from the quaint medieval picture of the reassembly of the body from its scattered components. In very general terms it is not difficult to imagine the pattern recreated (the body resurrected) in some other world."[13]

At this point we should note that the doctrine being proposed here has shifted in a very significant way. The old doctrine of resurrection of the flesh guaranteed personal survival because the resurrected body was physically identical with the one laid in the grave. Physical continuity supplied the link between the person who died and the one who was resurrected. But Polkinghorne's version of the resurrection envisages recreation of a *pattern* in some other world. This is open to a host of philosophical problems about the sense in which the recreation of a replica can count as the survival of the person who died.[14]

What would we say, for example, if the replica were created *before* my death? Would I then die happily knowing that someone was around to carry on, as it were, in my place? Would I think to myself that the replica really was me? Consider the possibility of cloning. Let us imagine that science reaches a stage where a whole adult human individual can be regenerated from a few cells of a person in such a way that the original—Jones I—and the copy—Jones II—are genetically identical, and that the clone knows everything that Jones I knows. We may imagine that the purpose of doing this is to give a healthy body to house the thoughts of the physically ailing, but brilliant Jones I. Now does Jones I die secure in the knowledge that he will live again? I would suggest that he might feel relieved to know that his life's work would carry on, and that his project would be entrusted to one incomparably suited to continue with it. He might also feel exceptionally close to Jones II and be deeply concerned for his welfare. But the other would not *be* him. In the end, Jones I would be dead and the other, Jones II, would carry on in his place. As far as Jones I was concerned, he himself would not live again, even though most other people would treat Jones II as if here were Jones I rejuvenated.[15]

If these intuitions are correct, then they suggest that whatever it is that we count as essential for being one and the same person, it is not a "pattern." And I would suggest that all theories of resurrection that speak of our rising with new and transformed bodies fall foul of what I term the replica problem. For without some principle of continuity between the person who died and the one who was resurrected, then what was resurrected would only be something very similar to the one who died, a replica, and not a continuation of the dead person.

The Soul

Such considerations have led theologians at least from Aquinas onwards to argue that any tenable resurrection belief hinges on a concept of the soul. For even if we hold to a belief in the resurrection of some "new and glorious body," then we need the soul to avoid the replica problem. There has to be a principle of continuity between this world and the next if what is raised to new life really is one and the same person as the one who died. Moreover, this principle of continuity must encapsulate enough of the real 'me' for both "old" and "new" versions to count as the same person. Might this requirement be fulfilled if we were to espouse a dualist concept of the person and say, with Descartes, that my essential personhood is to be identified with my mind, that is, with the subject of conscious experiencing?[16] However, I want to argue that not even this move is sufficient to rescue the Christian claim.

First, there are all the practical problems of which contemporary dualists are very much aware.[17] Our personal experience and emotions are intimately linked to our body chemistry. Indeed, the limits to what we are able to think at all are set by our genetic endowment; so that one man's physicochemical equipment enables him to be a brilliant mathematician, while another's lack condemns him to lifelong imbecility. If our diet is imbalanced and inadequate, or if certain of our organs are malfunctioning, then our bodies may be starved of essential nutrients or poisoned by the excessive production of some hormone. In such cases, the whole personality may be adversely affected. The "subject of my conscious experiences" would seem to be very much at the mercy of my physicochemical constitution.

A second difficulty lies in deciding which organisms count as having souls and which do not. And if God is to give eternal life to the former class and not to the latter, then even He has to be able to draw a line somewhere, and that nonarbitrarily.[18] The problem occurs both in considering the evolution of the species Homo sapiens and the individual development of human beings. Even if we ignore the problem of nonhuman animals and restrict the possibility of possessing a soul to humans, there are still insuperable difficulties.[19]

Consider first the evolutionary pathway that led from the early mammals to man. Somewhere along that line we would be fairly secure in denying that such and such a creature had any awareness of self. And it is also true to say that most normal adult humans possess such an awareness. But between these extremes lies a gray area. To have a nonarbitrary dividing line, it has to be possible for us to decide (at least in principle) where a sharp division can be drawn between the last generation of anthropoid apes and the first generation of true Homo sapiens. Are we to suppose that in one generation there were anthropoid apes who gave birth to the next generation of true Homo sapiens, and that the changes between one generation and the next were so great that the children counted in God's eyes as the bearers of immortality while their parents were "mere animals"? Yet unless dualists are prepared to fly in the face of evolutionary biology, how can they avoid this unpalatable conclusion?

The problems that we see in the evolution of the species is mirrored in the development of each fertilized human ovum. Somewhere in the path leading from conception to adulthood awareness of self develops. When exactly seems impossible to pinpoint (unless it turns out that awareness of self is a sort of quantum leap in a child's development).[20] Nor can the difficulty be evaded by claiming that each fertilized ovum is a potential human being and therefore potentially self-aware, not least because some genetic combinations become cancerous and are in no sense even potential human beings.

Just as there were religious difficulties arising for the dualist's position from the lack of sharp divisions in evolutionary development, so too there are religious difficulties here. For if, as Descartes would have us believe, it is the ability to doubt that guarantees the existence of the 'I', and if what survives is this subject of conscious experiences, then there is nothing to survive in any potential human being that has yet to develop the necessary level of mental life. Panpsychists apart, most of us would accept that a certain minimum of neurological equipment is a necessary condition of conscious experience. As Arturo Rosenblueth writes: "In the human species, the central nervous system, especially the cerebral cortex of the newborn baby, is very underdeveloped as compared with those of an adolescent or an adult. . . . The first signs of conscious behaviour do not appear until this anatomical and neurophysiological evolution reaches a sufficiently high level."[21]

If this is right, then would we have to imagine God greeting two mothers in heaven and saying to one, "The soul of your long-lost infant is now fully mature and waits here to be reunited with you"; while to the other he mutters, "Well, I am sorry about this, but your baby didn't quite make it because he failed to develop self-consciousness before he died"? Nor is the problem to be circumvented by claiming that what survives has nothing to do with neural equipment. It is rather the immaterial soul, which admittedly had yet to manifest its presence in the infant. For what content could be given to claiming that this tabula rasa was the real child? This theory of the soul fails to satisfy not just because it seems incompatible with our scientific knowledge, but also because it has some undesirable religious implications.

There are, in addition, some further objections of a more purely philosophical nature, which I think need mentioning at this point. The subject of my conscious experiencing is singularly unconvincing as a principle of continuity that guarantees persistence of the "same" person through change. Moreover, defining the "real" me in this way actually misses a lot of what most of us would want to say is a part of the "real" me. I shall begin by discussing the question of a principle of continuity.

One great problem with my awareness of self is its lack of persistence, its transitoriness. My stream of consciousness is far from being a constant or even ever-present (though varying) flow. When I am unconscious, in a dreamless sleep, or even in a vacant mood, it just is not there. Yet *I* do not cease to exist whenever my conscious mind is, as it were, switched off temporarily. Secondly, we have to face the problem that this awareness of self is ever-changing. What I was as a child is very different from what I, as I am in myself, am today; and if I live to be an old lady, doubtless the subject of my conscious experiences will look back with a mixture of wry amusement and nostalgia at that other her of forty years ago. Now it might be thought that this problem of continual change is no greater a problem for the notion of same 'self' than it is for the notion of same 'body' since the body is also in a continual state of flux. But I would suggest that what supplies continuity through change is matter. It may be that all my constituent atoms will have changed in the next few months, but they will not have all changed simultaneously. Moreover, the physically-based blueprints from the chemistry that keeps my body going are passed on from one generation of cells to another in a direct physical line of succession. Thus, I would argue that what keeps the subject of my conscious experiencing belonging to one and the same person is this physical continuity.

The essential requirement of physical continuity can be illustrated if we return to the clone example. Let us modify the thought experiment a little, and makes Jones II a copy of a perfectly healthy Jones I. And let us also stipulate that the two Joneses emerge from the cloning laboratory not knowing who is the original and who the copy. In other words, Jones I and II are, seemingly, wholly similar. Neither they nor we can tell which is which, unless we trace the histories of the two bodies to ascertain which grew from a fertilized ovum and which developed as the result of cloning. Now if we apply the implications of this to the question of what might live again after death, we see that being "the subject of my conscious experiences" is not sufficient to guarantee that I am one and the same person as the one who died. For what the clone example shows is that both Jones I and Jones II may believe (or doubt) equally that he really is the same person as Jones I while he relies solely on his personal experience of himself as Jones. Only when he traces the path of physical continuity can he know whether he truly is Jones I or not. (Of course, we might want to say that where there had been one person, Jones, there were now two distinct individuals, both of whom were physically continuous with the original. But in that case the possibility of defining 'same person' in terms of 'same stream of consciousness' does not even arise.)[22]

Thus I contend, a dualist definition of what I really am fails because it cannot provide adequate criteria for recognizing the 'same' person through change. I can think of no other case where we would even be tempted to accept something as transitory and ever-changing as 'consciousness of self' to be the essential criterion for defining what it is that an entity has to retain if it is to count as remaining the same individual through change.

I move on now to the problems that arise from the restrictedness of defining me as the subject of my conscious experiences. A great deal of what I am does not involve my conscious thoughts at all, even when I am fully awake. Take the familiar example of driving a car. When I was learning to drive, I certainly employed a great amount of conscious effort. But nowadays my conscious thoughts are fairly free to attend to other matters when I am driving, even though, of course, intense conscious attention instantly returns if danger threatens. I certainly do not want to say 'my body' drove here. *I* drove here, even though most of the time the subject of my conscious experiences was not much involved.

Moreover, we cannot ignore the possibility that the conscious subject might actually fail to recognize a significant part of all that I really am. To exemplify the point: imagine someone who believes himself to be a great wit, when most of his colleagues find him a crashing bore. If he were to arrive in the resurrection world without his familiar characteristics—clumsiness of speech, repetitiveness, triviality, self-centeredness—would he really be the person who had died? Yet could he bring these characteristics with him if the subject of his conscious experiences, the 'real' him, was wholly unaware of having been like this?

In sum, what I have been arguing against dualism is that this concept of the soul cannot bear the weight put on it. Yet it has to bear this weight if it is to be the sine qua non of my surviving bodily death. Considerations from the natural sciences and philosophy, and even religious implications, combine to render it far from convincing. But, it might be countered, no amount of argument on the basis of current scientific theory, philosophy, or religious sentiments can count against hard empirical fact. So what about the reports that exist of near-death experiences, which seem to show that some people really do have experiences apart from their bodies?

Near-Death Experiences

Let me begin by stating quite clearly that I shall not be concerned to discuss the merits or otherwise of individual cases. I am going to suppose, for the purposes of discussion, that there is strong, bona-fide evidence that some people come back from the brink of death fully convinced that they had left their bodies and had had apparently veridical experiences as if from a vantage point different from that of the body. The question then is, how do we interpret these "travelers tales."

I have three main points to make here. The first is that a present absence of satisfactory normal explanations for these cases does not imply that there are no such explanations ever to be found. We should not be hurried into a supernaturalist account merely because we can find no other, as if the God-of-the-gaps lesson had yet to be learned. And I note that at least one worker in this field, Dr. Susan Blackmore, argues for a psychological approach to explaining out-of-the-body experiences (OBEs).[23] Dr. Blackmore has spent the last decade researching OBEs and has moved from an initial belief that persons can leave their bodies to her present more skeptical position. She writes: "Everything perceived in an OBE is a product of memory and imagination, and during the OBE one's imagination is more vividly experienced than it is in everyday life."[24] One limiting factor, for our purposes here, in Dr. Blackmore's work is that she has been researching primarily "astral projection" rather than near-death experiences. And clearly, if there is such a thing as a quasi-independent human soul, it is at least possible that such a soul cannot actually leave the body while the body is not near death. In that case, all the research in the world into astral projection may be wholly irrelevant. But we should be prepared to explore naturalistic accounts of OBEs before embracing a supernaturalistic hypothesis.

My second point is that even if we take near-death experiences as supplying empirical proof of the existence, nay persistence, of the human soul or mind, that would not smooth out all the difficulties. All the problems that I have discussed earlier would still be there, awaiting some kind of resolution. And there would arise yet further problems. Take, for example, the question of how the soul actually "sees" physical objects while it supposedly hovers below the ceiling. William Rushton puts the point thus: "What is this out-of-the-body eye that can encode the visual scene exactly as does the real eye, with its hundred million photoreceptors and its million signaling optic nerves? Can you imagine anything but a replica of the real eye could manage to do this? But if this floating replica is to see, it must catch light, and hence cannot be transparent, and so must be visible to people in the vicinity. In fact floating eyes are not observed, nor would this be expected, for they exist only in fantasy."[25] And if it be countered that the soul perceives without using the normal phys- icochemical mechanisms, then we might ask why on earth did such a complicated organ as the eye ever evolve (or remain unatrophied) if human beings possess souls that can "see" without normal eyes. Moreover, one might expect that blind people, deprived of normal visual stimuli, would use this psychic ability, if it really existed. These, and kindred problems concerned with modes of perception, would need answers if we were to take seriously supernatural interpretations of OBEs.

Finally, I suggest that to accept the existence of some nonmaterial soul in man would be to embrace a notion fundamentally at vari- ance with other well-founded convictions about the nature of real- ity. For we would then have to allow for events happening in the world that rest on no underlying physicochemical mechanisms. Now I am very well aware that scientists are continually changing their theories to accommodate new data, and that from time to time some wholesale replacement of outmoded ideas has been neces- sary.[26] So, it might be asked, can we not envisage some new scientific outlook that embraces both the normal data and the paranormal? Just so. A new scientific outlook, which could encompass both normal and paranormal data, would clearly be more satisfactory than one which could in no way account for the paranormal. But it must be remembered that the whole scientific enterprise presupposes the existence of underlying mechanisms whose discovery enables us to understand the "how" of an event.[27] So it is hard to see how any unified scientific theory could embrace both the notion that most events in the world depend on underlying physicochemical mechanisms, and also that there are some events that do not utilize any such mechanisms at all. And if paranormal data are taken as support for the belief in the existence of nonmaterial entities (like souls) then these data fly in the face of normal science. Thus I concur with C. D. Broad that "It is certainly right to demand a much higher standard of evidence for events which are alleged to be paranormal than those which would be normal. . . . For in dealing with evidence we have always to take into account the antecedent probability or improbability of the alleged event, i.e. its probability or improbability relative to all the rest of our knowledge and well-founded belief other than the special evidence adduced in its favour."[28]

In sum then, it seems that at present paranormal data cannot be accommodated within naturalist science. But to move from that to claiming that we have empirical evidence for the existence of immaterial souls seems unwarranted, not least because to explicate the paranormal in terms of the activities of immaterial souls may appear to solve one explanatory difficulty, but only at the expense of raising a host of other problems.

Conclusion

When Christianity was originally formulated, man's entire world view was very different from our current beliefs. It was plausible to think in terms of a three-decker universe in which the center of God's interest was this Earth and its human population. The idea that God would raise man from the dead to an eternal life of bliss fitted neatly into this schema. However, the erosion of this picture, beginning from at least the time of Copernicus and Galileo, has cut the traditional Christian hope adrift from the framework of ideas in which it was originally formulated. What I have tried to show in this chapter is that various attempts, which have been made to try to accommodate some form of resurrection/immortality belief within our current world view, are inadequate and fail. I conclude, then, that a due consideration of man's place in nature leads us to the view that he belongs there and nowhere else.

NOTES

1. A sociological survey quoted by Daniel C. Batson and W. Larry Ventis in *The Religious Experience: A Social-Psychological Perspective* (Oxford: Oxford University Press, 1982), p. 225.

2. See, for example, John Polkinghorne, *The Way the World Is* (London: SPCK, 1983); and Russel Stannard, *Science and the Renewal of Belief* (London: SCM, 1982).

3. See, for example, Richard and Anthony Hanson, *Reasonable Belief* (Oxford: Oxford University Press, 1980), pp. 13ff.

4. It is to Cranmer's credit that he made the recitation of this creed easier for the English-speaking world by his deliberate mistranslation of "resurrectio carnis" as "resurrection of the body."

5. In more idiomatic English we usually say "resurrection of the dead."

6. Paul Badham, *Christian Beliefs about Life after Death* (London: SPCK, 1978), pp. 47ff.

7. R. Lawler, D. W. Whuerl and T. C. Lawler, *The Teaching of Christ: A Catholic Catechism for Adults* (Dublin: Veritas, 1976), p. 544.

8. Cf. Wolfhart Pannenberg, *Jesus-God and Man* (London: SCM, 1968), p. 82ff.

9. J. D. Bernal, *Science in History,* vol. 3, (Harmondsworth: Penguin, 1969), p. 902.

10. Augustine, *City of God,* bk. 22, chap. 20.

11. Cf. Paul and Linda Badham, *Immortality or Extinction* (London: SPCK, 1984), pp. 58ff.

12. Cf. Paul Badham, *Christian Beliefs about Life after Death,* chap. 4.

13. John Polkinghorne, *The Way the World Is,* p. 93.

14. Cf. Bernard Williams, *Problems of the Self* (Cambridge: Cambridge University Press, 1978).

15. I imagine that a very close relative like a wife or mother would find the situation emotionally very fraught!

16. Cf. René Descartes, *Discourse 4.* This is the view Paul Badham expresses both in his earlier work and in our joint book. At the time the latter was written, I was in close agreement with his position. But since then I have come to think otherwise.

17. Cf. Paul and Linda Badham, *Immortality or Extinction,* chap. 3.

18. Paul and I are still in agreement that the survival of every living organism that ever existed makes no kind of sense, religious or any other.

19. I think the problem of animals is a very real one. Cf. Paul and Linda Badham, *Immortality or Extinction,* pp. 48ff.

20. Quite how this could be I do not know.

21. Cf. Arturo Rosenblueth, *Mind and Brain* (Cambridge, MA: MIT Press, 1970), p. 27.

22. Cf. Bishop Joseph Butler's point that "though we are thus certain, that we are the same agents . . . which we were as far back as our remembrance reaches; yet it is asked, whether we may not possibly be deceived in it?" *Dissertation 1* "Of Personal Identity" paragraph 11.

23. Susan Blackmore, *Beyond the Body* (London: Heinemann, 1982), chap. 22.

24. Blackmore, p. 243.

25. Rushton is quoted in Blackmore pp. 227–28.

26. I devote Chapter 4 of my doctoral thesis *Emergence* (Ph.D. thesis, University of Wales) to this topic of change in science.

27. I exclude the "bottom line" on mechanistic explanations. It may be that there are some fundamental particles whose behavior is not further analyzable.

28. C. D. Broad, *Lectures on Psychical Research* (London: Routledge and Kegan Paul, 1962), p. 14.

13

The Logic of Mortality
ANTONY FLEW

"Whether we are to live in a future state, as it is the most important question which can possibly be asked, so it is the most intelligible one which can be expressed in language"—Bishop Butler (*A Dissertation of Personal Identity*).

The Initial Obstacle

Surely Butler was right. Can we not understand the hopes of the warriors of Allah who expect if they die in Holy Wars to go straight to the arms of the black-eyed houris in paradise? Can we not understand the fears of the slum mother kept from the contraceptive clinic by her priest's warning of penalties for those who die in mortal sin? Of course we can: they both expect—and what could be more intelligible than this?—that, if they do certain things, then they will in consequence enjoy or suffer in the future certain rewards or punishments. And, if this future life is supposed to last forever, then clearly the question whether or not it is fictitious (and, if it is not, the consequent problem of ensuring that we shall pass it agreeably) is of quite overwhelming importance. For what are threescore years and ten compared with all eternity?

But surely, urges the sceptic, something crucial is being overlooked? For this future life is supposed to continue even *after* physical dissolution, even *after* the slow corruption in the cemetery, or the swift consumption in the crematorium. So to suggest that we might survive such total dissolution is like suggesting that a nation might outlast the annihilation of all its members. Of course, we can understand the Myth of Er or stories of Valhalla. But to expect that after my death and dissolution such things might happen to me is to overlook that I shall not then exist. To expect such things, through overlooking this, is surely like accepting a fairy tale as history, through ignoring the prefatory rubric: "Once upon a time, in a world that never was. . . ."

The two previous paragraphs get us to the heart of the matter. Yet they are only the beginning rather than the end of the affair. It was in fact with substantially these same two paragraphs that, now all of thirty-three years ago, I first began to raise, about all doctrines of personal immortality or personal survival, some of what Bishop Butler—in the rather different context of the *Dissertation* from which the motto quotation is drawn—went on to deprecate as "strange perplexities." The continuing campaign, in which that brief but concentrated Note was only the first shot,[1] was and is a campaign to show how wrong Russell was to write, much too modestly that "a genuine scientific philosophy cannot hope to appeal to any except those who have the wish to understand, to escape from intellectual bewilderment"; for "All the problems which have what is called a human interest, such as, for example, the problem of a future life, belong in theory to the special sciences, and are capable, at least in theory of being decided by empirical evidence."[2]

Russell was wrong here. He was wrong in as much as there are quite possibly insoluble problems, problems of a philosophical rather than a purely scientific kind, which need to be resolved before any science, whether already established or yet to be, can be presented with an answerable question in this matter of the greatest human interest, an answerable question, that is, which is not answered with a decisive negative by everyone's prescientific knowledge of our universal human mortality. How, after all, did the men of the Medieval Schools become able to use "All men are mortal" as an uncontroversial stock example of a true, universal, contingent proposition?

The first two paragraphs got us to the heart of the matter, by establishing two fundamentals. One of these is that the essence of any doctrine of *personal* survival (or *personal* immortality) must be that it should assert that *we ourselves* shall in some fashion do things and suffer things after *our own* deaths (forever). It is this, and this alone, which warrants, or rather constitutes, what John Wisdom so correctly characterized as "the logically unique expectation."[3] It is important to emphasize that this is indeed of the essence: both because some doctrines employing the word "immortality" have from the beginning not been of this kind—Aristotle on the alleged immortality of the intellect, for instance—and because others, which started as genuine doctrines of personal immortality, have been so interpreted and reinterpreted that they have surreptitiously ceased to be anything of the such— "the death by a thousand qualifications," again.[4] It is also, it seems, sometimes necessary to point out that personal survival is presupposed by, and is no sort of alternative to, personal immortality: that in general, as in the particular case of the beheaded King Charles I, "It is the first step which counts."[5]

The second fundamental, which the first two paragraphs of this discussion force us to face is this. Any doctrine of personal survival or personal immortality has got to find some way around or over an enormous initial obstacle. In the ordinary, everyday understandings of the words involved, to say that someone survived death is to contradict oneself, while to assert that we all of us live for ever is to assert a falsehood, the diametric contrary of a universally known universal truth.

Ways Around the Barrier?

We may distinguish three sorts of ways in which we might attempt to circumvent or to overcome this formidable barrier, although the route-finding image becomes awkward when we notice that most living faiths have incorporated elements of more than one. I will, for want of any better alternative, once again employ the three labels: "Reconstitutionist," "Astral Body," and "Platonic-Cartesian."

1. The first of these cannot be better explained than by unrolling a pair of quotations, which I have often used before, but which will bear repetitions. One is an epitaph composed for himself by Benjamin Franklin. I copied it from a plaque erected not on but beside his grave in Christ Church cemetery, Philadelphia: "The body of B. Franklin, Printer, Like the Cover of an old Book, Its Contents torn out, And stript of its Lettering and Gilding, Lies Here, Food for Worms. But the work shall not be lost; for it will, as he believ'd, appear once more in a new and more elegant Edition Corrected and improved By the Author."

The other comes from "The Night Journey" (Chapter 17) in *The Koran,* in N. J. Dawood's Penguin Classics translation. As usual, it is Allah speaking: "Thus shall they be rewarded: because they disbelieved our revelations and said 'When we are turned to bones and dust shall we be raised to life?' Do they not see that Allah, who has created the heavens and the earth, has power to create their like? Their fate is preordained beyond all doubt. Yet the wrongdoers persist in unbelief" (p. 234).

This direct Reconstitutionist Way is blocked by the Replica Objection. This is: that the "new and more elegant Edition" would not be the original Founding Father, Signer of the American Declaration of Independence, but only a replica; and that Allah spoke more truly than his Prophet realized when he claimed, not the ability to reconstitute the same persons, but only the "power to create their like." The force of the Replica Objection is all the greater, and all the more decisive, in as much as the "new . . . edition" and "their like" are both to be the creations of a quasi-personal, rewarding, and punishing Creator, not just things that occur unintended.

It is clear that Aquinas, unlike some of our contemporaries who think to follow him, appreciated all this. But his Reconstitutionism incorporated an element of our third kind. For he believed that a soul, which is a substance, in the sense of something that can significantly be said to exist separately, yet that is most emphatically not in such separate existence a whole person, survives what would normally be called death and dissolution. This will eventually be— shall we say—incorporated into what might otherwise, had provision not been made for this element of partly personal continuity, have had to be dismissed as merely a replica of the original person.[6] About this Thomist response the only thing that we need to say here is that this sort of semi-soul, which is not by itself a whole person, must be exposed to all the objections that can be brought against a full Platonic soul, which is, or could be. Also, to the extent that the Thomist soul is not a whole person, its claim to constitute the essential link maintaining personal identity is bound to weaken.

2. To explain the Astral Body approach it is best to think of cinematic representations—as long ago in the movie version of Noel Coward's *Blithe Spirit*—in which a shadow person, visible only sometimes and only to some of the characters, detaches itself from a person shown as dead, and thereafter continues to participate in the developing action, at one time discernibly and at another time not. This elusive entity is taken to be itself the real, the essential, person.

It is not, however, essential that an Astral Body be of human shape; much less that, even after the traumatic detachment of death, it should remain—as in those decent old days it did—neatly and conventionally clad. The crux is that it should possess the corporeal

174

characteristics of size, shape, and position; and that—though eluding crude, untutored, uninstrumented, observation—it should nevertheless be in principle detectable. If it were not both in this minimum sense corporeal and in principle detectable, it would not be relevantly different from the Platonic-Cartesian soul. If it were not in practice excessively difficult to detect, no one could with any plausability suggest that such a thing might in fact slip away unnoticed from the deathbed.

The vulgar, materialist notion of souls—a notion which Plato derides at *Phaedo* 77D—satisfied the present, studiously undemanding specification for Astral Bodies; and that vulgar notion surely was, as near as makes no matter, that of Epicurus and Lucretius. There seems reason to believe too that many of the early Christian Fathers thought of souls as something less than totally and perfectly incorporeal.[7] So their souls also must for present purposes be classified as Astral Bodies.

The Way of the Astral Body runs between Scylla and Charybdis. For the more we make Astral Bodies like the ordinary flesh and blood persons from which they are supposedly detachable—in order to make sure that each person's Astral Body can be identified as the real and essential person—the more difficult it becomes to make out that it is not already known that no such Astral Bodies do in fact detach themselves at death. If, on the other hand, we take care so to specify the nature of our hypothesized Astral Bodies that falsification of the hypothesis that such there be, while still possible in principle, is in practice indefinitely deferred, then we find that we have made it impossibly difficult to identify creatures of too, too solid flesh and blood with any such perennially elusive hypothetical entities. Under these and other pressures those who have started to attempt the Way of the Astral Body tend so to refine away the corporeal characteristics of such putative bodies that they become indiscernible from Platonic-Cartesian souls. But, as and when more people begin to become aware of the difficulty—I would say the impossibility—of providing for the identification and reidentification of such entirely incorporeal souls, then we may expect to see a trickle of talent moving back in the opposite direction.[8]

3. The third, Platonic-Cartesian Way is, of course, the most familiar. It is based upon, or consists in, two assumptions. The first is that what is ordinarily thought of as a person is in fact composed of two utterly disparate elements: the one, the body, earthy, corporeal, and perishable; the other, the soul, incorporeal, invisible,

intangible, and perhaps imperishable. The second, and equally essential, is that the second of these is the real person, the agent, the rational being.

Traditionally these assumptions have been taken absolutely for granted; and, in discussions of survival and immortality, they still are. They are rarely even stated and distinguished, while still more rarely do we find anyone attempting to justify them. The founders of the British Society for Psychical Research hoped that its work might serve to verify what they feared that the advance of all the other sciences was falsifying, a Platonic-Cartesian view of the nature of man. In the middle decades of the present century, J. B. Rhine cherished the same hope, and believed that the work done in his laboratories at Durham, North Carolina, had indeed supplied the hoped for verification. This is neither the place nor the occasion for yet another demonstration that these desired findings were in fact presupposed in prejudicial misdescriptions of that work, rather than supported by it.[9]

But it is worth mentioning here and now that when Paul and Linda Badham construe out-of-the-body experiences as evidence for a Platonic-Cartesian view they make exactly the same mistake. If a patient claims to have "seen" something "when out-of-the-body," something that she could not have seen from her bed, then the more economical thing to say is that she "saw" that something clairvoyantly from her bed, rather than, equally clairvoyantly, from her temporarily detached soul.[10]

Far more impressive, as indicating the stubborn strength and widespread persistence of Platonic-Cartesian assumptions, is the spectacle of a long series of staunchly Godless mortalists claiming that they are themselves able not merely to conceive but also to imagine (image) their own disembodied survival. The latest such claimant to attract my own attention was J. L. Mackie. He made the claim on the very first page of a book in which he set out to reach atheist and presumably also mortalist conclusions.[11] The correct response is that, whatever the truth about what can or cannot be conceived, no one, surely, can distinguish an image of their own funeral from an image of themselves (but disembodied!) witnessing that funeral.[12]

Dualistic Fallacies

Whether or not these two assumptions, which together define the Platonic-Cartesian Way, can in the end be justified, it will not do, notwithstanding that this is what usually is done, to take them as from the beginning given, as if they either required no proof or had been proved already. The truth is that it is very far from obvious that disembodied personal survival is conceivable, that is, that talk of persons as substantial incorporeal souls is coherent. For person words in their ordinary everyday understandings—the personal pronouns, personal names, words for persons playing particular roles (such as "spokesperson," "bogey-person," "Premier," "aviator," etc.), and so on—are words employed to name or otherwise to refer to members of a very special class of creatures of flesh and blood.

In this ordinary, everyday understanding—what other do we have?—incorporeal persons are no more a sort of persons than are imaginary, fictitious, or otherwise nonexistent persons. "Incorporeal" in that expression is, if you prefer to be modestly and discreetly technical, an alienans adjective, like "positive" in "positive freedom," or "People's" in "People's Democracy." To put the point more harshly—and thus to provide an always welcome occasion for quoting "the Monster of Malmesbury"—to assert, in that ordinary everyday understanding, that somebody survived death, but disembodied, is to contradict yourself. Hence, in Chapter 5 of *Leviathan,* the incorrigible Thomas Hobbes was so rude as to say that, "if a man talks to me of 'a round quadrangle' or 'accidents of bread in cheese' or 'immaterial substances'. . . .I should not say that he was in error, but that his words were without meaning: that is to say, absurd."

1. My respected Keele successor, Richard Swinburne, recently thought to deflect the ferocity of such onslaughts by making the emollient point that no one has any business to argue, just because all the Xs with which they happen themselves to have been acquainted were 0, that therefore 0 is an essential characteristic of anything that is to be properly rated an X.[13] This is, of course, correct. Certainly it would be preposterous, and worse, to argue that because all the human beings with whom you had so far become acquainted had had black skins, therefore anyone with any other skin pigmentation must be disqualified as a human being. But incorporeality is a very different kettle of fish—or, perhaps we should say, no kettle and no fish. For to characterize something as incorporeal is to make an assertion that is at one and the same time both extremely comprehensive and wholly negative. Those proposing to do this surely owe it both to themselves and to others not

only to indicate what positive characteristics might significantly be attributed to their putative incorporeal entities, but also to specify how such entities could, if only in principle, be identified and reidentified. What sorts of predicates can these supposed subjects take and to just what are any attributes proposed as possible to be attributed?

2. The main reason why the need to attempt answers to these questions is so rarely recognized must be, surely, the easy and widespread assumption that common knowledge of the untechnical vernacular equips us with a concept of incorporeal persons, and hence that what ought to be meant by talk of the continuing identity of such entities is already determined. It is this assumption, as we have seen, which supports and is in turn supported by those reckless claims to be able to image personal survival in a disembodied state. The assumption itself is sustained by the familiarity both of talk about minds or souls and of talk about survival or immortality. Since both sorts of talk are without doubt intelligible, does it not follow that we do have concepts of soul and of mind, as well as of disembodied personal existence? No; or, rather, yes and no.

(a) Just because we can indeed understand hopes or fears of survival or immortality, it does not follow that we can conceive—much less image—existence as persons, but disembodied. No one has ever emphasized and commended incorporeality more strongly than Plato. Yet when, in the Myth of Er, Plato labors to describe the future life awaiting his supposedly disembodied souls, everything, which even that master craftsman of the pen has to say about them, presupposes that they will still be just such creatures of flesh and blood as we now, and he then (*Republic,* 614B ff.).

(b) On the other hand, the familiarity and intelligibility of talk about minds and about souls does entitle us to infer that we possess both a concept of mind and a concept of soul. But these semantic possessions are precisely not what is needed if doctrines of the survival and perhaps the immortality of souls or of minds are to be viable. The crux is that, in their everyday understandings, the words "minds" and "souls" are not words for sorts of substances, not words, that is, for what could significantly be said to survive the deaths and dissolutions of those flesh and blood persons whose minds or souls they are. To construe the question whether she has a mind of her own, or the assertion that he is a mean-souled man, as a question, or an assertion, about some hypothesized incorporeal substance is like taking the Red Queen's dog's loss of its temper as if this was on all fours with his loss of his bone; or like looking for the grin remaining after the Cheshire Cat has vanished. (If anyone really does want to hypothesize minds or souls as potentially explanatory scientific entities, then they will be faced with the same challenge as confronts the would be survivalist or immortalist: they will have, that is to say, to give meaning to 'mind' or 'soul' *as a substance word*.)

3. A more recent suggestion that this has already been done, and that a suitable sense is provided within our ordinary, nontechnical, everyday vocabulary, is found in Paul and Linda Badham's *Immortality or Extinction*.[14] To the assertion "that words like 'you', 'I', 'person', 'Flew', 'woman', 'father', 'butcher', all refer in one way or another to objects," they respond with what they rightly insist is more than "a purely grammatical point . . . that the word 'I' can never be so used, but must always relate to the subject" (p. 7). From this they proceed to infer that "What makes me 'me' is not my external appearance . . . rather it is that I am the subject of the thought, feelings, memories and intentions of which I am aware" (p. 10). This subject, it is assumed, could significantly be said to change bodies or even to continue to exist—and to have "thoughts, feelings, memories and intentions"—without any body at all: "The flames of the crematorium will not torture 'me' for 'I' shall not be there. Either I will cease to exist with my body or I shall continue to exist without it" (p. 11).

Now this, as British rally drivers used to say, is going a bit quick. In so doing, the Badhams have, surely, run out of road. Certainly, as Shakespeare realized, it is primarily because we are creatures endowed with conscience, in the sense of consciousness, that we are so strongly inclined to believe that talk of our disembodied survival is coherent:

> To die: to sleep;
> No more; and, by a sleep to say we end
> The heartache and the thousand natural shocks
> That flesh is heir to, 'tis a consummation
> Devoutly to be wish'd. To die, to sleep;
> To sleep: perchance to dream: ay, there's the rub;
> For in that sleep of death what dreams may come,
> When we have shuffled off this mortal coil,
> Must give us pause. . . .

Yes indeed. If it does truly make sense to say that the same person might survive as an incorporeal dreamer, disentangled from the mortal coils of flesh and blood, then it must be altogether reasonable to speak of death as the still undiscovered country. So Hamlet continues:

> The undiscover'd country from whose bourn
> No traveler returns, puzzles the will,
> And makes us rather bear those ills we have
> Than fly to others that we know not of?
> Thus conscience does make cowards of us all;. . . .[15]

Yet in the end, after the play is over, the prosaic objection must once more be put. After the death of Hamlet, where or what could Hamlet be? Who or what is the future dreamer—the putative he or she or it—whose possible nightmares—or should it be the possible nightmares of which?—the Hamlet of "too, too solid flesh" was anticipating with such trepidation? (All three available pronouns seem inappropriate, if not perhaps quite equally so; a fact that should perhaps be noted more often than it is, both in the present context and in that of theological discussion.)

How—to address the challenge directly to the Badhams—is the subject 'I' to be identified, if not always and only by reference to the sensations, desires, and thoughts of the object person who is at the same time the subject of those sensations, desires, and thoughts? However could it be identified thus separately, and hence as being presumably, separable, any more than mental images and bodily sensations, or "ideas and impressions," can be identified "loose and separate," and without reference to the people who are the subjects of such moments of consciousness?

4. The main reason, perhaps, why it is so often assumed either that these questions can be or that they do not need to be answered is that it is believed that we are, through our mastery of the vernacular, already fully equipped: not only with a concept of incorporeal persons, and some conceivable, if not of necessity in practice usable, means for their identification; but also, either with corresponding criteria for the reidentification of such entities as the same individuals, or else with some sort of waiver on these usual requirements of the ontological authorities.

Swinburne, for instance, who does to his credit recognize that there are serious and heavy problems about *The Coherence of Theism,* and who in that book labors long and hard to solve those problems, there quickly concludes "that the identity of a person over time is something ultimate, not analysable in terms of bodily continuity or continuity of memory or character" (p. 110). Given this conclusion, Swinburne allows—in the manner of a man making an unavoidable concession to the limitations of the human condition—that "We may use bodily continuity to reach conclusions about personal identity" (p. 109).

This will not do. For what we actually use bodily criteria for is to establish bodily continuity. And this is not just a usually reliable criterion for, but a large part if not the whole of what is meant by, personal identity. (It would be, wouldn't it, if persons just are, as I maintain that we all know that we are, a very special sort of creatures of flesh and blood?) Swinburne, like so many others, having first, by means already indicated, satisfied himself that persons are not essentially corporeal, goes on by way of two further and perennially persuasive mistakes to reach a further false conclusion, that personal identity is not the identity of any essentially corporeal entity.

(a) In the first place, I think that Swinburne, like so many others both overlooks the theoretical possibility and actual frequency of honest yet mistaken claims to be the same person as did this or suffered that, and fails to appreciate the decisive force of Bishop Butler's refutation of any analysis of "being the same person as did that" in terms of "remembering being the same person as did that."[16] In consequence, Swinburne is inclined to assume that, whatever difficulties other people might confront in trying to reidentify some putative person as the same as the one who did that particular deed, or who enjoyed or suffered that particular experience, the putative person in question must be in a position to know the true answer.

Of course, if there is or even could be a true answer, then the question to which it is a true answer must already have sense. It must, to particularize, make sense to say "that the identity of a [not essentially corporeal] person over time is something ultimate, not analysable in terms of bodily continuity or continuity of memory or character." It must, therefore, seem to Swinburne that he has deflected the impetus of Terence Penelhum's objections to the suggestion that disembodiable and disembodied persons can be thought of as incorporeal substances: "Beyond the wholly empty assurance that it is a metaphysical principle which guarantees continuing identity through time, or the argument that since we know that identity persists some such principle must hold in default of

others, no content seems available for the doctrine. Its irrelevance
... is due to its being merely an alleged identity-guaranteeing
condition of which no independent characterization is
forthcoming."[17]

Arguing against Penelhum, Swinburne mistakes it that the objection to giving an account of the identity of disembodied persons in
terms of memory claims is that such claims could not be checked,
which he contends that they could be. But the decisive objection,
put first and perfectly by Bishop Butler, is that true memory
presupposes, and therefore cannot constitute, personal identity:
when I truly remember my doing that, what I remember is that I
am the same person as did it.[18] So, until and unless sense has been
given to the expression "disembodied person," no problem of
discovering whether in fact X at time one was the same disembodied person as Y at time two can arise; and hence no unsequential
problem of whether any such putative discoveries could be
checked.

(b) Swinburne's second mistake here, and again it is an error in
which he has a host of companions, is a matter of method. In a
word, this seductive and popular mistake consists in the misuse of
possible puzzle cases, cases, which if they actually occurred, and
were thought likely to recur, would require us to make new decisions as to what in the future correct verbal usage is to be. What is
wrong is to assume that decisions, even the most rational decisions,
about responses to purely hypothetical challenges, and usually challenges that we have no reason or less than no reason to expect to
have to face in real life, must throw direct light on the present
meanings of the words concerned. These present meanings are, of
course, determined not by some hypothetical future but by actual
present correct usage, while our ordinary language provides us with
the concepts with which it does provide us because these were those
that were evolved in and adapted to the worlds in which our
ancestors lived—concepts not all of which will be equally well
adapted to the needs and the realities of our own world and the
worlds of our descendants.

It is, therefore, all very well to introduce bizarre cases in order to
stimulate a mind-flexing realization that, in a very different world,
we might evolve a very different concept of what would there be
called a person, along with correspondingly different criteria of
personal identity. Such speculations can also help us to see what are
those actual features of the world as it is to which our present

concepts are well adapted. But these puzzle cases, and the speculations that they provoke, cannot legitimately be employed to prove that our present concept of a person, and our present and corresponding criteria of personal identity, are other than they are. That present concept, as has been argued throughout, is a concept of a special kind of creature of flesh and blood, while, as I have argued more fully elsewhere, our present criteria for personal identity are, correspondingly, criteria for the reidentification of particular specimens of this kind—criteria, that is, for discovering whether this specimen here at time two is physically continuous with that specimen there at time one.[19]

The truly disturbing conclusion to be derived from a proper employment of puzzle cases is one to which Swinburne seems to have blinded himself. It is that it is possible to conceive, and even to imagine (image), situations giving rise to questions about personal identity to which, in the present meanings of the key terms, there could be no unequivocally true or unequivocally false answer. So not even the person or persons themselves could know that answer. Consider, for instance, the questions that would arise if someone were told that she was going to split like an amoeba—and did.[20]

The Non-Implications of Para-Psychology

Way back in our discussion of the third (Platonic-Cartesian) way, above, we noticed that, from the earliest days of the Society for Psychical Research many have hoped to be able to deploy the findings, or the alleged findings, of what is now called parapsychology in support of a Platonic-Cartesian account of the nature of man, and suggested, with particular reference to what are conveniently yet misleadingly called out-of-the-body experiences, that this is a false hope based in the main on systematically prejudicial misdescriptions of the data. It is time now, however briefly, to go over to the offensive.

Among those who believe that they have given sense to talk of incorporeal spirits and disembodied persons, it appears to be universally assumed that such beings could be said to acquire and to transmit information by Extra-Sensory Perception (ESP or, often and better, psi-gamma). The idea is that they would directly both acquire and transmit information "by telepathy," both between themselves and to and from normally embodied persons, and also acquire information, equally directly, "by clairvoyance" from the ordinarily sensible world of nonpersonal things. No one else ever seems to have noticed what can be seen as a corollary of the fact that psi-gamma, as at present defined, can only be identified by subsequent sensory checkups.

Suppose for a moment that there were such incorporeal subjects of experience, and suppose further that there was from time to time a close correspondence between the mental contents of two of these beings, although such a fact could not, surely, be known by any normal means to anyone in either our world or the next. Now, how could either of these two souls have, indeed how could there be, any good reason for hypothesizing the existence of the other; or of any others? How could such beings have, indeed how could there be, any good reason for picking out some of their own mental contents as—so to speak—messages received, for taking these but not those to be, not expressions of a spontaneous and undirected exercise of the imagination, but externally provoked communication input? Suppose these two challenging questions could be answered, still the third would be "the killing blow." For how could such beings identify any particular items as true or false, or even give sense to this distinction?

The upshot seems to be that the concept of psi-gamma is essentially parasitical on everyday, this-worldly notions, and that, where there could not be perception, there could not be "Extra-Sensory Perception" either. It is assumed too often and too easily that psi-capacities not only can be, but have to be, the attributes of something immaterial and incorporeal, mainly for no better reason than that they would be nonphysical in the quite different sense of being hard if not impossible to square with today's physical theories. Yet the truth is that the very concepts of psi are just as much involved with the human body as are those of other human capacities and activities. In the gnomic words of Wittgenstein: "The human body is the best picture of the human soul."[21]

Conclusion

Yet let us conclude not with a Wittgensteinian gnomon but a Chinese poem, sung, the translator tells us, only at the burial of kings and princes:

184

How swiftly it dries,
The dew on the garlic-leaf,
The dew that dries so fast
Tomorrow will fall again.
But he whom we carry to the grave
Will never more return.[22]

NOTES

1. It is most easily found as the final contribution—"Death"—in Antony Flew and Alasdair MacIntyre, eds., *New Essays in Philosophical Theology* (London: Student Christian Movement Press, 1955). But it was originally published in 1951, and, like the earlier pieces on "Theology and Falsification," in the long since defunct journal *University*. "Death" has, however, never been reprinted again, whereas the initial contribution to the "Theology and Falsification" symposium has now reappeared at least thirty more times—including translations into Italian, German, Danish, and Welsh. Nevertheless, by the time "Death" came to be included in *New Essays in Philosophical Theology,* it had an additional footnote listing four of my later contributions in the same area, three of which have since been reprinted in one or more philosophical anthologies. This should have been sufficient to show that I anticipated all my contemporaries and juniors by several years in raising and publishing such "strange perplexities" about the question of a future life.

2. Bertrand A. W. Russell, *Our Knowledge of the External World* (London: Allen and Unwin, 1922), p. 28.

3. See his "Gods," first published in the *Proceedings of the Aristotelian Society* for 1944-45, and reprinted in Antony Flew, ed., *Logic and Language: First Series* (Oxford: Blackwell, 1951).

4. Ponder here the shrewd and forthright protest of the Fundamentalist against "that weasel method of sucking the meaning out of words, and then presenting the empty shells in an attempt to palm them off as giving the Christian Faith a new and another interpretation," quoted by Walter Lippmann, *A Preface to Morals* (New York: Macmillan, 1931), pp. 30–31

   For a most relevant example of the sort of thing that that protest was a protest against, compare Dewi Z. Phillips, *Death and Immortality* (London: Macmillan, 1970). This slim volume makes particularly piquant reading for me. In it Phillips not only accepts all the points that I first began to raise twenty years before, but also assumes that all these points have always seemed equally obvious to all instructed Christians. Let me here assure him that at the time many very well instructed believers, some of whom had been most generous in their recognition of the intellectual force and moral passion of the challenge unleashed in "Theology and Falsification," put down both "Death" and the later "Can a Man Witness his own Funeral?" as disingenuous, factitious, and inconsiderable.

5. I deal faithfully with this shameful evasive maneuver in my "Survival," 1 (e), in Proceedings of the Aristotelian Society Supp. vol. 49 (1975); reprinted in Hywel D. Lewis, *Persons and Life after Death* (London: Macmillan, 1978).

6. See the *Summa Theologica,* III Supp. Q L 29 A2; especially Thomas's Reply to the first Objection.

7. See, for instance, the Reading from Tertullian in Antony Flew, ed., *Body, Mind and Death* (New York: Collier-Macmillan, 1964); also the observations thereon in the Introduction thereof.

8. See, for instance, Paul and Linda Badham, *Immortality or Extinction* (London: Macmillan, 1982). Given the present highly elastic interpretation of "Astral Body," their concern with post-Resurrection *"appearances"* may just possibly indicate a first extremely tentative move this way.

9. See my *A New Approach to Psychical Research* (London: C. A. Watts, 1953), chap. 9; reprinted in J. Ludwig, ed., *Philosophy and Parapsychology* (Buffalo: Prometheus Unbound, 1977). Or, for the same points made with reference to work with mediums, see "Is there a Case for Disembodied Survival?" in the *Journal of the American Society for Psychical Research* for 1972, reprinted in J. M. O. Wheatley and H. L. Edge, eds., *Philosophical Dimensions of Parapsychology* (Springfield, IL: C. C. Thomas, 1976).

10. Paul and Linda Badham, *Immortality or Extinction,* Part 3.

11. *The Miracle of Theism* (Oxford: Clarendon, 1983).

12. See my "Can a Man Witness his own Funeral," in the *Hibbert Journal* for 1956, reprinted in J. Feinberg, ed., *Reason and Responsibility* (Belmont, CA: Dickenson, 1971); W. J. Blackstone, ed., *Meaning and Existence* (New York: Holt, Rinehart and Winston, 1972); F. A. Westphal, ed., *The Art of Philosophy* (Englewood Cliffs, N. J.: Prentice-Hall, 1972); and P. A. French, ed., *Exploring Philosophy* (Morristown, N.J.: General Learning Press, 1975). P. A. French also includes a remarkably similar piece under his own name in another of his collections, *Philosophers in Wonderland* (St. Paul, MN.: Llewelyn, 1975). For final good measure, I myself added an improved rewrite to my *The Presumption of Atheism* (London: Pemberton/Elek, 1976), reissued in 1984 by Prometheus of Buffalo as *God, Freedom and Immortality.*

13. *The Coherence of Theism* (Oxford: Clarendon, 1977), p. 54.

14. See Note 8, above.

15. *Hamlet* 3 (i).

16. On this and related issues see my "Locke and the Problem of Personal Identity," first published in *Philosophy* for 1951, reprinted, in variously revised versions, in C. B. Martin and D. M. Armstrong, eds., *Locke and Berkeley* (New York: Doubleday, 1968); B. Brody, ed., *Readings in the Philosophy of Religion* (Englewood Cliffs, N.J.: Prentice-Hall, 1974); and my *The Presumption of Atheism.* (See Note 12, above.) This is the article, which in his book *Personal Identity* (London: Macmillan, 1976), Godfrey Vasey says "marks a turning point in discussions of personal identity" (p. 112). I will not resist the tempta-

tion to add my own opinion, that many of the later contributors to these discussions might have saved themselves and the rest of us from many errors had they attended, or attended more carefully, to that now ancient article. Such attention would at least have been an easy means of acquainting them with relevant key passages from the writings of such great men of old as Locke and Butler, Hume and Reid.

17. See his *Survival and Disembodied Existence* (London: Routledge and Kegan Paul, 1970), p. 70.

18. See, again, the article mentioned in Note 16, above.

19. Ditto to Note 18, above.

20. See both for a pressing of this disturbing conclusion and for the first introduction of this possible puzzle case, once again, my "Locke and the Problem of Personal Identity."

21. Ludwig Wittgenstein, *Philosophical Investigations,* translated by G. E. M. Anscombe, (Oxford: Blackwell, 1953), p. 278.

22. Arthur Waley, *170 Chinese Poems* (London: Constable, 1918), p. 38.

14

A Critical Outline of the Prima Facie Evidence for Survival
ARTHUR S. BERGER

Introduction

Until recently, death, like V. D., and other social diseases, was a pornographic subject not discussed in polite Western society. As Ernest Becker, the late Pulitzer prize-winning author, pointed out in *The Denial of Death,* society gives us many kinds of social games and activities into which we can escape in order to avoid thinking and talking about death.[1] Woody Allen personified the Western attitude toward death when he said on his fortieth birthday that he would gain immortality "not through my work but by not dying."[2] It was an attitude of evasion.

But about a decade ago, this attitude underwent a transformation. College courses and seminars on death and dying proliferated. More books and articles were published on these subjects than had been published in the preceding century. Western society decided to face death instead of looking away from it.

In spite of this Western about-face and the flood of literature concerning death, many people, among them the clergy and religious scholars, still do not know that, for over 100 years, groups of scientists and scholars have been doing research and collecting evidence on whether death is the final annihilation of the human being. To bridge this gap in knowledge, this chapter: (1) describes some of the reasons for the resistance to a fuller understanding and acceptance of survival research and evidence; (2) notes the relationship between religion and evidence; and (3) offers an outline and critical commentaries of six kinds of the latest prima facie survival evidence plus a reference to the evidence of the future.

Resistance to the Evidence

The story that the philosopher Ducasse used to tell in his delightful French accent illustrates the problem. A student came to his professor with a seashell that did not fit into any scientific classification. After studying it for a little while, the professor threw the shell on the floor, crushed it under his shoe and exclaimed: "There is no such shell."[3] Thus, we see that in science as well as in philosophy whenever phenomena do not fit into or come into conflict with basic assumptions, these phenomena are resisted or ignored.

In the case of human survival after death, the fundamental assumption against which survival evidence must always force its way was expressed by the British philosopher Antony Flew in the preceding chapter in which he equated "I" with his physical body and asserted that death was the "enormous initial obstacle."[4] With Flewian logic, the widely held corporealist theory of human nature was urged. We are the same as our bodies. Death simply finishes us and there is no effective way past the obstacle it creates. The survival question cannot arise. It is not an open question. Any empirical evidence concerning survival, as well as any effort, such as is currently being made by the Survival Research Foundation to investigate this evidence, is treated as the professor treated the shell. No one denies that the theory presented by Professor Flew is a rational one. Indeed, it could not have had a more rational exponent. But the first inquiry is whether the theory is true. It may be completely untrue. It is logically possible to take a dualistic view of the human being. The person can be seen as a compound of a physical body and another component that is the vehicle of attitudes, thoughts, and memories. Death need not be an enormous obstacle at all. It may be just the starting point.

On such a view, the survival question becomes very open and not closed, and its investigation and evidence warrant the closest scrutiny. Second, the Flewian assumption that we are identical with our bodies begs the question of whether we are more than just bodies of flesh. The evidence to be presented here might be interpreted by reasonable people, if certain tests (to be described) were passed, as indicating that we are more than physical bodies and some element of us continues beyond death.

Other assumptions blocking acceptance of survival research and evidence are: (1) that the whole subject suffers from the bad odor of fraud and charlatanism; (2) that the phenomena may be curious but generally trivial and not worth the trouble of knowing about; and (3) that the investigations are conducted or supported by soft-headed and gullible people. These assumptions can only be attributed to ignorance. Since the founding of the English Society for

Psychical Research in 1882 and the American Society for Psychical Research in 1885, many eminent scholars and scientists have been associated with the two societies. The list of members and presidents of both organizations includes the physicists Sir William Barrett, Sir Oliver Lodge, and Lord Rayleigh; the biologists Hans Driesch and Sir Alister Hardy; the statesmen Arthur Balfour and William E. Gladstone; the chemist Sir William Crookes; the lawyers Richard Hodgson and W. H. Salter; the medical doctors Montagu Ullman and Ian Stevenson; the psychologists William James, Gardner Murphy, William MacDougall, and Robert H. Thouless; the philosophers Henry Sidgwick, Henri Bergson, H. H. Price, C. D. Broad, and F. C. S. Schiller; the astronomers Camille Flammarion and F. J. M. Stratton; and the physiologist Charles Richet. Other members were Alfred Tennyson, John Ruskin, Mark Twain, and Lewis Carroll.

The recital of this honor roll does not mean that psychical research, or parapsychology as it is also called, has had and now has the endorsement of scholars and scientists in general. Indeed, the contrary is true. But the honor roll does reply to the criticisms of psychical research. Respected scholars and scientists with reputations to protect would not actively support fraudulent activities. The charge that the phenomena are trivial is answered by the distinguished people who have attached to the phenomena investigated the greatest importance for science, religion, and philosophy. And the enumeration of critical and sceptical people associated with the work of the society contradicts the criticism that those doing or supporting this work are soft-headed. On the contrary, such strict canons of evidence have been applied that William James observed that if he had to point "to a scientific journal where hard-headedness and never-sleeping suspicion of sources of error might be seen in their full bloom, I think I should have to fall back on" the publications of the English and American societies for psychical research.[5]

Religion and Evidence

Materialists and some philosophers who consider the survival question ridiculous may be inclined to close their minds to research and evidence bearing on the survival question. But when religious people do so, their resistance is difficult to understand. That human destiny lies beyond the flesh and the fleeting moment is a doctrine of many of the leading religions of the world. In none of them is death final extinction. All posit some vital component within the human body of flesh. In Christianity and Judaism, it is the soul; in Islam the Ruh; in Brahmanism, the Atman; in Buddhism, a complex of impersonal states or activities; and in Unification theology, it is the spiritual self. This death-conquering element separates from the physical body, persists beyond its death, and enters into another kind of existence.

Strong empirical evidence of the survival after death of the human consciousness would fit in squarely with and undergird this doctrine to which a formidable number of people have hinged their hopes, attitudes, and activities. Such evidence would not supplant religion; it would not have any relation with such doctrines as love, salvation, heaven, or hell, for example. But it would be invaluable to religion. Convincing findings that a human consciousness had survived the blow of death would be an almost lethal dose from which materialism might never recover. Such findings would supply the fundamental precondition of the eternal life promised by Western religion or the rounds of lives promised by Eastern religion. Such evidence would demonstrate also that the religious teaching of a future life was consistent with scientific findings and was credible.

Latest Types of Survival Evidence

Early attempts to collect survival evidence clustered mainly around apparitions of the dead and communications with the dead through mediums such as Mrs. L. E. Piper, who was carefully investigated by both the English and American Societies. Contemporary investigations have a broader range. The paranormal phenomena bearing on survival and now being investigated are divided into two types: physical and mental.

Physical Phenomena

No scene is more associated with Spiritualism than that of people sitting with their hands on a table in a dark seance room. Soon the table begins to shake, rise, and move although no one seems to be pushing or controlling it. Table-turning or -lifting is only one of the phenomena that played a large part in the Spiritualist movement and that the Spiritualists claimed showed the existence of a spirit world. Other kinds of physical phenomena included levitations (in which human bodies or physical objects rose or floated in the air), materializations (in which spirit forms, faces, and hands were seen), immunity to injury from fire or holding hot coals, apports (in which objects such as musical instruments or flowers appeared in a closed room), spirit photographs, slate-writing, ectoplasm (or the discharge of a substance from the body of a medium), and percussive noises such as knocking sounds. With one exception, the current literature of parapsychology is silent concerning all these phenomena. It is considered that the observations of the phenomena probably were faulty and can be attributed to trickery.

Poltergeists

The exception is the poltergeist, the kind of case in which knocking or banging noises are heard, objects fly through a room, cups and dishes fall from shelves, pictures turn on walls, and doors and windows open by themselves.

Because of the possibility that a deceased human agency might be behind these disturbances they have excited attention. Parapsychologists have studied records of these cases[6] and investigated them on the spot in the United States[7] and Europe.[8] Generally, however, the results have been disappointing for anyone seeking survival evidence. Researchers have concluded from the cases investigated either that they could be attributed to faulty observation by untrained people or to fraud or to recurrent spontaneous psychokinesis (RSPK) in which psychokinetic forces from a living person are theorized to have influenced physical objects in the neighborhood of the person.[9]

Nevertheless, while these explanations seem reasonable for some poltergeist cases, they need not apply, for example, to a case in which trained observers could find no living agent to be the focal point of the outbreaks. The search has continued for this kind of case, which might suggest a deceased human agency.

In 1980, I investigated a series of disturbances in a house in Durham, North Carolina, occupied by a husband, wife, infant child, and the husband's brother. The disturbances consisted mainly of objects being moved. Certain volumes of an encyclopedia set had been pulled out of a shelf and arranged systematically on the floor at an angle; pillows had been removed from the couch in the living room and been carefully rearranged on the floor; fragile glass globes had been taken out of a chandelier and placed on a dining room table without breakage. This controlled and careful arrangement of objects and lack of breakage suggested intelligence and purpose. It was not the blind kind of energy that explodes in the unconscious and aimless RSPK projected by a living agent. The case looked like evidence of a deceased human agency until I was able to account for it on normal grounds. It seemed probable that, although the wife and husband's brother were innocent, the disturbances had been brought about by the deliberate acts of the husband and child in the case.[10]

About the same time that I was investigating the Durham disturbances, however, investigators from the American Society for Psychical Research were investigating poltergeist phenomena in a gift shop in an old farmhouse in New Jersey.[11] Tools and a filing cabinet drawer moved; electrical systems, such as an adding machine and burglar alarm and music system, operated without reason or malfunctioned; footsteps, flapping noises, and human voices were heard; apparitions were seen. These disturbances had been continuing for a period of at least five years. In order to try to identify a deceased person who might be the cause, the investigators brought along sensitives when they visited the gift shop. One was able to describe rather accurately a woman, later identified as a spinster named Hester, who had lived in the house for 90 years until 1949. Carefully, the investigators removed fraud or normal causes as explanations for what was happening. Of all the witnesses they interviewed, it was not possible to isolate any one person whose presence was necessary to the production of the phenomena. In fact, electrical systems like the burglar alarm malfunctioned when the house was empty. The case strongly suggested a situation in which the poltergeist agent could not have been any living person. It stands as the most recent prima facie evidence of a deceased agency, possibly the dead Hester, although her identification as the agent was not clearly established. The case demonstrates the need for not approaching poltergeist cases with hasty generalizations about them, such as malobservation, trickery, or RSPK, and the further need to continue to investigate them because any given disturbance may be another source of survival evidence.

Electronic Voice Phenomena

That people who have died are able to communicate with the living by using electronic equipment has been asserted from time to time by individuals who favor the survival hypothesis—or who wish to sell books. According to Walter F. Prince, a noted parapsychologist around the time of the Great War, *Thy Son Liveth* by Mrs. L. N. Geldert was a book written for the latter purpose, "a book," he said, "made to sell."[12] In the book, the author claimed that her son, after being killed in France, used an abandoned wireless telegraph in a trench to send her a message. She received it, she wrote, on a dismantled wireless set in her home in New York. Prince dismissed the claim as "a fabrication pure and simple."[13]

In recent years, however, two developments in instrumental communicatons claimed to be from the dead have received more attention from parapsychologists than the impatient Prince was prepared to give 65 years ago. Reports of phone calls from the dead, for instance, were the subject of a two-year investigation.[14] In spite of this devoted research, however, the cases, which depend almost entirely upon the uncorroborated testimony of the people receiving the calls, lack the evidential value that is necessary for this kind of phenomenon to merit serious interest.

A second phenomenon of physical effects received on electronic equipment does seem worthy of attention. The first indication that inaudible, strange, paranormal voices and rappings were being recorded in experiments with a tape recorder seems to have been given in 1959 by Raymond Bayless, a parapsychologist.[15] He and an associate recorded over one hundred mysterious voices, one saying, "Merry Christmas and Happy New Year to you all." In the same year, Friedrich Jurgenson, a Swedish singer, claimed that he had recorded the voice of his dead mother. Jurgenson's experiments stimulated the interest of Konstantin Raudive, a Latvian psychologist, who began to conduct experiments of his own. By 1971, the year in which he published *Breakthrough* to describe methods of recording voices, he had already recorded more than 70,000 of them.[16] The publicity resulting from his book caused Peter Bander, who recommended that *Breakthrough* be published in Great Britain and America and wrote the preface to it, to caution people not to be misled into the belief that they would be able to reproduce such experiments at will. Machines still had to be invented and methods discovered that would produce immediate results. "Dial M for Mother," warned Bander, "is still something very much in the future."[17] In spite of this warning, housewives, students, scientists and others in Great Britain, the Continent, and America set about to reproduce the experiments. With microphones, diodes, or interfrequency methods, hundreds of these experimenters began to assert that they had achieved positive results and were recording electronic voices.

But David Ellis, a Perrott-Warwick student at Trinity College, Cambridge, who investigated the subject carefully is not at all convinced that the voices are genuinely paranormal.[18] The so-called voices might be the result of wishful thinking or of imposing some arbitrary meaning or interpretation on random noises. The problem of deciphering the "voices" amid the white noise that accompanies them is great and becomes greater because the voices are faint, speak rapidly, softly or in whispers or seem to be polyglot.

Other authorities, such as Richard Sheargold, the British investigator, are persuaded, however, that the phenomena are paranormal and objective. Joel Honig, an American authority associated with the Survival Research Foundation and who visited Raudive, is also so persuaded. I, too, can attest that at least one voice I heard was an objective fact. The question then becomes: From where do the voices originate? The explanation that they come from persons who are present during the experiments does not apply in most cases. A theory that they are stray fragments of radio broadcasts picked up by a tape recorder also can be excluded in many cases since some voices have been recorded in Faraday cages where radio signals cannot penetrate and since some voices seem to answer questions put by the experimenters or engage in responsive conversations with them. The theory that they originate from nonhuman intelligences in space also seems unlikely because many voices are recognizably human, speak in the languages of this planet, express human thought-forms, and none appear to be conveying interplanetary messages.

Two viable theories remain. Many experimenters join the late Raudive in asserting that the phenomena are voices of people who once lived on this planet, are now on "the other side," and are trying to communicate with the living to tell them that survival is a reality. In Raudive's reported recordings, for example, the "voices" say: "The dead live, Konstantin," "We are," "Please believe." After the death of Margarete Petrautski, a secretary for Raudive and Zenta Raudive, his wife, a voice was registered on tape. It called out "Zenta," gave the name "Margarete" and said in German "Imagine, I really exist."

But a theory put forward by Professor Hans Bender, a German parapsychologist, disputes this spiritistic interpretation. He postulates some variant of psychokinesis in the phenomena. The electrical impulses generated by the subconscious minds of the experimenters are being converted by psychokinesis into voices on the tapes.

It is not at all clear to parapsychologists that any breakthrough in survival evidence has really been achieved. Apart from some of the objections already noted, another serious one is that the voices give virtually no particulars that would enable the experimenters to identify a purported communicator. Without an indication of personal identity, the phenomenon is a vacuous one.

Ambiguous and controversial though this latest phenomenon may be, it would be dogmatic to try to avoid or dismiss the claim made by its supporters that it is survival evidence. Some electronic researchers, therefore, like Alexander MacRae of Scotland and George Meek of America, are attempting to design and develop more sophisticated electronic and audio equipment to see if the evidential value of the phenomenon can be improved. Objective and controlled investigations to test which of the rival theories is correct are underway also. I am conducting experiments now that will be mentioned when future evidence is discussed in which experimenters with tape recorders are asking questions to which they themselves cannot respond. Should the answers be discovered on their tapes at the conclusion of the experiments and if they can be verified as the right answers, we should be in a better position to determine the origin of the voices and to assess the values of this intriguing but still inconclusive survival evidence.

Mental Phenomena

Among the various types of mental phenomena on which the latest survival evidence depends are reincarnation-type cases, out-of-the-body experiences, visions of the dying and drop-in communicators.

Reincarnation-Type Cases Cases in which claims are made by some individuals that they remember having lived on this planet before and in which the details they could not have known normally but remember can be corroborated should be very meaningful for both Brahmanism and Buddhism. Reincarnation is a major teaching of both religions. It is still not widely accepted in the West, however, although some Christians are giving serious thought to reincarnation and although Eastern beliefs in karma and reincarnation are steadily gaining in influence among the general public.

Strong evidence of reincarnation would be of great import to the

196

survival hypothesis and to all who are interested in it, Christians or not, for such evidence is different in one vital respect from all other survival evidence. While other evidence may suggest that a person may have reason to hope that he will survive his future death, reincarnation-type evidence suggests that someone has already survived one death in the past and has been reborn in a different body.

When mature persons claim memories of past incarnations, a reasonable inference would be that they might have obtained knowledge in a normal way concerning the details of the lives of the dead persons they say they were. But when children of tender years say they remember having lived before in locations distant from their present homes and provide information about these lives, which investigators can verify, the evidence takes on a more imposing aspect. A case from Lebanon that Ian Stevenson, Director of the Division of Parapsychology at the University of Virginia, investigated is an example of such a case.[19]

When Imad Elwar was two years of age, he was walking down a street in his village of Kornayel. The child ran over to a strange man who came from the distant village of Khriby and who was also walking down the street. The child threw his arms around the stranger. "Do you know me?" asked the man. "Yes," said the child. "You were my neighbor." The man had been a neighbor of Ibrahim Bouhamzy who had died some years before. It was this event that convinced the family of Imad that many of the claims he had been making about a former life he had lived as a member of the Bouhamzy family in the village of Khriby and about events and people he had known might be true after all. Imad's father had called him a liar until the recognition of the stranger. When the case came to Stevenson's attention, he went to Lebanon to verify the statements Imad had made and to observe if the child was able to recognize people and places in the village of Khriby. Of forty-seven items of information Imad had given about his former life before he and Stevenson went to Khriby, such as the fact that he had a woman named Jamile, that she was beautiful and wore red clothes, forty-four were verified as correct. Of sixteen items of information Stevenson had tabulated in Khriby of recognitions there by Imad, such as recognizing where Ibrahim Bouhamzy had lived or identifying the sister of the dead man, fourteen were correct.

In many cases, however, the family of the child and the family of the person the child claims to have been have met before an investigator can arrive. The evidence becomes doubtful because how many of the child's "memories" of a prior life are the result of true memory and how many the result of the meeting may be difficult to separate. Cases would be more reliable if what a child remembered were written down and investigators began their work before the meeting of the two families. Several such cases appear in Stevenson's most recent series of case reports.[20]

One is that of Jagdish Chandra of India. Jagdish's father, a lawyer, carefully recorded his son's statements that, in a prior life, he was Jai Gopal, that he had lived in the city of Benares, and that his father had been Babuju Pandey. In all, thirty-six items of information were recorded. At least twenty-four were verified prior to the meeting of the families.[21]

The cases are offered by Stevenson as "suggestive" of reincarnation but, from a critical point of view, they are also "suggestive" of other interpretations such as fraud, cryptomnesia, and ESP. The least likely of these is fraud. The children and their families usually have little to gain from the claims. The painstaking care with which Stevenson's investigations are conducted also tend to lessen the possibility. It is more difficult to eliminate cryptomnesia and still more difficult to discard ESP. A child could have obtained information about a deceased person at some previous time and since forgotten it. If, as mentioned earlier, this seems less probable in the case of a child between two and four years of age than in the case of an adult, it is still possible that a family member might have picked up the details of someone's life by normal means and passed them on to the child either accidentally or deliberately. It is also very hard to combat the final suggestion that the details of any case might have been acquired by extrasensory powers exercised by the child. In rebuttal one can only say that the child claiming to remember a past life has never demonstrated any paranormal gifts at other times. And, if the child had such powers, why were they used only in this case and with respect to the one deceased person the child claims to have been? .

The reincarnation-type cases would be stronger if, besides giving items of information, which might be attributed to normal or paranormal means of acquisition, a child showed behavior traits and patterns pertinent to the prior life claimed, such as a dislike of certain foods or an interest in certain activities. In the case of Jagdish Chandra, Stevenson emphasized the child's fondness for sweets and an insistence on customs observed by Brahmins.[22] (Jagdish Chandra was not a Brahmin but Jai Gopal had been and had liked sweet foods). In his latest cases, Stevenson is therefore paying considerable attention to behavior as another strong indicator of reincarnation.

Out-of-the-Body Experiences The experience of perceiving the world and one's own physical body from a point in space outside that physical body is termed an out-of-the-body experience (OBE). Other names for this sensation are "astral projection" or "travelling clairvoyance." The experience can be induced deliberately by some people or may occur spontaneously, often when people are ill, under anaesthesia, or on the verge of death.

Is the OBE a rare experience, limited to one place or time or to odd people? Apparently not, for out-of-the-body experience has been reported in all cultures. It was known in ancient times. St. Paul alludes to it (2 Cor. 12:2). It is surely known in modern times. Robert Crookall, a well-known OBE researcher, collected 160 first-hand descriptions of the experience in 1960[23] and 222 more experiences in a later book.[24] A random mail survey was taken of 300 students at the University of Virginia and 700 adult residents of Charlottesville, Virginia.[25] Fourteen percent of the townspeople and 25 percent of the students claimed at least one out-of-the-body experience. This result fits in with other surveys.

There seems little reason to doubt that the OBE is a real experience. The issue is how to understand it. If it is, as it is described in psychiatric terms, a "complex psychosensorial hallucinatory perception of one's own body projected into the external visual space" or if it is an altered state of consciousness in which imagination and memory are at work, then the OBE is not a paranormal phenomenon and has no bearing on the survival question.[26]

But if it is a genuine separation of some conscious and remembering part of the physical organism, it would be of enormous importance to the central teachings of Christianity, African religions, Judaism, Hinduism, and Islam because it would tend to show that the human being may possess a soul or spiritual self.

Would it be important for the survival problem as evidence of survival? People who have had the OBE are convinced that their souls are immortal. Crookall writes that if "astral projection is true and soul is distinct from body, survival is to be expected."[27] Many parapsychologists, however, cannot bring themselves to agree. The OBE is not convincing survival evidence to them because, although it may be true and may indicate the existence of an independent conscious entity, the separation and functioning of this entity takes place while the physical body is alive and all its systems are functioning. The OBE may thus depend entirely on the life of the physical body. It may be that the death of the physical body would entail also the death of the entity whether consciousness at the time of death were separated from it or contiguous with it.[28]

Nevertheless, the OBE is indirect and important evidence of survival. Any experimental showing of the existence of an ecsomatic, observing, and conscious element capable of leaving, operating, and functioning independently of the physical body, even while the body is alive and well, would be a great stride forward in knowledge and would suggest the means by which survival after death might be realized.

A crucial question is: What real indications do we have of an objective separation from the physical body of such an element? Instances of an objective separation have been reported by witnesses. One is the classic Wilmot case in which S. R. Wilmot and a fellow-passenger traveling on a ship from Liverpool to New York saw the figure of Wilmot's wife enter their stateroom in her nightgown and walk to Wilmot's berth to kiss him. At the time, Mrs. Wilmot, who confirmed that she had left her body and crossed the sea to visit her husband in his cabin, was physically in Connecticut.[29] Other instances of witnesses claiming to have observed another person during an OBE are given in the parapsychological literature.[30]

In further support of the objective separation during an OBE of an observing component of the physical body, parapsychologists have collected and presented cases in which extrasensory information was obtained during the OBE. For example, after Mr. De Forest tried to project himself into the apartment of a young lady friend, he found himself in a strange apartment, saw wallpaper with a green leaf design on it, went through a doorway and saw a girl sleeping on a divan with a bandanna on her head. The details of the apartment he described and in which he had never been were confirmed by the girl who, at the time of his alleged OBE, had been asleep on a divan with her hair up and a bandanna on her head.[31]

The latest attempts to detect the presence of an objective element of the human body during an OBE have been made in a laboratory setting. Using a subject who claimed the ability to induce an OBE, Robert Morris, a parapsychologist, arranged for an experiment in which the subject was to visit a location one-half mile from the subject's room. In this location animals, human beings, and mechanical devices were set up. The subject's task was to make himself known to the animals or human beings and to affect the apparatus while he was out-of-the-body. The human detectors were not told when any OBE was to take place. During the periods when OBEs were claimed, the most promising results were with a kitten. During the OBE, it became very quiet and did not meow at all in contrast to the control non-OBE periods when it was very active and meowed 37 times.[32]

In a more recent experiment, a psychic was to induce an OBE and, in that state, go to a room in which he was to perceive certain target pictures. In order to do so, he had to look through a viewing window in such a way that his OBE component would be located within a shielded chamber. Equipment, which consisted of sensor plates suspended from metal strips, had been installed in the chamber. Attached to the strips were strain gauges capable of detecting any movement in the sensor plates in the area in front of the viewing window. When the subject was supposed to be having his OBE and was correctly describing the target pictures, the sensor plates became active, and they were significantly more active when there were hits on the targets than when there were misses.[33] In the words of one of the experimenters: "This suggests to us not only that there is a physical effect at the location to which [the subject] projects when he is out-of-body, but that the out-of-body experience might be a fluctuating process, e.g., that there are times when a person might be more out-of-body (for example, during hits on visual targets) than he is at other times (during misses)."[34]

Additional data are badly needed to support the objectivity of the out-of-the-body experience and the interesting possibility that an OBE projection may be more complete at times and less so at other times. These data may be supplied as new experimental approaches, inspired by the present findings, are tried in the future.

Visions of the Dying The out-of-the-body experience is closely related to the visionary experiences of persons on the verge of death but who did not die and to such experiences of dying patients who actually died. It seems to be a characteristic of these experiences. A recent study has shown that about 37 percent of the people who have had near-death experiences have had the sense of detachment from the physical body.[35] A number of dying patients also described an OBE.[36] For convenience, we shall consider together both near-death experiences and the visions of terminally ill patients because the findings of researchers investigating both kinds of cases are very similar.

Raymond Moody, Jr., conducted interviews of people who were resuscitated after having been believed or declared dead by medical personnel or had verged on death because of sickness, accident, or injuries.[37] He found a striking similarity among the accounts and was able to pick out many recurring elements. One chief element was meeting deceased persons who came to help. In Moody's words, quite a few people told him that at some point after they thought they had separated from their physical bodies, "they became aware of the presence of other spiritual beings in their vicinity, beings who apparently were there to ease them through their transition into death."[38] Kenneth Ring, a Professor of Psychology at the University of Connecticut, analyzed the cases of people who recounted near death experiences. He found eight who reported seeing the spirits of the dead, generally relatives whom they recognized.[39] Another common element in the accounts studied by Moody was the encounter with a very bright light or a "being of light."[40]

Karlis Osis and Erlendur Haraldsson, two parapsychologists, reported research they had done with terminally ill patients.[41] Their research was based on questionnaires sent to doctors and nurses. A pilot study made first by Osis in America led to a transcultural analysis through another study by Osis in America and a similar one by the two parapsychologists in India. Questions were asked specifically about patients who had reported seeing apparitions. The common element found, which harmonized with Moody's and Ring's findngs, was that dying patients saw people that others around the patients could not see. Of the sample studied, 91 percent identified the apparitions as dead relatives of the patients.[42] In one case, an American cancer patient, entirely clear and rational otherwise, seemed to see another world. "He would look up at the wall, eyes and face would brighten up as if he saw a person—he'd speak of the light and brightness. He saw people who seemed real to him, said 'Hello,' and 'there's my mother.' He gestured, stretched out his hands after it was over, closed his eyes and seemed very peaceful.[43]

The purpose of the apparitions reported in the cases of the dying patients echoed what nearly dying people had told Moody and Ring. The purpose was to "take the patient away" and to act as helpers to guide the patients to another world. One such case involved an eleven-year-old girl who was dying of heart disease:

"She was having another bad episode with her heart, and said that she saw her mother in a pretty white dress and that her mother had one just like it for her [the patient]. She was very happy and smiling, told me to let her get up and go over there—her mother was ready to take her on a trip."[44] The girl died four hours later.

In addition to relatives, terminally ill patients saw religious figures. Christians saw Jesus and the Virgin Mary, Hindus saw Yama, the god of death, or Krishna, one of Yama's messengers.[45]

Another element in the cases of the dying was the way that they reacted to the "take away" apparitions. Despite pain and melancholy, they reacted positively. The sensation was one of elation or serenity.[46] Similarly, in Ring's analysis of near-death experiences, 60 percent of the people he interviewed had such profound sensations of peace and contentment that it was impossible for them to describe their feelings.[47] Of the dying patients, 72 percent wanted to accompany the apparitions.[48]

This kind of evidence of survival makes sense. If survival after death in another world is a reality, then it seems reasonable to expect that close relatives or religious figures would be there to greet us and to act as our guides. The experience should also be accompanied by the greatest feelings of peace and joy. Nevertheless, it does not make sense to regard as survival evidence the reports of their experiences by patients who verged on death or the reports of the experiences of actually dying patients unless other possible causes for these experiences can be excluded. It is possible that both classes of experiences can be explained on naturalistic grounds; that is, there may be good psychological, physiological, or pharmacological reasons that can be given for them. Religious beliefs, wishful thinking, or medications such as morphine might easily facilitate the experiences. Other important medical factors are disturbance of brain function and cerebral anoxia, which are known causes of hallucinations and which probably occur in nearly dying and dying patients before they sink into unconsciousness.

Although the two classes of experiences would seem to corroborate one another, the important issue concerning this type of apparitional experience remains whether it is simply an hallucination unrelated to reality or whether it is a genuine perception of another reality in which components of deceased persons have persisted after death. Until this issue is resolved, the near-death experience would not seem to qualify as survival evidence. We cannot extrapolate from this experience what may actually happen after death. The

Survival Research Foundation, however, is now engaged in systematic efforts to collect data for this class of case, which may help clarify and resolve this crucial issue.

The apparitional phenomena occurring in the experiences of terminally ill patients may stand on a better footing as evidence, however, because of the contentions of Osis and Haraldsson that they have excluded medical and other possibilities and that patients who are dying and actually die become more aware than others of another world and the beings who inhabit it. Their approach was to divide hallucinations into three classes: of living people, of dead ones, and of religious figures. It was reasoned that hallucinations of living people would not have anything to do with survival after death but that visions of the dead and of religious figures might. The two researchers set out to compare the hallucinations of normally healthy people with those of dying people. On the basis of 877 cases, they found that 83 percent of the terminally ill patients in the American sample and 79 percent of those in the Indian had visions connected with survival after death. Only 17 percent in the American sample and 21 percent in the Indian sample had visions of living people, which would relate to this world and not to another. With regard to the hallucinations of people in good health, in one survey 32 percent of them had visions of dead or religious figures and in another survey only 22 percent had such visions. In one survey, 67 percent and in another, 78 percent, had visions of living people but which had no bearing on another world. In other words, the data collected seem to show a great preponderance of survival-related visions of dead people and religious figures in the experiences of terminally ill patients as compared to normally healthy persons. These data may imply that, when people are really dying and do die, death may allow them to get a clearer glimpse of a postmortem world and that they may be able to see spirits or beings who exist there better than those people who are healthy or come close to death but do not die. The researchers stated as their conclusion: "This evidence strongly suggests life after death—more strongly than any other alternative hypothesis can explain the data."[49]

"Drop-In" Communicators As shown by Saul's visit to the woman at Endor in order to reach the dead Samuel (1 Samuel 28:3–19), spirit communications through mediums are one of the ancient and traditional forms of communicating with the dead. Some of the best survival evidence in the history of parapsychology has come

from mediums such as Mrs. Piper, the medium from Boston who was considered to be the greatest medium of her era. Richard Hodgson, who managed the American Society for Psychical Research after its founding, was a sceptic when he began his sittings with her. But when communications were received through Mrs. Piper from his dead friend, George Pelham (a pseudonym), Hodgson wrote a lengthy report in which he expressed the belief that the medium had received genuine communications from the spirit of his friend "G. P."[50]

That was back in 1897. Mediumistic evidence has lost much of its force since then, however. It has been undermined by the argument that mediums possess almost limitless telepathic powers to acquire facts about the dead from the minds of the living who know the information and that mediums also possess equally limitless clairvoyant powers to "read" documents in which the information communicated is written. This argument, which Professor Hornell Hart named the "Super ESP" theory, can be explained more concretely in this way: If a medium conveys to us facts relating to a dead person, which the medium could not have known normally, e.g., the deceased John Doe liked to take pictures, this information is worthless as survival evidence unless it can be corroborated.[51] In order for it to be corroborated, some living persons must know that John Doe had an affinity for picture-taking or there must be a record somewhere to this effect. If, after enlisting the help of the CIA, British Intelligence, and the KGB, and employing our own sleuths to locate such sources of information, we discover that John Doe's third cousin living on a remote Pacific Island can corroborate the fact reported about Mr. Doe, or, failing the discovery of the cousin, there is brought to our attention an advertisement in the yellow pages of a 1956 telephone directory that reads: "John Doe: Your photographer for weddings and bar mitzvahs" and that also corroborates the reported fact, we have given the evidence a value it did not have before; but we have also given life to the Super ESP theory. We would find ourselves in what has been called "the typical Catch-22 situation; the moment you have succeeded you have failed."[52]

A great weakness of the Super ESP theory is that it goes far beyond the experimental data because such unlimited ESP powers have never been demonstrated by research. But it is a theory many parapsychologists find more acceptable than a theory of survival after death because we have good evidence that ESP exists but not such good evidence that the spirits of dead people do.[53] The Super ESP theory is a monster that waits at every turn for those seeking survival evidence. The first effort made to skirt it was to try to eliminate the possibility that a family member or friend who knew about the life of a deceased person was with a medium at the time of an alleged communication. This attempt consisted of substituting for the family or friend some person or "proxy" who had no knowledge of any details about the dead person's life and who was merely acting on behalf of the family or friend and trying to get information from a deceased communicator. Many proxy sittings were held, some of which supplied impressive material, but the Super ESP theory turned out to be resourceful and flexible.[54] It was now stretched to suppose that mediums had used their ESP to work through the proxy to the family or friend who had requested the sitting. A new strategy was required. So later a whole series of people was interposed between the medium and the original sources of information in order to create multiple barriers for the medium's ESP and to obtain evidence that would point more clearly to a dead person and not any living person as the source of information.[55] But this brave effort really to strain the Super ESP theory produced no positive results worthy of note.

The latest attempt made to thwart the "Super ESP" monster, however, has produced survival evidence that does merit serious consideration. It consists of "drop-in" communicators: deceased persons not only unknown both to the medium and persons present, but obviously, in contrast to proxy sittings in which the dead are sought on behalf of absent family members or friends anxious for their appearance, in the cases of the "drop-ins" uninvited and unexpected.

Alan Gauld has reported ten drop-in communicators whose statements about their lives have been verified.[56] One of these cases was that of "Harry Stockbridge" who was known neither to anyone sitting with the medium nor to the medium. He said that he had been a Second Lieutenant in the Northumberland Fusiliers and that he had been killed on July 14, 1916. His unit had been a Tyneside Scottish battalion. He described himself as tall, dark, thin and said he liked to frequent Leicester. Very evidential statements like these were verified by Stockbridge's relatives who had no prior contact with the medium or the sitters.[57]

In addition to Gauld's reports, Stevenson recently reported another drop-in case of a communicator named Robert Passanah, who gave details about his life that could be corroborated and Stevenson added that he had collected 60 more such cases.[58]

These cases are an important class of survival evidence because they seem to corner the Super ESP monster, which must now be forced to defend itself by explaining (a) why the medium's ESP came to focus specifically on special communicators, like Harry Stockbridge, who have made an appearance; (b) how, without the least clues to go on, the medium's ESP has been able to range over the world to locate the minds of living people who knew information relevant to the particular communicator as well as to locate this information amid veritable mountains of papers, such as newspaper obituaries and death and other records; (c) how the medium's ESP has been able further to sift through these sources of information and pick out just those specific details relating to the particular communicator; and (d) how the medium's ESP has been able to assemble all these details on the spot into an intelligible message seeming to come from a human intelligence.

But the drop-ins, although bringing out the numerous faults of the Super ESP theory, have a built-in fault of their own. The one fact that tends to undermine them is that all the details relative to drop-in communicators were corroborated in the past and will be corroborated in the future only because some living person knew or will know them or some document attested or will attest to them. The Super ESP theory may be cornered by the drop-ins, but it will never be subdued by them. There always will exist in this class of cases sources of information on which this monster can feed and sustain its strength.

So another method of trying to subdue it is needed. This method, to be described in the next section has been designed and may point more clearly to information that has come telepathically from the mind of a deceased person rather than telepathically from the minds of living persons or clairvoyantly from documents in existence.

A Future Type of Survival Evidence

Objections to the value of mediumistic communications do not rest solely on the argument that facts may have been acquired by the medium's ESP, which has drawn them from the minds of living persons or from papers in which the relevant details are contained. Another objection is that some mediumistic communications purporting to have come from the dead have come from people who were very much alive and well at the time.[59] Moreover, communications seeming to have come from actual communicators have come from imaginary ones like "Philip" whom a group in Toronto invented.[60] In the light of these objections, before mediumistic evidence can be accepted, we must make fairly sure that no existing sources could have furnished the medium's ESP with facts pertinent to a deceased person purporting to communicate and that the communicator is a real person who once lived and died and is not a "thought form" of sitters who have conceived the communicator in their fervid imaginations.

A large-scale, long-term, worldwide research program to render these objections less tenable and to obtain stronger survival evidence in the near and distant future is now underway and has attracted considerable attention in Great Britain,[61] on the Continent, and in America.[62,63] (The Survival Research Foundation, P.O. Box 8565, Pembroke Pines, Florida 33084, U.S.A., is conducting this program and invites participation in it.)

Those participating in the program and interested in producing better survival evidence for scientific, religious or personal reasons, merely arrange posthumous experiments with the intention of communicating after death certain specific information. These experiments consist of a dictionary test I have designed[64] and other cipher and lock tests.[65] In these tests, key words known only to the persons arranging the experiments and not recorded in any way are used to encipher test messages or to set locks. The test message, undecipherable without the key, or the test lock, which cannot be opened without it, are left with the Survival Research Foundation. It is these keys that the persons expect to communicate posthumously. Psychics attempt by telepathy to obtain the keys from these persons while they are alive. If they do not succeed during the participant's lifetime, but, after death, the keys that decipher messages or open locks should be communicated through a medium they could not be attributed to any "thought form" of the experimenters at the Survival Research Foundation and could not be explained as having come from any existing sources of telepathic or clairvoyant knowledge. Any mediumistic communication that resulted in the deciphering of a test message or in the opening of a lock would constitute excellent empirical evidence of the survival of the person who left the message or lock. And if message-deciphering or lock-opening keys should be communicated and imprinted on a tape during electronic experiments, they could not be attributed to the subconscious minds of the experimenters or explained as the result of psychokinesis. The receipt of keys in this way also would point to the personal indentities of the communicators.

The aim of the program is to see whether multiple successful experiments using mediums and tape recorders can be conducted. Such successes would be formidable objective survival evidence.

Conclusion

A recent cartoon showed two prisoners spreadeagled and manacled six feet above their dungeon floor. Their situation was quite hopeless. Nevertheless, one prisoner says to the other, "Look, I've got this idea. . . ." The survival problem has placed researchers in a similar position. Yet they have not given up. They keep getting ideas and collecting evidence to try to solve the problem.

Not one type of the latest evidence they have collected, or all types together have decisively solved or come close to solving it. In every case the evidence must be considered simply prima facie, that is, it may allow an inference of survival but does not compel it.

But even before this inference can be made, these types of evidence must pass a series of tests to our satisfaction.

It is apparent that these tests are analagous to the canons of evidence applied in a court of law. Indeed, the philosopher Broad once commented that "the best type of investigator for this purpose [of appraising paranormal phenomena] would be a person with the training of a judge or a police magistrate."[66] And Stevenson wrote that for decades parapsychologists have used the methods of lawyers.[67]

If these tests are passed so that an experience or event is entitled to the status of survival evidence, then its acceptance is another matter. Materialists and corporealists, although with little justification, probably will go on offering the same kind of resistance to it that the professor displayed when his student brought him a shell that did not fit into his scheme of things. But such evidence and its investigation should be accorded the most serious attention by all who take a dualistic view of the human being as a compound of a physical body and another element like the soul or spiritual self. If dualists are of a scientific or philosophic turn of mind, they will realize that no science or philosophy that leaves out of account evidence that human survival after death may be a reality can stand for long. If dualists affirm religious convictions and ties, they may have even stronger motives for being open and sympathetic to survival investigation and evidence since, as mentioned, such investigation and evidence may verify and reinforce their hopes and beliefs for a future life.

NOTES

1. Ernest Becker, *The Denial of Death* (New York, The Free Press, 1973).

2. Woody Allen quoted in Herman Feifel, "Death in Contemporary America," in *New Meanings of Death* (New York, McGraw Hill, 1977).

3. C. J. Ducasse, "Some Questions Concerning Psychical Phenomena," *Journal of the American Society for Psychical Research* 48 (1954) p. 3–20.

4. See chap. 13.

5. William James, *The Will to Believe and Other Essays in Popular Philosophy and Human Immortality* (New York, Dover Publications, 1956). *The Will to Believe* first published in 1897, *Human Immortality* in 1898, pp. 303–4.

6. Alan Gauld and A. D. Cornell, *Poltergeists* (London: Routledge and Kegan Paul, 1979).

7. William G. Roll, *The Poltergeist* (Metuchen, N.J.: Scarecrow Press, 1976).

8. Hans Bender, "New Developments in Poltergeist Research," in William G. Roll, R. L. Morris, and J. D. Morris, eds., *Proceedings of the Parapsychological Association* (1969), 6 Duke Station, N.C., pp. 81–102.

9. D. J. West, *Psychical Research Today* (London: Gerald Duckworth Co., 1954).

10. Arthur S. Berger, Joyce Berger, and William G. Roll, "A Poltergeist in Durham" in William G. Roll and John Beloff, eds., *Research in Parapsychology 1980* (Metuchen, N.J.: Scarecrow Press, 1981), pp. 57–58.

11. Karis Osis and Donna McCormick, "A Poltergeist Case Without an Identifiable Living Agent," *Journal of the American Society for Psychical Research* 76 (1982), pp. 23–51.

12. Walter F. Prince, "Additional Notes on Two Books," *Journal of the American Society for Psychical Research* 14 (1920), p. 615–626.

13. Walter F. Prince, "Additional Notes on Two Books," p. 622.

14. D. Scott Rogo and Raymond Bayless, *Phone Calls from the Dead* (New York: Berkley Publishing Co., 1979).

15. Raymond Bayless, "Correspondence," *Journal of the American Society for Psychical Research* 53 (1959), pp. 35–38.

16. Konstantin Raudive, *Breakthrough,* (New York, Taplinger Publishing Co., 1971).

17. Peter Bander, *Voices from the Tapes,* (New York: Drake Publishers, 1973), p. 9.

18. David J. Ellis, *The Mediumship of the Tape Recorder* (Pulborough, West Sussex, England: D. J. Ellis, 1978).

19. Ian Stevenson, *Twenty Cases Suggestive of Reincarnation* (New York: American Society for Psychical Research, 1966) 2nd rev. ed., (Charlottesville, VA: University Press of Virginia, 1974).

20. Ian Stevenson, *Cases of the Reincarnation Type,* vol. 1, *Ten Cases in India* (Charlottesville, VA: University Press of Virginia, 1975).

21. Ian Stevenson, *Cases of the Reincarnation Type,* p. 165.

22. Stevenson, p. 168.

23. Robert Crookall, *The Study and Practice of Astral Projection* (Hyde Park, N.Y.: University Books, 1960).

24. Robert Crookall, *More Astral Projections* (London: Aquarian Press, 1964).

25. John Palmer, "A Community Mail Survey of Psychic Experiences," *Journal of the American Society for Psychical Research* 73 (1979), pp. 221–51.

26. N. Lukianowicz quoted in Nils O. Jacobson, *Life Without Death?,* English Translation Sheila La Farge, (New York: Dell Publishing Co., 1973), p. 98.

27. Robert Crookall, *More Astral Projections,* p. 12.

28. C. J. Ducasse, *A Critical Examination of the Belief in a Life after Death* (Springfield, IL: Charles C. Thomas, 1961), p. 164.

29. Frederick W. H. Myers, *Human Personality and its Survival of Bodily Death,* 2 vols. (London: Longmans, Green & Co., 1903) vol. 2, pp. 682–5.

30. Hornell Hart, "Six Theories about Apparitions," *Journal of the American Society for Psychical Research* 50 (1956), pp. 153–239.

31. Hornell Hart, "ESP Projection: Spontaneous Cases and the Experimental Method," *Journal of the American Society for Psychical Research* 4 (1954), pp. 123–46.

32. Robert L. Morris, "PRF Research on Out-of-Body Experiences, 1973" *Theta* 41 (1974), pp. 1–3.

33. Karlis Osis and Donna McCormick, "Kinetic Effects at the Ostensible Location of an Out-of-Body Projection During Perceptual Testing," *Journal of the American Society for Psychical Research* 74 (1980), pp. 319–29.

34. Karlis Osis and Donna McCormick, "Current ASPR Research on Out-of-Body Experiences," *ASPR Newsletter* (1980), vol. 6, no. 4, pp. 21–22.

35. Kenneth Ring, *Life at Death: A Scientific Investigation of the Near-Death Experience* (New York: Coward, McCann & Geoghan, 1980).

36. Karlis Osis and Erlendur Haraldsson, *At the Hour of Death* (New York: Avon Books, 1977), pp. 168–69, 178–79.

37. Raymond A. Moody, Jr., *Life after Life* (New York: Bantam Books, 1975).

38. Raymond A. Moody, Jr., *Life after Life,* p. 55.

39. Kenneth Ring, *Life at Death,* pp. 67–68.

40. Raymond A. Moody, Jr., *Life after Life,* pp. 58–59.

41. Karlis Osis and Erlendur Haraldsson, *At the Hour of Death*.

42. Karlis Osis and Erlendur Haraldsson, *At the Hour of Death*, p. 64.

43. Osis and Haraldsson.

44. Osis and Haraldsson, p. 67.

45. Osis and Haraldsson, p. 64.

46. Osis and Haraldsson, p. 69.

47. Kenneth Ring, *Life at Death*, p. 39.

48. Karlis Osis and Erlendur Haraldsson, *At the Hour of Death*, p. 67.

49. Osis and Haraldsson, p. 3.

50. Richard Hodgson, "A Further Record of Observations of Certain Phenomena of Trance," *Proceedings of the Society for Psychical Research* 13 (1897), pp. 284–582.

51. Hornell Hart, *The Enigma of Survival* (Springfield, IL: Charles C. Thomas, 1959).

52. William G. Roll, "The Catch-22 of Survival Research," *Theta* 6 (1978), (2, 3) p. 24.

53. Alan Gauld, "The Super-ESP Hypothesis, *"Proceedings of the Society for Psychical Research* 53 (1961), pp. 226–46.

54. C. Dayton Thomas, "A Proxy Case Extending over Eleven Sittings with Mrs. Osborne Leonard," *Proceedings of the Society for Psychical Research* 43 (1935), pp. 439–519.

55. Karlis Osis, "Linkage Experiments with Mediums," *Journal of the American Society for Psychical Research* 60 (1966), pp. 91–124.

56. Alan Gauld, "A Series of 'Drop-in' Communicators," *Proceedings of the Society for Psychical Research* 55 (1971), pp. 273–340.

57. Alan Gauld, "A Series of 'Drop-in' Communicators," pp. 322–27.

58. Ian Stevenson, "A Communicator Unknown to Medium and Sitters," *Journal of the American Society for Psychical Research* 64 (1970), pp. 53–65.

59. S. G. Soal, "A Report on Some Communications Received through Mrs. Blanche Cooper," *Proceedings of the Society for Psychical Research* 35 (1925), pp. 471–594.

60. Iris M. Owen and M. H. Sparrow, "Generation of Paranormal Physical Phenomena in Connection with an Imaginary 'Communicator'," *New Horizons* 1 (1974), pp. 6–13.

61. *Psychic News*, September 11, 1982, front page headline "Britain Joins US in New Survival Research Project;" *The Unexplained* 9, issue 8 (1982), "Key to the Afterlife?"; *ASSAP News* 3 (1982).

62. The general science magazine in America, *Omni* January 6, no. 4 (1984), "Codes from Beyond," p. 94.

63. Arthur S. Berger, "Better than a Gold Watch: The Work of the Survival Research Foundation," *Theta* 10, no. 4 (1982), pp. 82–84; "Project: Unrecorded Information," *The Christian Parapsychologist* 4 (1982), pp. 159–61.

64. Arthur S. Berger, "The Development and Replication of Tests for Survival," *Parapsychological Journal of South Africa* 5, no. 1 (1984), pp. 24–35.

65. Robert H. Thouless, "A Test for Survival," *Proceedings of the Society for Psychical Research* 48 (1948), pp. 253–63; Frank C. Tribbe, "The Tribbe/Mulders Code," *Journal of the Academy of Religion and Psychical Research* 3 (1980), pp. 44–46; Oan Stevenson, "The Combination Lock Test for Survival," *Journal of the American Society for Psychical Research* 62 (1968), pp. 246–54.

66. C. D. Broad, *Lectures on Psychical Research,* p. 9.

67. Ian Stevenson, *Twenty Cases Suggestive of Reincarnation,* p. 4.

15

Current Western Attitudes to Death and Survival

DAVID LORIMER

"No choice is uninfluenced by the way in which the personality regards its destiny, and the body its death. In the last analysis, it is our conception of death which decides our answers to all the questions that life puts to us. That is why it requires its proper place and time—if need be, with right of precedence. Hence, too, the necessity of preparing for it."—Dag Hammarskjold.[1]

In the turmoil of a disintegrating and transforming social scenario, Western man is struggling to come to terms with his own physical mortality in the light of spectacular technological progress; he is striving to formulate a coherent and constructive response to the limitations and possibilities of earthly existence. It is, therefore, timely, I think, to take stock of current Western positions on death and survival and to attempt to give some overall perspective to the debate. We can no longer afford to emulate the philosophical, emotional, or psychological ostrich. With our heads firmly embedded in the sand we are in fact a good deal more vulnerable than we realize.

Although I am principally concerned with Western attitudes, there has, of course, been a great increase in the knowledge and influence of Eastern cultures; these will invariably be touched on at various points in our discussion. Many factors must be taken into account in the consideration of our theme, so that I have divided my analysis into six sections: historical influences, cosmological views, the current philosophical positions on body, mind, and death, psychical research, the near-death experience, and finally the plethora of social factors.

Historical Influence

Since the present can only be fully appreciated as a creative outgrowth from the past, it is vital to understand the interplay and significance of the thoughts of our ancestors. At the end of *Man and His Destiny in the Great World Religions,* Brandon concludes:

If the civilisations of mankind thus represent the effort made for social and economic security, its religions signify an agelong quest for spiritual security. Conscious of the transitoriness of all phenomena, man is acutely aware that he too is subject to the disintegrating process of time and that the end of his present form of existence is inevitable. Consequently, by virtue of his constitutional inability, except in rare instances, to accept the prospect of personal annihilation, man instinctively seeks some state in which he will be secure from the everlasting menace of time's destructive logic. [2]

Brandon's observations are at once empirical and psychological: empirical in his capacity as a student of comparative religion, and psychological in that he makes a near-universal deduction about the human condition, implying a degree of wish-fulfillment that we shall encounter elsewhere. The conclusion of Frazer's three-volume study of immortality in primitive societies bears out the pattern suggested by Brandon:

It is impossible not to be struck by the strength, and perhaps we may say the universality, of the natural belief in immortality among the savage races of mankind. With them a life after death is not a matter of speculation and conjecture, of hope and fear; it is a practical certainty which the individual as little dreams of doubting as he doubts the reality of his own existence. [3]

Such certainty is based on a theory of a soul that separates itself from the body during dreams of illness, and is permanently severed from it at death. Survival is envisaged as a rather pallid persistence of the individual, who retains the trappings of his earthly social status; it was not unusual for servants to be buried along with their masters, so that service could be continued in the afterlife. [4]

The Old Testament and the early Greeks also believed in an attenuated form of existence beyond the grave. This was based on the analogy of declining physical strength; weakness in old age was extrapolated to a picture of shadowy enfeeblement, as depicted in Book 12 of Homer's Odyssey, where the denizens of the underworld are obliged to drink sheep's blood before having sufficient strength to communicate. In the Old Testament, there is the additional factor of Sheol being a place where the dead are cut off from God; they are left to lament the passing of their days on earth.

The psychology of the Orphics, Pythagoreans, and Platonists

was radically different. Far from glorifying the athletic prowess of youth and singing of the pleasures of a sensual existence, they regarded physical life as an exile, an imprisonment of the immortal soul in the cage of a mortal body. Death was considered as the soul's release from such cramping confines into a state where it would be possible to breathe more freely. Some commentators argue that these conceptions demonstrate the unmistakable influence of Eastern philosophy, especially since they include the ideas of karma and reincarnation.[5] In any event such a view is now widely disseminated in the West by numerous groups including Theosophists and Anthroposophists. We shall also see how it constitutes the basis of the modern dualist position on the mind–body problem, although without the religious overtones that continued in the Christian Platonic tradition.

The key event in the New Testament is, of course, the resurrection, prefigured in Ezekiel at a time when there was a growing sense of individual destiny and hence personal moral responsibility reflected in the crystallization of some kind of postmortem judgment. Christian eschatology is developed in the Gospels, the letters of Paul (notably 1 Corinthians 15), and in Revelation. In the gospels there is the resurrection of Jesus himself "the first fruits of the dead," the apparent vanquisher of death; in him existed the possibility of a similar triumph for his followers. Jesus himself enlarges on the theme of the Last Judgment with its decisive division of the sheep from the goats, of eternal bliss from everlasting torment, thus arousing the contrary emotions of longing and dread. Although Paul's terminology is confusing, he does anticipate that the dead will sleep until the Second Coming, at which point they will be roused by the last trump, judged, and subsequently consigned to heaven or hell. Revelation conjures up the majestic return of Christ as universal judge, a scene dramatically portrayed over the portals of so many French cathedrals.

The crude literal view of bodily resurrection came into collision with the Platonic idea of the immortality of the soul and gave rise to numerous acrimonious disputes. On the one hand, theologians like Tertullian (with Augustine, Aquinas, Luther, and Calvin following in his footsteps) argued that with God all things were possible, and that if he had created the world out of nothing and reconstituted the phoenix from its ashes, the bodily resurrection of man would be the work of a moment. On the other hand, Origen, more sympathetic to the Platonic scheme, maintained that the idea of resurrection was preposterous and unreasonable. One more general observation can be made of both conceptions, regardless of their form: that they presuppose the final vindication of earthly injustices through divine intervention and retribution.

In the Atomists, such as Democritus and Epicurus, we encounter for the first time a systematic materialism. We find in Lucretius the fullest exposition of this philosophy, which anticipates the arguments of Hume and twentieth-century identity theorists. The Atomists observed that the difference between a live body and a dead one was the absence of breath and heat; they therefore conceived of a soul consisting of atoms of air and fire. From here is but a short step to asserting the nonexistence of such an ethereal substance, especially in the light of the close correlation between the physical body and mental states. Lucretius concludes that, with the loss of air and heat from the body, there can be no sensation and therefore "no other self to remain in life and lament to self that his own self has met death."[6]

The pivotal philosopher of the scientific outlook is Descartes, who, significantly, was a mathematician as well. He shifted the focus away from God to man and tried to start his reasonings from a bedrock of certainty, which, by definition, is only attainable in mathematical calculation and abstraction. It is ironic that although neither Descartes nor Newton were materialists, their philosophies were among the most powerful impulses in this direction: no man can know what use his successors will make of his theory. Descartes conceived of mind as immaterial and unextended interacting with matter, which is extended in space. More importantly still, he regarded the body as a complicated machine and animals as automata. Subsequent concentration on quantifiable external aspects of the universe gradually eroded the primacy of mind, so that it was widely regarded as completely dependent on the body and brain, hence perishing with it. By stressing the common features and origin of men and animals, Darwin encouraged the extension to man of the Cartesian contention of the body as a machine. Monod is one of the most articulate modern proponents of this theory, explaining evolution simply in terms of Chance and Necessity.[7]

Marx and Lenin adopted materialism in their scheme of secular salvation, using Darwin as a court of appeal. For them it was clear that without what Marx called "the tedious notion of personal immortality," there was no sense in investing hope outside time. Hence all hopes had to be centered on a desacralized paradise on earth in the future. If Marx followed Smith in attributing pride of place to economic motives, Watson and Freud pursued another line. Watson's model of human behavior was based on the mechanical stimulus-response model of causality. Freud, for his part, advanced a theory of motivation stressing the central importance of sexuality and childhood experiences. From his experiences of wish fulfillment in dreams, he deduced that the desire for immortality was itself a form of wish fulfillment, a childish illusion, which did not merit the serious attention of a rational man; it was a hangover from a bygone age of superstition—man should now stand on his own feet instead of resorting to psychological crutches. The anthropologist Malinowski shared Freud's opinion and analyzed the beliefs of primitive societies in this light. This proudly self-sufficient pose is still popular among materialist rationalists who like to see themselves as the vanguard of progressive thought, but it confuses psychology with logic. The desire for immortality has no bearing on the question of its truth or falsehood.

Cosmological Shifts

The etymology of the word "concept" is revealing: in Latin it means "to seize with," a tool used to organize and classify our knowledge and perception. The word "perspective" implies a way of seeing, and, likewise, the word "theory" is derived from the Greek *theorein* meaning to see. All these words come together in the overall term *Weltanschauung,* uneasily rendered into English as "world-view." "To have a *'Weltanschauung',"* claims Jung, "means to create a picture of the world and of oneself, to know what the world is and who I am."[8] Nor can we choose not to have a *Weltanschauung;* this would simply indicate that we were unaware of it, not that it did not exist. Jung goes on to make the important points that "the fatal error of every *Weltanschauung* so far has been that it claims to be an objectively valid truth and ultimately a kind of scientific evidence of this truth"; its basic error is "its remarkable tendency to pretend to be the truth of things themselves, whereas actually it is only a name which we give to things."[9] The abstraction of one aspect of the world is mistakenly assumed to correspond to the whole of reality.

A corollary of the fixed *Weltanschauung* is the rigid manner in which it assimilates new contents into the framework of the existing theory, even if this procedure requires some Procrustean mental contortions. Such a tendency was noticed by Bacon over 300 years ago and has resulted in some notable bigotry and resistance to new theories:

The human understanding, when any proposition has once been laid down (either from general admission or belief, or from the pleasure it affords) forces everything else to add fresh support and confirmation; and although most cogent and abundant instances may exist to the contrary, yet either does not observe or despises them, or gets rid of or rejects them by some distinction, with violent and injurious prejudice, rather than sacrifice the authority of its first conclusions."[10]

This inherent conservative tendency of what James and Jung would call "apperception"—the assimilation of new material to existing thought patterns—creates violent clashes and upheaval at the crisis of a "paradigm shift."[11]

The medieval Christian *Weltanschauung* placed God at the center of metaphysics, with man and the earth at the center of the universe. Human life possessed a context and a significance in the vast divine plan. Death was the gateway to another life, whether of the blessed or the damned. Although it was regarded as a misfortune (the French word *malheur* indicating a connection with evil), Christianity was able to explain suffering, sin, and death through the all-embracing dogma of original sin.[12] Ariès delineates two stages of what he calls "tame death" associated with medieval Christian society. The first he characterizes by the phrase *"et moriemur"* pointing to "the familiar resignation to the collective destiny of the species."[13] The second develops out of the first and is typified by *"la mort de soi,"* a move towards the individual dimension of the collective fate. At both stages death is familiar rather than remote, it is not hushed up or wrapped in awestruck secrecy. The deathbed scene involved a public ceremony presided over by the dying person himself. It was very important that he should retain the initiative and remain the active central figure in the process. Later emphasis on the individual brought into play the ideas of postmortem judgment and death as a final and critical test without, however, robbing the dying of their dignity. It seems that the horror of physical death was absent, although there was a fear of hell and of being buried alive.[14]

The essence of the Cartesian-Newtonian *Weltanschauung* was its emphasis on the individual particle or unit. Even if political and scientific developments have tended to reduce the significance of the individual in relation to the size of society and the universe, he remained the basic building block. Here Ariès discerns a new pattern, which culminates in the modern notion of "forbidden death." Preoccupation moves from *"la mort de soi"* to *"la mort de toi,"* the death of the other. Death is exalted and dramatized, it is represented as a break, a rape, or a tearing away of the living into the realms of the dead; the Grim Reaper avidly pursues and eventually corners his quarry. The death of the other is unacceptable, the occesion for much sorrow, regret, and anger experienced by the bereft survivor. The emerging importance of the survivor had profound implications for the way in which the dying person was treated. The initiative gradually passed from the individual to his family, who started expressing themselves on his behalf, encroaching on his role and hence on his dignity. The familiarity of death recedes in front of triumphant scientific advance, retreating into the hospital where a hushed silence descends to muffle any untimely outcry. (The current position will be more extensively treated in the sixth section of this chapter.)

Current Philosophical Positions

The modern debate revolves around the exact nature of the relationship of consciousness to the brain. There are two mutually exclusive theories: the monistic materialist hypothesis following in the trail of Lucretius and Hume, and the dualist interactionist view deriving from Plato and Descartes.

The materialist central state or identity theory is popular among philosophers of mind. It asserts that mental states correspond with brain processes, and that brain and mind are consequently different aspects of a unity that language has unfortunately distorted. Frequent swipes of Occam's razor are made at dualist opponents who attempt to defend their position. Proponents of the identity theory appeal to close correlations between the chemical effect of drugs and alcohol on the brain and consciousness, suggesting that no distinction need be drawn; and in brain damage, consciousness seems to be permanently impaired. Psychic phenomena are by and large ignored or explained away. It is quite clear, according to this view, that consciousness is produced by the brain; there is therefore no reason to suppose that it will survive bodily dissolution. It is a curious feature that this viewpoint is shared by those who still believe in bodily resurrection on the grounds that the Bible insists that the whole man is remade, and that a nonphysical body is inconceivable and unidentifiable.

The dualist/interactionist approach has been most vigorously defended by Popper and Eccles.[15] Not all of its supporters are convinced that consciousness does survive bodily death, but the theory is certainly compatible with such a possibility. Among early supporters of the theory in its modern form at the turn of the century were the philosophers James, Bergson, and Schiller. They did not deny the dependence of consciousness on the brain but argued that the crucial point was the nature of such a functional dependence—was it productive, as maintained by the identity theorists above, or could it be transmissive? Bergson saw the brain as a kind of telephone exchange, which filtered, selected, and even on occasion obstructed messages from the mind. Arguments about the effects of drugs or brain damage were equally explicable on the basis of the transmission theory—the instrument was affected more or less drastically so that it was impossible to express the messages adequately or clearly. Neuroscientists Sherrington and Penfield subscribed to this view,[16] and a variant has been developed by Pribram.[17] Among psychologists, Burt and Jung outlined similar theories, and among prominent philosophers, Price and Broad.[18] Many of the above-named are past presidents of the Society for Psychical Research, whose investigations over the past hundred years have furnished a great deal of material indicating the possibility of consciousness operating independently of the brain; indeed, many cases, if taken at face value, can only be coherently explained by such a hypothesis, unless one resorts to the all-encompassing Super ESP theory in a desperate bid to shore up the crumbling materialist edifice.

Psychical Research

The Society for Psychical Research was founded by a group of Cambridge intellectuals in 1882 with the aim of investigating in a detached and thorough fashion reports of experiences ostensibly inexplicable in terms of the then-current mechanistic framework. One of the first significant productions was the 1886 *Phantasms of the Living,* in which over 700 cases of telepathy, clairvoyance, hallucinations, and apparitions were scrupulously examined, involving hundreds of exhaustive interviews with the experiencers and others implicated in the instances cited. The authors excluded or relegated to an appendix any cases on which some doubt might be cast, and went to great lengths to analyze possible alternative explanations and prevent fraud. The cumulative weight of evidence convinced them of the genuine occurrence of the phenomena under consideration. Reactions to the book ranged from the credulous through the discriminating to the sceptically incredulous, and were typical of the range of opinion elicited by such books even today. Since, by definition, no cast-iron certainty is attainable in this field owing to the anecdotal nature of the material, the reliability of the witnesses, and the unrepeatability of the cases in question, the sceptic can always logically invoke fraud or self-deception, even where this seems highly unlikely. A refined justification of scepticism can be found in the concept of antecedent probability, by which the probability of an occurrence is measured against the knowledge that is held to be reasonably certain. Thus, a man who believes that all information must come through the senses will put at zero the probability of any case of extrasensory perception. Any explanation whatever, even fraud and self-deception on a hitherto unimaginable scale, is less unlikely than such an eventuality. It is easy to see that we are back with the problem of a closed *Weltanschauung,* which forgets that it represents an abstraction of reality rather than reality itself. We cannot set predetermined boundaries on what may or may not occur and why.

Apart from the out-of-body experiences, and apparitions of the dead and the living investigated by the early researchers, the principal source of evidence indicating the possible survival of consciousness has been mediumistic communications purporting to originate from those beyond the grave. Disagreement over the interpretation of such messages and the ostensible identity of the communicators has been even more widespread than over other phenomena. Five broad categories of explanations can be distinguished: fraud and deception, multiple personality, clairvoyance or telepathy in association with the sitter, retrocognition combined with Super ESP, and the spiritualistic explanation, which accepts the phenomena at face value. A full discussion of the competing hypotheses falls outside the scope of this chapter, but a few observations are in order. One needs to guard against the tendency to interpret all cases in the light of one particular theory, since there are indications that all five approaches are appropriate in certain instances. Some forms of direct voice mediumship are inadequately accounted for by fraud or multiple personality, where the voice is known to the sitter but completely unknown to the medium (although theoretically this might be a fraud perpetrated by a discarnate entity). In some instances there is no sitter, so that telepathy and clairvoyance are eliminated. In the best documented cases, the Super ESP hypothesis is the only plausible alternative to the spiritualistic interpretation. Each person must then make an assessment of the probabilities for himself.[19] The conundrum that many investigators reach has been neatly expressed by Murphy, who claimed that the evidence could not be by-passed, nor could conviction be achieved. James thought that the Almighty had tantalizingly arranged for the subject to remain baffling, while Broad, after a lifetime's careful thought and research, felt that he would be more annoyed than surprised to find himself surviving death. Among thorough investigators who reached a negative conclusion was Dodds, while Hart, whose *Enigma of Survival* remains a classic, comes down conclusively in favor of survival.[20]

Near-Death Experiences

Since the publication of Moody's *Life after Life* in 1975, the near-death experience (NDE) has emerged as a study in its own right, where it had previously been classified as a special case of an out-of-body experience.[21]

Technically the experience is a by-product of advances in resuscitation techniques. There is an International Association for Near-Death Studies in the United States, which has its own journal, *Anabiosis,* and other studies have appeared since Moody's pioneering work: one by Rawlings, with an evangelical leaning, and two more technical and scientific studies by Ring and Sabom.[22] The similarity of material in all of these studies cannot be written off as mere coincidence. Moody, Rawlings, and Ring describe a "core experience," which, if carefully analyzed, exhibits similar if not identical characteristics. A broad distinction has been drawn between the "autoscopic" and the "transcendental" experience. In the first kind, the patient has an out-of-body experience and may well hear himself pronounced dead by the doctor as well as witness events that take place while he is apparently unconscious. The deeper transcendental experience entails passing through a tunnel and emerging into the light, where the patient perhaps encounters an angelic being (possibly his higher self in a sense) and experiences a feeling of oneness with life as well as an insight into its ultimate meaning. At some point he decides to return to his physical body and once again "wakes up," often distressed to return from an ocean of peace and serenity to the racking pain of his accident or operation. Grof has done some fascinating work with terminal patients who were under the influence of LSD, which has precipitated an NDE exhibiting patterns typical of mysticism, birth, or initiation.[23]

The interpretation of NDE's must distinguish between the experiencer and the investigator or reader. For the experiencers the most common consequence is the removal of the fear of death and a conviction that they have had a preview of the transition. Those resuscitated who reported no experience did not change their attitude to death. One further significant shift tended to occur in the scale of values and priorities of experiencers: they were now less worried about material advancement of well-being and more concerned with spiritual knowledge and with loving their neighbors. This indicates both a philosophical and an ethical change. Many readers have been impressed by the coherence and cogency of the studies, especially when cases are accompanied by veridical perception of events that the person could not have known from the vantage point of a virtually dead body on a bed. Even those who put a wish fulfillment construction on the experiences cannot adequately account for this. As more studies of NDEs appear in the years to come, they can expect to play a growing part in attitudes to death and survival, in spite of the obvious fact that those who have been resuscitated have not actually died. When NDEs are taken in conjunction with postmortem mediumistic descriptions of the process of physical death, a strong argument for survival can be constructed.[24]

Socially Unacceptable Death

The reviewer who described death as "the one certain, inescapable and tragic event which comes equally to us all and makes us all equal when it comes" was making a more significant statement than he realized—especially with his choice of the word "tragic."[25] Newspapers loosely characterize violent deaths as tragic accidents, and in doing so hark back to the primitive notion that all death was in a sense accidental (unless deliberately caused by a sorcerer). The reality of their own death is as unreal to many people as the likelihood that they will contract some smoking-related disease or that they will be killed in an automobile accident—such events always happen to other people.

In formulating an attitude towards death and survival, there are many criteria and sources of information on which one can draw, some of which we have discussed in previous sections: philosophical or political convictions, scientific disciplines, religious traditions, and the phenomena of psychical research. Individuals may well incorporate more than one of these categories into their view. For the vast majority, however, none of these areas is relevant. Unless a death occurs in the family, they remain unconcerned about death and its implications and quite ignorant of data that might enable them to arrive at an informed opinion. Death is a temporary intrusion into their lives, a stone thrown into a pool that soon returns to its customary placidity; while those whose lives are profoundly affected, on the other hand, do not always know where to turn for help.

What are the characteristics of our society that make it so difficult for people to come to terms with death? The prevalence of secular ideologies such as Marxism and/or nationalism may have fired a small minority with an intense sense of purpose in striving towards the ideal society of the future, but such frameworks are unable to give a profound meaning to individual suffering. They are only able to hold out the prospect of a glittering future, which may have little relevance to the immediate concerns of the individual. The context of his life is limited to the space-time dimension; he is a speck in space, a dispensable cog in the advancing wheel of time. The tentacles of materialist utilitarianism reach out to the very fringes of society: your happiness will undoubtedly be increased (as if it were quantifiable in any case) by the possession of the latest gadget—and if you do not buy it, your status will decline. Consumerism claims to satisfy every present wish, urging the purchaser to make sacrifices towards acquiring the product, or enticing him with irresistible credit terms. Material preoccupations loom so large that they obscure the entire horizon and perspective, inflating the ego, and draining the natural sense of affinity and compassion for others. The rats press ahead. On our screens we are daily sickened by monstrous and deplorable acts of terrorism and violence, but we can switch them off. We unconsciously identify with our own soldiers in warfare, excusing their atrocities as necessary evils while roundly condemning those perpetrated by our evil-intentioned aggressive opponents. The nuclear sword of Damocles now hangs ominously over us; humanity is staring at itself in a mirror and does not relish the sight.

The threat provokes more often than not the same sense of helplessness, despair, and resignation that we experience in the face of death. The reverberations of the arms race have been accompanied by a crisis of economic confidence triggered by the oil price rise of 1973—the West has never quite recaptured the postwar euphoria. With increasing numbers of unemployed in our relatively affluent society, questions about the wider meaning of life assume greater importance. Death challenges the entire context.

Typical surveys of beliefs in a life after death estimate that between 30 and 40 percent of the respondents have no such expectation. We saw how in the Middle Ages death was a public ceremony over which the dying person would preside; then gradually how this initiative was wrested from him and how he was encouraged to play a more passive role than his surviving family (this shift applies mainly to the more wealthy families).[26] Meanwhile there arose a science whose aim was not to explain why but rather how—a science whose central tenets were prediction and control, and which achieved spectacular results in so many fields, including the medical. Allied to a utilitarian ethic it brought unheard of prosperity in its wake (together with the disadvantages noted above). Epidemics were subdued, infant mortality declined, longevity increased. But at the end of the road stood death—not any more the Grim Reaper, but the more insidious cancer and heart disease welling up from within rather than striking from without, unseen by-products of our way of life. What medicine could not control struck deep as failure, engendering a sense of guilt and inadequacy in the doctor. Death is discreetly denied, unnamable, a clammy invisible hand, forbidden territory, a morbid and unmentionable topic of conversation.

Slowly a conspiracy was formed against death, a great lie sprang up as a protective wall behind which timid human beings could cower, pretending that death was not camped outside. The genesis of the conspiracy has been vividly and brilliantly portrayed by Tolstoy in a series of short stories. It became customary for the doctor, not the priest, to assume the unpleasant responsibility of informing the patient that he would soon die. He was concerned to protect his own feelings and those of the patient and family; behind his obvious reluctance was "the love of the other, the fear of hurting him and depriving him of hope, the temptation of protecting him by leaving him in ignorance of his imminent end."[27] It is important here that the hope referred to is not transcendental but earthly; for the atheist this is the only hope allowed, one that can make death seem tragic and meaningless. Ariès gives a penetrating analysis of the progress of the conspiracy, a comedy in which life goes on as usual with everyone pretending that nothing has changed. The dying person is dominated by his family, becoming entirely dependent on them physically, emotionally, and psychologically: "The day will come when the dying will accept this subordinate position, whether he simply submits to it or actually desires it. When this happens—and this is the situation today—it will be assumed that it is the duty of the entourage to keep the dying man in ignorance of his condition."[28]

Their dissimulation, arising from their own unresolved attitudes to death, removes from the sick person most of the warning signs, which might enable him to prepare for the event; and when he eventually does find out, or when his own intuition prevails over the loving pretense, he is likely to feel betrayed and even more helpless or angry.

Ariès wryly remarks that Tolstoy's Ivan Ilyich would today have been sent to a hospital: "Perhaps he would have been cured, and there would be no novel."[29] Owing to the necessity of sophisticated equipment and highly trained personnel in modern medicine, death has for the most part been transferred to the hospital. This has had two far-reaching consequences, one for the patient and the other for the doctors. The patient, already in a dependent position vis-à-vis his family, now finds control of his fate diminished still further, except in so far as pain is removed. In extremis, he can be given sedatives, fed intravenously, and plugged into a life-support machine. At this point the doctors have to make an unenviable decision: when is it really impossible to resuscitate the patient or keep him alive? What, moreover, is the exact definition of death? Such dilemmas are rendered all the more acute if the doctor himself is a materialist with no belief in the possibility of survival. The doctor cannot control death itself but can influence the duration of dying, the point of admission of defeat and failure, the rejection and defensive depersonalization of the patient.

Evasion and denial are inevitably reflected in attitudes towards funerals and mourning. The most common complaint against the crematorium is that it is impersonal, even undignified. No sooner is one funeral over than the next procession is waiting outside. The body of the loved one moves along a production line, reduced to the contents of an urn. The substance has evaporated, the body has been radically nullified, effaced. One implication of this, noted by Ariès is that "cremation excludes a pilgrimage."[30] Few people care to visit an urn, while many would still tend a grave, and hence the memory of the deceased. Past rituals of mourning had served as a kind of social catharsis for the grief of the family. Certain procedures and visits were imposed and expected; and until the nineteenth century the tone was restrained. During this period, however, ostentatious mourning was not uncommon, often vulgarly out of proportion with real feelings, even if such a display did indicate that the death was unacceptable. Today, the pattern is one not simply of restraint but positive repression of emotion and grief: "too evident sorrow does not inspire pity but repugnance, it is the sign of mental instability or bad manners: it is morbid."[31] Mourning is shameful and solitary, it is a disease for which the family is put in quarantine. We look the other way.

The pioneering crusader against this attitude has been Elizabeth Kübler-Ross. When she began work with dying patients in the 1960s, it was in the teeth of great suspicion and hostility. Her efforts to talk to, support, and learn from the dying were dismissed as morbid—ironically, since her prime concern was to return some sense of dignity and initiative to dying, to bring the whole subject, emotional tangles and all, out into the open. She began to run seminars on death and dying with terminally ill patients, and developed workshops to enable people to face and integrate their feelings about death. Then in 1977 she founded Shanti Nilaya, a nonprofit organization dedicated to the promotion of physical, emotional, intellectual, and spiritual health. Death is not to be regarded as a threat but as a challenge to live life to the full in an attitude of unconditional love, which will nullify much of the anguish and remorse experienced by survivors who reproach themselves in some way for the death: if only they had done this and said that, things might have been different. Unconditional love is total acceptance of the other as he or she is, not as one would like them to be; it can remove the burden of "if only" guilt, permitting a spontaneous and creative adaptation of energies to fresh challenges as they arise.

Conclusion

We have now examined a number of the factors relevant to a discussion of current Western attitudes to death and survival, together with their sociological background. It is surely imperative for all human beings to have an informed opinion on the subject, or else run the risk of living on the basis of false premises or values—an avoidable situation that they may come to regret. I would anticipate that Western people will become more informed about, and less afraid of, death in the next twenty years, as a result of three main factors: the continuing work of Shanti Nilaya in preparing people to face their deaths and hence questions relating to the meaning of life; further research into states of consciousness during the NDE and into mystical experience; and finally the development of electronic equipment that may render "communication" with discarnate entities more coherent and convincing. I would also anticipate a resurgence of interest in Platonic philosophy and continued search for spiritual knowledge in the esoteric traditions of the West. Taken together these factors indicate a profound shift of preoccupations away from the exclusively material towards a more spiritual, integrated, and compassionate perspective. It is an inspiring prospect.

NOTES

1. Dag Hammarskjold, *Markings* (London: Faber, 1966), p. 136.

2. S. G. F. Brandon, *Man and His Destiny in the Great World Religions* (Manchester: University Press, 1962), p. 384.

3. Sir James G. Frazer, *The Belief in Immortality,* vol. 1, (London: Macmillan, 1913), p. 468.

4. Sir James G. Frazer, *The Golden Bough,* vol. 4, (London: Macmillan, 1937), p. 104.

5. Sir Sarvepalli Radhakrishnan, *Eastern Religion and Western Thought* (Oxford University Press, 1939), p. 138.

6. Lucretius, *On the Nature of Things,* Bell edition, (1933), p. 87.

7. Jacques Monod, *Chance and Necessity* (London: Fontana, 1974).

8. Carl G. Jung, *The Structure and Dynamics of the Psyche,* vol. 8. of *Collected Works* (London: Routledge and Kegan Paul, 1969), p. 368.

9. Carl G. Jung, *The Structure and Dynamics of the Psyche,* p. 378.

10. Francis Bacon, *Novum Organum,* bk. 1, sec. 55.

11. Thomas J. Kuhn, *The Structure of Scientific Revolutions* (Chicago: University of Chicago Press, 1970).

12. Philippe Ariès, *The Hour of Our Death* (London: Penguin, 1981), p. 605.

13. Philippe Ariès, *Western Attitudes Toward Death from the Middle Ages to the Present* (London: Marion Boyars, 1976), p. 55.

14. Philippe Ariès, *Western Attitudes Toward Death from the Middle Ages to the Present,* p. 41.

15. Sir Karl Popper and Sir John Eccles, *The Self and its Brain* (London: Routledge and Kegan Paul, 1984).

16. Sir Charles Sherrington, *Man on His Nature* (Cambridge: Cambridge University Press, 1942); Wilder Penfield, *The Mysteries of Mind,* (Princeton: Princeton University Press, 1975).

17. Karl Pribram, *Languages of the Brain* (London: Prentice Hall, 1971).

18. Sir Cyril Burt, *ESP and Psychology,* ed. Anita Gregory, (London: Weidenfield and Nicolson, 1975); and *Psychology and Psychical Research,* (London: Society for Psychical Research, 1968); C. D. Broad, *Lectures on Psychical Research,* (London: Routledge and Kegan Paul, 1962); H. H. Price, "Survival and the Idea of Another World," *Proceedings of the Society for Psychical Research* 50, pt. 180 (1953); Carl G. Jung, *Synchronicity,* vol. 8 of *Collected Works* (London: Routledge and Kegan Paul, 1969).

19. David Lorimer, *Survival?* (London: Routledge and Kegan Paul, 1984).

20. E. R. Dodds, "Why I Do Not Believe in Survival," *Proceedings of the Society for Psychical Research* 51 (1934).

21. Raymond Moody, *Life after Life* (New York: Mockingbird Books, 1975).

22. Maurice Rawlings, *Beyond Death's Door* (London: Sheldon, 1979); Kenneth Ring, *Life at Death* (New York: Coward, McCann and Geoghagan, 1980); Michael Sabom, *Recollections of Death* (London: Harper and Row, 1982).

23. Stanislaw Grof and Joan Halifax, *The Human Encounter with Death* (London: Souvenir Press, 1978).

24. David Lorimer, *Survival?,* chap. 12.

25. John McManners, *Times Literary Supplement,* 14 December 1979, p. 112.

26. Philippe Ariès, *The Hour of Our Death,* p. 138.

27. Philippe Ariès, *The Hour of Our Death,* p. 561.

28. Philippe Ariès, *The Hour of Our Death,* p. 562.

Contributors

Dr. Linda Badham, Co-author of *Immortality or Extinction?*, sixth form tutor, and teacher of Mathematics at Aberaeron School, Aberaeron, Dyfed.

Rev. Dr. Paul Badham, Co-author of *Immortality or Extinction?*, Senior Lecturer in Theology & Religious Studies, and co-ordinator of the MA program in Death and Immortality, St. David's University College, Lampeter, University of Wales.

Professor R. Balasubramanian, Director of Advanced Studies in Philosophy, University of Madras, India.

Dr. Arthur Berger, President of the Survival Research Foundation, Florida.

Professor Saeng Chandra-Ngarm, Professor of Religion, Chiang Mai University, Thailand.

Rabbi Daniel Cohn-Sherbok, Director, Centre for the Study of Religion and Society, University of Kent, Canterbury.

Rev. Dr. Mariasusai Dhavamony, Professor of History of Religions and Hinduism, Gregorian University, Rome, Italy.

Professor Antony Flew, Professor of Philosophy, York University, Ontario, Canada.

David Lorimer, Author of *Survival: Body, Mind and Death in the Light of Psychic Research,* and Director of the Scientific and Medical Network, Gloucester, U.K.

Dr. Thomas McGowan, Associate Professor of Religious Studies, Manhattan College, New York City, U.S.A.

Dr. Sulayman S. Nyang, Associate Professor of African Studies, Howard University, Washington, U.S.A.

Professor Kofi Asare Opoku, Reader in Religious Studies, University of Calabar, Nigeria.

Dr. Bruce Reichenbach, Professor of Philosophy, Augsburg College, Minneapolis, U.S.A.

Professor Salih Tug, Professor and Dean of the Faculty of Theology, University of Marmara, Istanbul, Turkey.

Index

Index

Index

Index

man
  Advaita view of 110–112
  Buddhism view of 130
  Islamic view of 72–75
Martin, C. B. 186 (16)
Marx 217, 218
Mbiti, John S. 20 (10, 12), 21 (25), 22
McCormick, Donna 210 (11), 211 (33, 34)
McDermott, James P. 156 (28, 29)
McGowan, Thomas 2, 231
McManners, John 230 (25)
Meir, R. 25
mental phenomena 196–199
metaphysics, Buddhism and 141–143
Midrash Proverbs 35 (23)
Misra, G. S. P. 154 (5)
Monod, Jacques 217, 229 (7)
Montefiore, C. G. 35 (24)
Moody, Raymond A. 202, 211 (37, 38, 40), 223, 230 (21)
Morgan, Kenneth W. 84 (13)
Morris, J. D. 210 (8)
Morris, Robert L. 200, 210 (8), 211 (32)
mortality, logic of 171–187
Mugambi, J. 20 (8), 22
Muhammad 73–76, 78, 79, 86, 89, 90
Murchland, Bernard 68 (9)
Murphy, Gardner 190, 223
Myers, Frederick W. H. 211 (29)

Napoleon 45
near-death experiences 166–168, 223–224
Neuner, J. 50 (14)
Newton 217
nirvana 137–139
Nketia, Joseph 20 (7)
Noss, John B. 91 (1, 3)
Nyang, Sulayman 2, 232

Ochs, Robert J. 69 (29)
Opoku, Kofi Asare 1, 20 (3, 6), 21 (24), 22, 232
Osis, Karis 202, 203, 210 (11), 212 (33, 34, 36), 211 (41–46, 48, 49, 55)
Otto, Rudolf 8 (4)
out-of-body experiences 199–201
Owen, Iris M. 212 (60)

Palmer, John 211 (25)
Pandey, Babuju 198

Pannenberg, Wolfhart 158, 169 (8)
para-psychology 183–184
Parrinder, Geoffrey 22
Passanah, Robert 206
Pelham, George 205
Pelikan, Jeroslave 69 (33–36)
Penelhum, Terence 181, 182
Penfield, Wilder 221, 230 (16)
Petrautski, Margarete 195
phenomena, physical 191–207
philosophical positions, current 220
Pieper, Josef 54–56, 62, 68 (14–18, 20), 69 (27), 70 (47)
Piper, L. E. 191, 205
Plato 175, 178, 220
Polkinghorne, John 160, 161, 169 (2, 13)
poltergeists 192–193
Popper, Karl 221, 230 (15)
Pribram, Karl 221, 230 (17)
Price, H. H. 190, 221
Prince, Walter F. 194, 210 (12, 13), 230 (18)
psychical research 221–223
Puranic idea of death 98–99

Quinn, Edward 69 (21)
Quran tradition 71–85

Radhakrishnan, Sarvepalli 229 (5)
Rahner, Karl 54, 57, 58, 61, 69 (28, 29), 70 (44)
Raudive, Konstantin 194, 195, 210 (16)
Raudive, Zenta 195
Ravleigh, Lord 190
Rawlings, Maurice 223, 230 (22)
Ray, Benjamin C. 18, 21 (22), 23
real and the unreal, the 112–117
Reichenbach, Bruce R. 4, 10, 49 (10), 156 (24), 232
Reid 187 (16)
resurrection
  of the body 158–161
  versus immortality 59–62
return of the dead 14–16
Rhine, J. B. 176
Richet, Charles 190
Ring, Kenneth 202, 203, 211 (35, 39), 212 (47), 223, 230 (22)
Rogo, D. Scott 210 (14)
Roll, William G. 210 (7, 8, 10), 212 (52)

Index

Index

Whuerl, D. W. 169 (7)
Williams, Bernard 45, 50 (20), 169 (14)
Wilmot, S. R. 200
Winston, Clara 68 (14)
Winston, Richard 68 (14)
Wisdom, John 172

Wittgenstein, Ludwig 184, 187 (21)
world religions, teaching of 1–3

Zahan Dominique 13, 20 (1, 2), 21
(13), 23
Zimrah, Ibn Abi 32